African Theatre
11

T0341276

Series Editors
Martin Banham, James Gibbs,
Yvette Hutchison, Femi Osofisan
& Jane Plastow

Reviews Editor
Jane Plastow
Workshop Theatre, School of English, University of Leeds LS2 9JT, UK

Associate Editors
Omofolabo Ajayi-Soyinka
Dept of Theatre, 1530 Naismith Dr, University of Kansas, Lawrence, KS 66045–3140, USA
Awo Mana Asiedu
School of Performing Arts, PO Box 201, University of Ghana, Legon, Ghana
Eckhard Breitinger
Forststr. 3, 95488 Eckersdorf, Germany
David Kerr
Dept of Media Studies, Private Bag 00703, University of Botswana, Gaborone, Botswana
Amandina Lihamba
Dept of Fine & Performing Arts, PO Box 3505, University of Dar es Salaam, Tanzania
Patrick Mangeni
Head of Dept of Music, Dance & Drama, Makerere University, Kampala, Uganda
Olu Obafemi
Dept of English, University of Ilorin, Ilorin, Nigeria

Published titles in the series:
African Theatre in Development
African Theatre: Playwrights & Politics
African Theatre: Women
African Theatre: Southern Africa
African Theatre: Soyinka: Blackout, Blowout & Beyond
African Theatre: Youth
African Theatre 7: Companies
African Theatre 8: Diasporas
African Theatre 9: Histories 1850–1950
African Theatre 10: Media & Performance
African Theatre 11: Festivals

Forthcoming:
African Theatre 12: Shakespeare in & out of Africa

Articles not exceeding 5,000 words should be submitted preferably as an email attachment.

Style: Preferably use UK rather than US spellings. Italicise titles of books or plays. Use single inverted commas and double for quotes within quotes. Type notes at the end of the text on a separate sheet. Do not justify the right-hand margins.

References should follow the style of this volume (Surname date: page number) in text. All references should then be listed at the end of article in full:
Surname, name, date, *title of work* (place of publication: name of publisher)
Surname, name, date, 'title of article' in surname, initial (ed./eds) title of work
(place of publication: publisher).
or Surname, name, date, 'title of article', *Journal*, vol., no: page numbers.

Reviewers should provide full bibliographic details, including extent, ISBN and price.

Copyright: Please ensure, where appropriate, that clearance has been obtained from copyright holders of material used. Illustrations may also be submitted if appropriate and if accompanied by full captions and with reproduction rights clearly indicated. It is the responsibility of the contributors to clear all permissions.

All submissions should be accompanied by a brief biographical profile. The editors cannot undertake to return material submitted and contributors are advised to keep a copy of all material sent in case of loss in transit.

Editorial address
African Theatre, c/o Workshop Theatre, School of English,
University of Leeds, Leeds LS2 9JT, UK • j.e.plastow@leeds.ac.uk

Books for Review & Review articles
Professor Martin Banham, Reviews Editor, *African Theatre,*
4 Oakwood Gardens, Leeds LS2 2JE • martinbanham@btinternet.com

African Theatre 11
Festivals

Volume Editor
James Gibbs

Reviews Editor
Martin Banham

JC JAMES CURREY

James Currey
is an imprint of Boydell and Brewer Ltd
PO Box 9, Woodbridge, Suffolk IP12 3DF, UK

and of

Boydell & Brewer Inc.
668 Mt Hope Avenue, Rochester, NY 14620, USA
www.boydellandbrewer.com
www.jamescurrey.com

The publisher has no responsibility for the continued existence or accuracy of URLs for
external or third-party internet websites referred to in this book, and does not guarantee that
any content on such websites is, or will remain, accurate or appropriate.

British Library Cataloguing in Publication Data
available on request from the British Library

ISBN 978-1-84701-057-5 (James Currey paper)

Papers used by Boydell and Brewer are natural, recyclable products
made from wood grown in sustainable forests

Typeset in 10/11 pt Monotype Bembo by Long House, Cumbria, UK
Printed in Great Britain by CPI Group (UK) Ltd, Croydon, CR0 4YY

Contents

Notes on Contributors

Andrew Buckland has enjoyed a career as a versatile man-of-the-theatre. He has latterly moved into university teaching and currently provides leadership for the Drama Department at Rhodes University, Grahamstown. In the interview in this volume, he reflects on various aspects of his career and on the state of theatre in Africa as he has experienced it.

Yatma Dieye was awarded a first degree in English and Spanish from Cheikh Anta Diop University, Dakar, in 1978, and has since earned qualifications in phonetics, English language, translation and teaching from the Universities of London and Michigan, and Morey House College of Education. She is primarily a teacher and translator and is based in Rufisque.

Patrick-Jude Oteh trained at the University of Ibadan and lives and works in Jos, Plateau State, Nigeria. Having already earned a bachelor's degree in Theatre Arts and a master's degree in International Law, he is currently a doctoral candidate in the University of Ibadan. Patrick-Jude Oteh is the founding Artistic Director of the Jos Repertory Theatre and, during 2011, was Summer International Fellow at the John F. Kennedy Centre for the Performing Arts in Washington DC. He is involved in the formation of the first Arts Management Centre in Nigeria and writes a regular column on Arts Management for the *People's Daily Newspaper*.

James Gibbs no longer teaches or lectures but he retains his interests in African theatre and literature. His publications include a study of Wole Soyinka and a collection of essays on Ghanaian theatre, *Nkyin Kyin*. His *Bibliography of Ghanaian Theatre* is available on line thanks to the Jahn Library.

Robert Mshengu Kavanagh was born in Durban, in 1944, and educated in Cape Town, Oxford, and Leeds. He is an arts educator and theatre academic; a practitioner and writer. Kavanagh has worked in South Africa, Ethiopia and Zimbabwe. He co-founded Workshop '71 and the

Zimbabwean arts education trust, CHIPAWO, of which he is currently Director. His publications include *South African People's Plays*, *Theatre and Cultural Struggle in South Africa*, *Making People's Theatre* and *Ngoma: Approaches to Arts Education in Southern Africa*.

Amy Niang is a Lecturer in International Relations at the University of the Witwatersrand, Johannesburg. Her research interests include the Mossi State over an extended period approached partly from an anthropological point of view. Her analyses of contemporary Senegalese politics have appeared, inter alia, on-line in *Pambazuka News* and in *African Arguments*.

Sonali Pahwa studies youth theatre, arts in development, drama therapy, and women's Internet practices in Egypt. She gained a PhD in cultural anthropology from Columbia University, and now teaches at Northwestern University in Qatar.

Victor Yankah lectures in Theatre at the University of Cape Coast, where his specialised area is Theatre for Development. He is also a playwright, and in 2011, was awarded a Post-Doctoral Fellowship by the American Council of Learned Societies' African Humanities.

Ahmed Yerima was formerly the Director-General of the National Theatre and National Troupe of Nigeria, and is a former Director-General of the Abuja Carnival. He currently teaches theatre studies at the Redeemer's University in Lagos. Like Yankah, he is a playwright as well as a teacher.

Obituary
Efo Kodjo Mawugbe

During decades when serious concerns about the state of the Ghanaian theatre were expressed, Efo Kodjo Mawugbe, who has died at the age of 57, defied the pessimists with his creativity and productivity. A towering figure in the Ghanaian theatre, Mawugbe's lasting legacy to African theatre will only be adequately felt when more of his work is propelled into print and it is wonderful that this volume includes one of his plays. However, from the record of his achievements that is already in the public domain, Mawugbe's resourcefulness, his openness to trends in African theatre, his command of language, and his desire to contribute to current debates are vividly apparent.

Mawugbe's parents were support staff at the University of Science and Technology, Kumasi, and his early formal education was gained partly at Weweso Local Authority School. From Kumasi, he was sent to one of the foremost schools in the Volta Region, Mawuli, for his secondary schooling and there he benefitted from an environment in which theatrical productions were encouraged. He acted from his first year at the school and before he left had seen one of his own texts brought to life on stage.

Between 1975 and 1978, Mawugbe studied for a first degree in the School of Performing Arts, Legon, and he returned to the School in 2006 as a mature student to complete an MFA in playwriting. His educational achievements also included a certificate from the Ghana Institute of Management and Public Administration (GIMPA, 1991), and he was singled out to benefit from opportunities to study abroad. He attended the Banff Arts Centre Management Course in Calgary (1995), completed an attachment programme in Theatre and Events Organisation at the ETA Creative Arts Foundation, Chicago, and earned a certificate in Theatre Management and Audience Development (UK).

Mawugbe's employment record shows that after graduation from Legon, he taught briefly at the Ghana Empire School and then, from 1979 to 1984, was Senior Research Assistant in the Centre for Cultural Studies, at 'Tech' in Kumasi. He subsequently held a series of positions in the cultural arena, frequently shouldering administrative and leadership responsibilities. He undertook a wide variety of tasks as festival organiser, teacher, mentor, journalist, and all-round man-of-the-theatre. He was familiar with new technology and as 'at home' in a TV studio as on stage. His easy familiarity with different Ghanaian cultures and languages was shown by the way he was adopted in different places, and by the way his day name was variously spelled. He was Kodjo, Kojo and Kwadwo.

Titles of works and descriptions of ventures from his last years reveal his creative use of theatre and the theatrical. They include: *The Independence Story*, 'a re-enactment of events leading to Ghanaian Independence' (1997, see also 2007); *Slave Route March*, 'an Emancipation Day Celebration' (1998); *Educating the Ghanaian Children*, 'a Mock Parliamentary Debate on Child Education' (1999); *Tata Amu*, 'a stage biography of Ephraim Amu' (1999); *Oral Tradition, Oral Heritage*, 'a children's drama' (2003); *Free Juice For All*, 'a collaborative work' (2006), and *Cinderama*, 'a production to empower Ghanaian children' (2010).

The process of establishing Mawugbe's dramatic oeuvre continues, but the list as it stands is already hugely impressive. It includes: *Sweet Temptations* (1977), *A Calabash of Blood* (1978), *Aluta Continua* (1979), *The Unbending Branch* (1980), *In the Chest of a Woman* (1984), *Constable No Rank* (1986), *You Play me I Play You* (1989), *The Events* (1989), *Take me to the Altar* (1990), *The Royals* (1992), *G-Yard People* (1994), *Check Point Charlie* (1995), *Queen Zariba of Zariba*(1995), *The Last Saturday* (1995/6), *Poverty Club* (1997), *Ananse-Kweku-Ananse* (2003), *A.P.T.S.* ('Acquired Prison Traumatic Syndrome') subsequently known as *Prison Graduates*, and published in this volume under that title, (2005), and *Once Upon a Time in Lagos* (2006).

At the time of Efo Kodjo Mawugbe's untimely death on 14 September 2011, *In the Chest of a Woman* was the only title in print.

James Gibbs

Introduction

JAMES GIBBS

In deciding on an editorial approach to this volume on African Theatre Festivals various possibilities were considered. For example, given that African Theatre needs to be marketed through interest in relatively few, high-profile names, the possibility of tracing the impact of festivals on individual playwrights was suggested. One can, for example, imagine following Wole Soyinka through the festivals in which he participated and at which his work was produced. This would include the National Students' Drama Festival (London, 1958, on the fringe of which *The Swamp Dwellers* was produced), the Commonwealth Arts Festival (UK, 1965, that prompted the premiere of *The Road* in London) and the Premier Festival Mondial des Arts Nègres, (Dakar, 1966, where *Kongi's Harvest* was staged and where Soyinka sat on the film panel). And it would have to move up to FESMAN 2010 at which there was a production in French of *Death and the King's Horseman*, and then on to analyse his contribution to recent Lagos Black Heritage Festivals. While such an approach was not followed in the end, there is material in this volume for those interested in Soyinka, and his fraught relationship with Festac '77 comes through.

Another route into exploring the organisation and impact of international theatre festivals in Africa would have been to trace the involvement of a particular acting group in a series of festivals. For example, it would have been possible to follow Abibigromma, the company attached to the National Theatre in Accra, from one celebration to another and that would have shed light on the demands made and the experiences offered by different festivals. The Abibigromma Company participated in the Cairo International Festival of Experimental Theatre (CIFT) in 1996, and went on from Egypt to visit four other countries.

While aware of those approaches, this volume assembles contributions on particular festival traditions – together with an interview that allows reflection on Southern African experiences. The Festivals considered are amongst those with the highest profiles in the continent and raise issues of ideology, viability and sustainability. Coverage in this volume of African

Theatre is selective rather than comprehensive, but, I think the results shed light from a variety of angles on the major and recurrent concerns linked to a Festival Culture.

When Robert Mshengu Kavanagh's contribution arrived in my in-box, I realised that it should stand at the front of this volume. Tightly focused on Zimbabwe, the paper repeatedly grapples with matters that surface in other parts of the continent. For example, while all African countries draw on indigenous festival conventions and also engage with imported theatre festival traditions, makers of the new Zimbabwean theatre learned from and reacted against a culturally influential settler community with an established tradition. Politically, too, Zimbabwe has experienced in extreme forms the conflicts that surfaced in other countries: the Chimurenga was a peculiarly Zimbabwean conflict, but other African nations had to wage their own chimurengas. The prejudices of Robert Mugabe challenged the Zimbabwean festival culture in clearly identified ways, but other national traditions have been come up against their own Mugabes.

Kavanagh's deep commitment to the theatre in Zimbabwe gives his contribution particular authority – and enables him to illustrate the points he makes with relevant personal experiences. Near the beginning of his article, he refers to indigenous traditions of communal celebration and then moves on to the essential ingredient for a progressive policy concerning festivals: an 'integrated strategy for the development of the arts'. He shows himself acutely aware of the incentives and opportunities offered by festivals, and he is also aware of the need for support that will contribute to 'artistic production as a process'. He engages with the fundamental elements involved in promoting sustainable theatre traditions, including training, venues, facilities, sponsorship, and 'above all audience'. He also looks closely at funding, and the conditions attached to it. In the course of a clear-sighted analysis, he runs through the possible sources of financial support for theatre, referring, for example, to arts councils, the corporate sector, UN agencies, Scandinavian donors, the mass media, and the boxoffice, and he takes into account the 'possibilities of overseas performance' that exposure at a festival might lead to. Kavanagh points out that, while those struggling to create a sustainable, popular theatre tradition are starved of funds, money is made available for festivals. In a list that includes receptions, fees, travel, accommodation, and subsistence - for visiting artists - he indicates where the festival money goes. His analysis exposes the gap between the meagre benefits that local theatre groups derive from participating in festivals and the well-remunerated opportunities offered to outsiders, particularly those from funding countries. In his conclusion, as throughout his contribution, Kavanagh sets festivals in the context of the needs of local theatre-makers.

Kavanagh's paper is followed by five contributions that look at three linked events: le Premier Festival Mondial des Arts nègres (variously capitalised, Dakar, 1966,) the Second World Black and African Festival of Arts and Culture (Lagos 1977 and also known as 'Festac '77') and le troisième Festival Mondial des Arts nègres, also referred to as the Third Festival of Black Arts and Cultures, as the Third World Festival of Black Arts and Cultures and as FESMAN (Dakar, 2010). There have been three in the last forty-six years; a gap of thirty-three years between editions two and three. It is difficult to predict with any certainty when the next one will take place, but Brazil 2014 has been mentioned. The first contribution in this volume, by Ahmed Yerima, on Festac, takes us to the heart of the 'legacy issue' as far as festivals are concerned: 'They come, they go. What do they leave behind?' In the case of Lagos, the most obvious legacy has been the Bulgarian-designed, Bulgarian-built National Theatre at Iganmu. It seems that while the building provided a focal point for the celebration in 1977 it was neglected in the post-Festac period, the fabric deteriorated, and, for a time, the 'iconic' complex was 'For Sale'. Yerima opens his chapter with comments from three of those who provided leadership for the Festival that hint at fissures between them. However, once in his stride, the author's most telling words come from from Soyinka about theatre architecture. After a visit to Uganda in 1962, the playwright found imitation without substance, describing the National Theatre building in Kampala as 'a miniature replica of a British provincial theatre'. His warning did not prevent Nigeria opting for a grandiose version of a Bulgarian sportscomplex some fifteen years later. One area in which I looked for close critical analysis was the production of *Langbodo*, the major local theatrical contribution to Festac '77. As Yerima points out, considerable resources were made available for that festival entry. I was sorry not to secure a follow-up contribution that adequately explored its contribution to the Festac legacy.

Yerima's chapter is followed by an annotated bibliography that tells part of the story of Festac through an itemisation of newspaper articles and other sources. This list includes a brief foray into Soyinka's writings, contributed to the Festac Colloquium, and then looks back on the festival experience. Concern with Festac '77 is followed by a contribution from Yatma Dieye who makes unfailingly unfavourable comparisons between the first and third editions of the Festivals, the Dakar contributions. She draws attention to popular sentiment in Senegal and the very different national moods in which the festivals were held. Those deeply-felt comments lead into an essay by Amy Niang who sets Fesman 2010, or 'the FESMAN' as she prefers, in the context of Senegalese dynastic politics. She refers to funding issues, artistic questions and political dimensions. The fact that the monstrous African Renaissance Monument, constructed by North Korea at a cost of perhaps $27 million, now looms over Dakar, attracting criticism for a variety of reasons and entangled with former President Abdoulaye Wade means that there is a ready symbol for his legacy, or as Niang might put it 'a synecdoche for the wasteful ways of the Wade's 10-year administration'. A less tangible but equally unhappy legacy of Wade's cultural ambitions is the controversy to which Niang refers over the fate of art works transported to Dakar for exhibition and then impounded by shippers on the grounds of unpaid bills.

The fourth item on Fesman 2010 consists of a list of performances presented during the Festival. Like the bibliography on Festac, this offers relatively raw data that readers are encouraged to process. While recognising the depth of knowledge and the planning that went into the drama programme, there will be those who sense imbalances. It brings into the spotlight the theatre curator, Kwame Kwei Armah, and the reference to him provides a hook on which to hang the trenchant comments about festivals expressed by his near namesake, Ayi Kwei Armah. No discussion of festivals in Africa would be complete without acknowledgement of the Ghanaian novelist's dismissive reference to the 'festival game' and his description of major international arts festivals as 'wasteful demonstrations of intellectual bankruptcy'.

I have already had occasion to mention PANAFEST, first held quite near Ayi Kwei Armah's birthplace in 1992. Kwesi Yankah's close analysis of the roots of this festival and of its evolving format reveal the powerful background influences of those interested in tourism income and others concerned about 'diasporean relations'. Indeed, among the editorial issues confronted in preparing this volume has been the question of how to spell 'diasporean'. It appears that various forms are currently in use in this relatively new interest area. 'Diasporan' is favoured in some US academic publications, while 'diasporian' has a hold in certain parts of the Ghanaian press, and some prefer to stick with 'diaspora Africans' and 'diaspora identity'. Whatever usages eventually emerge as the most widely accepted, the point is that the African Diaspora represents a constituency and a challenge that, as Yankah indicates, is shaping PANAFEST. Further research into the evolution of this festival is encouraged by the bibliographies that include 'PANAFEST through the Headlines'. This material should be read in conjunction with two pieces linked with Efo Mawugbe who was a back-stage presence at the festival from its inception. His untimely passing occasions the obituary at the front of this volume, and the cooperation of his literary executors means that we have the privilege of including his play, *Prison Graduates* in the text.

Although several important theatre festival traditions have flourished in North African countries, including the politically radical festivals held in Algeria, coverage in this volume is limited to Egypt and to the Cairo International Festival of Experimental Theatre (CIFT). Sonali Pahwa's contribution draws attention to issues that have already surfaced, such as the links between a festival and an influential individual. She also notes the desirability of striking a balance between performance and discussion at festivals, and indicates how international theatre, by its very nature, encourages particular kinds of drama, notably physical drama.Pahwa's paper refers to the cost of staging international festivals and, once again, to their legacies. Political events sometimes overwhelm theatre festivals, and the impact of CIFT will have to be periodically reassessed in the wake of the January 25 Revolution. The 'Arab Spring' led to the cancellation of CIFT

2011, but the 'copy-cat' festivals that have emerged may turn out, in the long run, to be a significant legacy. They may be the harvest from the establishment of the international theatre tradition in Cairo.

Africa West and South remain twin sources of theatrical inspiration for the continent and it is appropriate that an account of the Jos Theatre Festival in Nigeria and an interview with Andrew Buckland, now teaching in Grahamstown, are included in this volume. Work created for the Jos Theatre Festival (JTF) is already familiar to readers of this journal since *Our House* was included in *African Theatre 7: Companies*. That play formed part of one of the six theatre festivals that Patrick-Jude Oteh and the team at Jos have managed to organise in a city that sits astride the faultline between Muslims and Christians. Oteh's narrative shows how important flexibility has been in establishing and maintaining a theatre tradition, and how essential diplomacy is when one has to negotiate with outside agencies. JTF has managed to work with local supporters and with international funders – who, of course, have their own agendas, and it was encouraging to hear that, despite continuing civil strife, the 2012 Festival did take place. At a late hour, it was possible to include a list of the productions put on in the course of that event. The continued existence of the Festival speaks of dedication and commitment, and of belief in the survival of theatre.

In his thoughtful responses to questions, Andrew Buckland throws light on the roles theatre festivals have played in his career. Because he is at pains to draw attention to the privileges he has enjoyed, Buckland sometimes obscures his own resourcefulness and plays down his industry. To get a fuller sense of the vigorous theatre he has created, readers are encouraged to follow up references through, for example, Google Images.

The 'reach' of the volume is extended and 'rounded off' by a book review section that includes responses to important academic studies as well as reactions to recently published playscripts.

REFERENCES

http://www.efa-aef.eu/newpublic/upload/efadoc/2/for%20members%20only%202.pdf,
http://kadmusarts.com

Festivals as a Strategy for the Development of Theatre in Zimbabwe
1980–2010

ROBERT MSHENGU KAVANAGH

Because of Zimbabwe's recent history many might consider the development of theatre in that country and the role played by festivals in it to be a special case. However, it is possible that the question of festivals as a strategy for the development of theatre in the Zimbabwean context may suggest parallels to readers in other countries in Africa and elsewhere.

The well-known Zimbabwean playwright and authority on various aspects of arts and culture, Stephen Chifunyise[1], writes a weekly column in *The Herald* newspaper called 'Theatre Corridors'. On 2 December, 2010, he wrote an article headlined 'Festival showcases future dance stars'. He was referring to the Jikinya National Primary Schools Traditional Dance Competition. In the following week, he went on to discuss festivals in general in his column and provided a useful survey of those currently existing in Zimbabwe. There are four international festivals: the Harare International Festival of the Arts (HIFA), the Zimbabwe International Film Festival (ZIFF), the International Images of Women in Film Festival (IIFF) and the Buddyz Annual Festival of the Arts (BAFA), which is largely a regional festival founded in 2006 by the Patsimeredu Edutainment Trust, which brings together in Harare community-based theatre initiatives from all over the country and the Southern African region. Local festivals include Chimanimani in Zimbabwe's Eastern Highlands, Intwasa (Bulawayo, founded 2005) and the Rushinga Annual Arts Festival (see below). There are also a number of festivals featuring music from mbira to jazz and gospel. In addition, Zimbabwean theatre groups have participated in international theatre festivals including the Edinburgh Festival, the World Festival of Children's Theatre and the Images of Africa Festival (Denmark, 2006).

Chifunyise's articles beg the following question: what is the role of arts or theatre festivals, especially international festivals, as a strategic element in the development of the arts in society, with Zimbabwe as a case study? This question is the subject of this chapter.

1

Rushinga Annual Arts Festival – a festival with a difference?

Rushinga is a very small and remote rural centre in the far North East of Zimbabwe, not far from the border with Mozambique. The festival is the brainchild of the local MP, Lazarus Dokora, who is also Deputy Minister in the Ministry of Education, Sport, Arts and Culture. The aim of the festival, which was first staged in 2007, is to 'unlock the value of culture in the development agenda for Rushinga constituency'. It is a component of what is called the Rushinga Constituency Education Dialogue Series, and 'comprises workshops, performing arts competitions and exhibitions'. It 'has become a source of skills development' and access to markets. The festival 'enables the community to take pride in its language, systems and beliefs and provides platforms for sharing of knowledge'. Participation is open to all in the community. On display are decorative reed mats, basketry, wood carving, crocheted items, batiks, sculpture and ceramics. Performances include poetry, drama, traditional dance, choral music, gospel music, music bands and gymnastics. There are also debates and competitions for beauty or trials-of-strength.

The role of an arts festival

Definitions of the word 'festival' have the following components in common: joy; celebration; a regular occurrence; marking an event; and an organised programme of events or performances. The celebratory component suggests that the function of a festival is to mark a success, achievement or the successful completion of some task or process. Not included in many definitions is the fact that a festival often features an exhibition or showcases the fruits of whatever is being celebrated. Many of these festivals involve an element of competition. Those who have contributed outstandingly to the success or social achievement being celebrated at the festival are singled out for honours or prizes. Significantly, as in the Festival of Dionysus in ancient Athens which developed into a competition for writers of tragedy, the competitive element seems to have been a later introduction. As the festival format develops, often quite gratuitous elements may be introduced, such as the competition between dance groups in the case of the Ngoni in Zambia, which bears no direct relation to what is being celebrated by the festival – harvest time – except for the fact that it contributes to the celebrations.

In Africa the festival format that immediately springs to mind is that of Harvest or First Fruits' Festivals, which are to be found in the traditional cultures of peoples all over the continent and elsewhere. In southern Africa, for instance, it is found in the *incwala* in Swaziland, the Zulu *umkhosi* in South Africa, the *ngoni* of Zambia and the *ngoma* in Tanzania. In *Kongi's Harvest*, Wole Soyinka depicts a Yam Festival, as celebrated in many cultures in West Africa. In the context of Africa, therefore, an arts festival, like a Harvest Festival, might be regarded as the celebration and showcasing of an artistic harvest. However, one cannot expect to bring in a heavy crop if one does not sow. In other words, for an arts festival to be an organic component of the national development of the arts in a given society, it should derive from or grow out of a process of fertile artistic production. Thus, before a festival comes the process of artistic production, with the role of the festival being to provide a framework for the celebration as well as exhibition of the fruits of all labour.

This would imply that an integrated strategy for the development of the arts requires an investment in artistic production before that in festivals. Funding, resources and training must be made available to the producers, i.e. the artists, first. A strategy of arts development that relies on festivals without prior investment in artistic production is likely to be ineffective – or even counterproductive. Artists need to be supported so that they are able to produce mature works that will then be showcased and appreciated at a festival. In short, funding for artistic production should precede funding for festivals.

However, the role of the festival is not passive in its relation to production. The very fact that artists have a festival to focus on, where their work will be showcased, appreciated and possibly receive an award, stimulates production. However, festivals can go further in assisting this development. So far our discussion has concentrated on the festival as end product. But the process of artistic production is exactly that – a process. It continues at and after the festival. Before the event it provides something for artists to work towards. At the festival it provides not only the opportunity to display creative products but also, where the festival has a workshop component and critical seminars, to share skills, learn from other artists and, particularly for directors, an opportunity to discuss their work and have it subjected to criticism. There are opportunities for networking and setting up partnerships or synergies with other artists, attracting promotional attention and setting up performances or funding for the future.

Obviously it is in the interest of festivals to feature original, high-quality works. A far-seeing festival strategy therefore includes playing an active part in the process of artistic production – by commissioning works, providing training opportunities and, if possible, even funding for artistic production. Thus, a festival can and should support and facilitate artistic production as a process before, at and after the festival itself.

When training, artistic production, festivals, promotion and audience-creation form part of an integrated strategy, a festival can play a dynamic and beneficial role in the development of the arts in a society. But when they do not, festivals can easily do the opposite. This article explores such as case in Zimbabwe.

The development of theatre in Zimbabwe

In order to examine the function of festivals, and international festivals in particular in the national development of the arts and theatre in Zimbabwe, a brief description of theatre in Zimbabwe from Independence in 1980 to 2010 is required.

For the development of a theatre culture, tradition or industry – when theatre production is consistent, widely distributed, viable, dynamic, provocative and popular – the following are required: an enabling national policy, training, appropriate venues and facilities, sponsorship and/or funding, investment capital and, above all, an audience.

In Zimbabwe the development of theatre and the arts in general has never been included in what government and the society as a whole refer to as 'development', which is assumed to be about the economy, health, agriculture, scientific and technological education, and so on. As a result none of the above requirements for the development of a viable theatre were put in place to any meaningful extent. While there is theatre in Zimbabwe, it would not be true to say that Zimbabwe has a national theatre culture, tradition or industry according to the criteria listed above.[2] Theatre certainly does not command a national audience in the way that music or television does, and there is little national interest in or demand for it.

There have been one or two opportunities to rectify this situation. There was the golden (and missed) opportunity in the 1990s afforded by Norwegian funding for the arts, which provided support for, among other things, the key area of audience-creation through the establishment of community venues and programmes of regular performances.[3] Unfortunately, there have also been measures that have made the situation worse. These include a disastrous circular to headmasters of schools from the Ministry of Education, Sport and Culture, banning theatre groups from taking their performances to schools at a time when many full-time theatre groups survived on this activity.[4] The hyperinflationary chaos and the 'Murambatsvina' clean-up operation in particular ejected theatre and other arts organisations from their offices at the National Sports Stadium.[5] There were the sanctions, which included the withdrawal of project support for the arts by northern-hemisphere funding agencies, with the exception of an extremely restricted range of creative output with donor-driven objectives such as promoting AIDS awareness and even regime change.[6]

The upshot of all this was to produce the theatre scenario that obtained until recently. What was once 'community theatre' – where performances took place in community halls in the high-density suburbs or were toured all over the country by itinerant full-time theatre groups – contracted into a scattering of closed-door commissioned performances for development agencies.

After the collapse of the 'enclave theatre' or 'Little Theatre' – terms used to describe those enterprises run by the settler populations that had flourished in white Rhodesia – few actual theatres remained operational in Zimbabwe. The Repertory Theatre ('Reps') in Harare, which has traditionally been the cultural flagship of the white community, was one exception. The theatres in Kadoma, Masvingo, Bulawayo and Mutare remained operational and available for performances. Others, such as that in Gweru, decayed. The only new theatres that were developed in the period after independence were the tiny Theatre-in-the-Park in Harare Gardens, where Rooftop Productions managed to keep a more or less consistent programme of local material going, and Amakhosi's Township Square in Bulawayo. Over the Edge (founded in 1994), CHIPAWO (1989), and its professional youth theatre – The New Horizon Theatre Company (2004), while not having their own venues managed to produce and perform a consistent theatre repertoire. Schools continued to produce their plays but the University of Zimbabwe, a national centre of theatre and cultural activity in the 1980s and early 90s, offered little (until recently) with the exception of student class productions.

This was a bleak scenario. Yet anyone reading Stephen Chifunyise's survey of festivals could be forgiven for imagining the opposite. While festivals thrived and proliferated, theatre production and public attendance languished.

Theatre production and finance

The finance required for funding a professional theatre production usually comes in three forms – grants, investment capital and/or revenue from the box office.

In terms of grants, the Zimbabwean government made no provision for funding the arts outside the tiny administrative budget it gave to the National Arts Council of Zimbabwe. The National Arts Council never had the capacity – or possibly the will – to fund theatre productions. With the partial exception of Bulawayo, city authorities, unlike their counterparts elsewhere in the world, did not promote their cities or serve their citizens by developing and supporting the arts. On the contrary, I was told by the director of the Festivals that the City of Harare expressed scepticism as to the value to the city of the Harare International Festival of the Arts (HIFA). I know from personal experience that when, in January, 2011, the Flatfoot Dance Company, a visiting South African children's dance group, asked for permission to do free performances in the city squares and streets of Harare, the Custodians of the City demanded payment and the idea was abandoned. Local authorities in Zimbabwe are traditionally impoverished but they do have the ability to support theatre production in kind, for example in the use of venues. Few did. Few in fact acknowledged the importance of arts and culture in the life of their communities.

The corporate sector in Zimbabwe, in contrast to their colleagues south of the Limpopo, followed the policy of the government and few companies ever acknowledged the importance of the arts to society or financed them. In the days before independence an exclusive, white corporate world did support minority white arts – for example, the National Theatre Festival organised by the National Theatre Organisation (NTO). After independence, white business did virtually nothing to assist in the development of majority arts or theatre, although they continued to support what activities the white community sustained. However, the corporate sector experienced rapid and substantial indigenisation, both in terms of black-owned business and black leadership of formerly white-led sectors such as banking. This new indigenous sector has not in the main come to value the arts sufficiently to contribute to their advancement apart from commissioning performances for their functions. Those that have supported the arts, such as Delta Beverages, were involved in business that had some relation to entertainment and culture. Delta Beverages, whose products included 'Chibuku', thick brown millet beer, was the major funder of the National Arts Council's projects, including the Neshamwari traditional dance competition, Jikinya and the National Arts Merit Awards (NAMA).

United Nations Agencies commissioned theatre performances for functions, or supported the arts as they related to their core business. For example UNDP supported an Artists Against Poverty project in 2003. However, international financial backing fell away. During 2005-6, the Swedish International Development Authority (SIDA) phased out its contracts with cultural partners, including the major producers of theatre, Rooftop, Amakhosi and CHIPAWO. The Culture Fund of Zimbabwe was set up, but, although it did its best, it could not significantly impact on arts development. The resources available to the fund were too small and it had limited ability to stimulate theatre production and performance. As mentioned above, the Norwegian Agency for Development Co-operation (NORAD) had earlier made funding available for the arts through the Ministry of Education, Sport and Culture, and its support for arts organisations continued. However, with the notable exception of its commemoration of the Ibsen Centenary in collaboration with CHIPAWO (2006), their support did not impact significantly on theatre.

From about 2000 support for theatre production from foreign govern-ment aid agencies and NGOs was confined either to theatre as a development tool, almost exclusively HIV/AIDS related, or as an instrument of political influence or regime change. In addition to the aid agency funding for development related projects, mentioned above, another external contribution should be noted: production funding from various embassies for the promotion of the literature and culture of their donor countries.

Investment capital is predicated on the likelihood of profit and for this there needs to be the prospect of attracting an audience that is able and prepared to pay an economic price. However, in a situation where there was no marketable mass and no widespread theatre culture or industry, there was little prospect of it.

In addition to the aid agency funding for development related projects, mentioned above, another external contribution should be noted: production funding from various embassies for the promotion of the literature and culture of their (donor) countries.

In many countries, playwrights, artists and directors are able to sustain themselves through television work. In Zimbabwe this has not been the case. The Zimbabwe Broadcasting Corporation never had the money to pay reasonable fees for local programmes. Independent local producers were generally forced to fund their productions themselves or to look for sponsors. The latter rely on advertising and as more and more of their consumers began to abandon Zimbabwe Television (ZTV) for Digital Satellite Television (DStv), it became increasingly difficult to find sponsorship for national broadcasts. The best deal that could be struck with ZTV was to agree to provide the programmes without charge while the ZTV finance and advertising department agreed not to charge for 'flighting'.

Finally, at the box-office: a paying audience for theatre hardly existed. One exception was the Reps Theatre, which is an amateur club, drawing its audience largely from the white community. In the main it stages popular musical programmes from Britain or the United States. But, even where a paying audience exists, for the theatre to be viable, the audience must pay a viable price. And there's the rub. The example of Rooftop helps to make this clear. The Theatre-in-the-Park featured three clearly differentiated types of production. There were plays on topical and social Zimbabwean themes, which reflected contemporary life and there were donor-driven, political plays. In the middle were the plays of Stephen Chifunyise. The former were to a large extent well-acted and popular and a paying theatre audience was visibly in the making as young Zimbabweans crossed over from the Central Business District to Harare Gardens after work to enjoy a theatre experience which they could relate to – often featuring actors and actresses from Zimbabwe television soaps and other programmes. Yet Rooftop did not develop this potential. Instead it was the donor-supported 'regime change' plays that largely characterised its repertoire. Examples include *Super Patriots and Morons*, *Ivhu Versus the State* and *The Good President*, the last of which was written and directed by Cont Mhlanga, the founder of Amakhosi, a playwright and director from whom one might have expected better. His earlier play, *Workshop Negative*, also an anti-ZANU-PF piece, was well acted and theatrically powerful.[7] Many of these 'political' plays were shallow, sloganising and poorly scripted. Apart from the opening nights, when representatives of the donor community, Western diplomatic missions, NGOs and their sympathisers were present, they did not attract audiences. This apparent paradox could only be explained by the fact that the plays that pulled in a paying Zimbabwean audience did not yield viable revenue – or at least revenue commensurate with what the foreign donor agencies were able to provide.

This leaves the possibility of overseas performance. Unlike South Africa, Zimbabwe has not had much success with theatre exports, surely as a consequence of the lack of investment in the development of theatre outlined above. The international spotlight that fell on Zimbabwe because of the reclamation of the land was a unique opportunity for the country's theatre artists who were prepared or able to exploit this issue in an entertaining and theatrically skilful way. One or two plays by Rooftop Promotions had some success. For instance, Stephen Chifunyise's *Strange Bedfellows*, not in the 'regime change' mould but rather dealing with racial issues, toured widely in Europe. However, no Zimbabwean play ever experienced the kind of international success achieved by South Africans with plays such as *Sizwe Bansi is Dead*, *The Island*, *Woza Albert!*, *Sophiatown* and *Sarafina* during the Apartheid years. In fact, Zimbabwean efforts to capitalise on the opportunity offered by foreign markets were generally too weak theatrically to succeed. Sympathetic audiences outside the country may applaud the rhetoric but if the script, the acting and the directing are poor the play's commercial potential is limited.

To recapitulate, for the development of a strong, viable and high-quality theatre, a production must be financed. In Zimbabwe it was not. Outside the donor-agenda, there was very little money for independent theatre production.

But this is not to say that there was no money at all for theatre and the arts in Zimbabwe. True, there wasn't much, especially after the imposition of sanctions and there has been even less since the world recession. But there was money. Why was it not available for independent theatre production?

Funding for festivals

Funding that might have gone into theatre production, performances, touring and audience-creation, was going to festivals, in particular international festivals. It was foreign embassies and development agencies, the only meaningful source of funding for independent theatre in Zimbabwe, who were most attracted to international festivals. But they were not the only ones who found this activity an attractive proposition. Theatre companies applied annually to organisations such as UNESCO and various development NGOs and were told there was no money. Yet all these institutions contributed regularly to either one or all of the international festivals – HIFA, ZIFF and IIFF. Many theatre companies and organisations report how their efforts to raise production funding from these sources were met with the response that owing to the recession there had been cuts in funding and what was left over was earmarked for one or other international festival.

The result was that many plays never reached the stage. This was particularly frustrating for aspiring playwrights. Other productions never got beyond the preview stage or an opening performance as they failed to attract funding for performances and touring and nothing more was heard of them.

Yet the festivals, in particular the international festivals, continued to survive. Under what circumstances and for what ends did the festivals receive funding?

New Horizon Theatre Company

Produced three plays in 2010, all of which secured limited funding through their place in the promotion of the national literature and culture of foreign countries – *The Post Office* (India), *The Most Wonderful Thing of All* (Norway) and *Mutambo wa Panyika* (Spain). Rabindranath Tagore's *The Post Office* was worked up to preview stage with initial support from the Indian Council for Cultural Relations. It was never performed after preview. *The Most Wonderful Thing of All*, an interrogation of New Horizon's own Zimbabwean version of Ibsen's *A Doll's House* (2008), was funded by the 'Ibsen through African Eyes' Festival and Workshop in Lusaka in October. After the Harare preview and performance in the Lusaka playhouse, one or two commissioned performances in Zimbabwe, it was not seen again. *Mutambo wa Panyika*, a production in Shona of the Spanish playwright, Calderon della Barca's *Life is a Dream*, was a partial exception. Funded to opening performance by the Embassy of Spain, it has had limited performances since – in Harare and Masvingo.

Financial support for festivals

Festival fund-raisers in Zimbabwe would claim that things were tough, that there was no money. Their assessment was relative. Festivals, especially international festivals, require a lot of money. Though tough, the fact remained that, while independent professional production and performances were starved of funds, festivals did secure support – and in the process they siphoned off whatever resources there might have been for training, production, performance and audience-creation. It is obvious that this impacted negatively on production and performance. What is not so obvious is that it also impacted negatively on the festivals themselves and their usefulness as agents of artistic and theatre development.

One of the reasons for this is that foreign funders, embassies, United Nations Agencies and corporates have one thing in common – their need for mileage, in the form of profile, publicity, impressive reports and concrete outcomes. Festivals and workshops are easier and better mileage in these terms than sustained developmental assistance to the arts.

However another reason is that an international festival is an opportunity for donors to showcase the cultural products of their own countries. Thus, though funding goes ostensibly to a Zimbabwean festival, in actual fact the bulk of the money supports the exportation of their own cultural products. The money is spent on fees, travel, accommodation and subsistence of artists from the donor countries. Local corporates, who invariably claim that they have no money, wishing to associate their brand with international big names, scramble to fund international acts. Just as curiously, foreign development organisations which do not normally include theatre in their portfolios, find money for international performances or films at international festivals.

Thus not only is local production and performance generally not supported before and after festivals but even during festivals almost all the funding and sponsorship goes to foreign participants. In this way funding for festivals has more to do with the support of the arts in donor countries than it has to support of the arts in Zimbabwe.

Sponsorship for local artists at HIFA (2010)

All international participants were sponsored. The following (and many other) local ones were not: African Destiny, Solomon Chimbetu, Mawungira eNharira, Hope Masike, Chitungwiza Harmony Singers, Douglas Vambe.

The Coca Cola Green is a sort of Third World events venue, virtually reserved for local productions, especially traditional dance. Few if any of the performances in this venue were sponsored.

Yet participation in international festivals is highly sought after by some – though not all – local artists. So what does a participating local artist get out of taking part – often without any sponsorship – in an international festival? HIFA offers the very big names a fee. Others have to content themselves with a share of the box office and a chance to be seen by audiences that might not otherwise attend their productions. Theoretically there is a chance they might be noticed by foreign visitors and this may result in further opportunities. However, especially in the case of theatre performances, they perform only once or twice and in some cases never again outside the festival. To do so, they would need production funding as opposed to festival funding.

Because the festivals do not have any independent funding and because the funding they do get is not adequate, they are forced to rely completely on what performances their funders choose to offer. This applies not only to foreign participants but also to local entries where items supported by a festival funder have in most cases to be accepted and applicants who are not supported in this way have very little chance. The arts education organisation CHIPAWO, with which I have worked for many years, participated in the festival on a number of occasions – but each time because it was supported by a festival funder, such as MS Zimbabwe (Danish Association for International Cooperation) or the Norwegian Embassy. When CHIPAWO applied independently, its applications failed. It is relevant to note that the British Council annually funds courses or workshops for Zimbabweans, selected by itself, on aspects of theatre. These workshops are run by resource persons flown out from the UK. The student work produced at the workshop is showcased at the festival, even if this means four or five plays. The Council has also inaugurated the HIFA Direct programme – whatever this programme produces is guaranteed to be performed at HIFA.

Thus the festival content to a large extent reflects the interests and tastes of the foreign funder rather than works of relevance to the national development of the arts and theatre in Zimbabwe.

Needless to say, in a situation like this, a festival like HIFA had little or no funding to spare for supporting local arts or theatre production. Very few if any works were commissioned by the festival itself and certainly there was nothing left over to plough back into the training or the production costs of local theatre.

Festivals and the development of theatre

So almost all of whatever money might have been available for the independent local arts in Zimbabwe – in other words the arts not specifically tailored to the development or political agenda of the foreign donors – went to international festivals. Of that, the lion's share went to foreign artists. Obviously this had a profound impact on the development of the arts and theatre in Zimbabwe. Instead of funding for productions that would be performed over an extended period to audiences in many different parts of the country, a lot of money has been spent in a very short period on performances that the vast majority in the country and even in Harare did not have either the opportunity, the time or the money to enjoy.

*Financial implications of funding international festivals in
in Zimbabwe*

- A festival requires a lot of money.
- The money is consumed in a very short space of time
- Few people can attend events on weekdays
- Attending events is time-consuming and expensive
- Festivals are in the capital city and do not reach the majority of
  the people in other parts of the country

International festivals in Zimbabwe cater for a tiny minority which
has the time and the money to travel to the capital and move from one
production to the next not only at weekends but on weekdays.

Conclusion

In a situation like that in Zimbabwe between 1980 and 2010, the tendency
to support international festivals can hardly be said to have had a positive
impact on national arts development and, in the case of HIFA, on national
theatre development.

But as we have seen, festivals are a valid and effective strategic component
of national theatre development. They are – but only if the strategy ensures
a balanced and integrated development of the various components of theatre
production, namely training, creativity, performance, festival promotion and
audience-creation, and funding that supports that strategy. To ensure this,
there needs to be a national dialogue and strong national institutions which
can advocate and educate government, social partners, funding agencies and
the arts sector itself as to the importance of such a strategy and the negative
effects of prevailing practice.[8]

NOTES

1   Stephen Joel Chifunyise, Zimbabwe's most prolific playwright, was educated in Zambia,
    where he played an important part in the development of theatre. In Zimbabwe, he rose
    to the position of Permanent Secretary in the Ministry of Education, Sport and Culture. A
    notable African Resource Person in arts, culture, the media, cultural policy and intangible
    cultural heritage, he is co-founder and Chairman of CHIPAWO and Principal of the
    Zimbabwe Academy of Arts Education for Development.
2   This assessment relates to Zimbabwe in the period after independence. In pre-colonial
    society, theatre cultures did exist, even according to the criteria listed above. The fact that
    they do not today is an indication of the failure of the state to build a modern culture on
    the basis of earlier and indigenous forms.
3   This was mismanaged by ministry and artists and withdrawn. One infamous illustration of

the Ministry's attitude at that time was the comment made by the ministry official charged with administering the Norwegian assistance. He said to the present writer: 'You can't give money to artists. They will just squander it.'

4   It is true that it was still possible to perform in schools after the issuance of the circular by requesting and being given a letter from the Ministry or the relevant provincial educational authority. Not only was this time-consuming but it was also difficult owing to an attitude in government that such performances had no educational value and that being given permission to do so was a privilege. One such response, in this case from the Harare Regional Director to a request to perform an adaptation of Henrik Ibsen's *A Doll's House*, followed by teacher-led discussions on the gender, culture and law issues the play raised, was to demand a written justification as to why something of this kind should be allowed to take place in schools.

5   The National Theatre Organisation had collapsed a few years earlier and the only theatre associations still functioning in the country were the Zimbabwe Association of Community Theatre and the Zimbabwe Association of Theatre for Children and Young People. ZACT never revived and ZATCYP survived only tenuously, eking out a sparse and semi-reclusive existence.

6   The issue of sanctions against Zimbabwe is contested, with Europe and foreign media referring to them as targeted travel restrictions which only (at the time of writing) affect the President and those closely associated with ZANU-PF. This version of the truth is often inadvertently contradicted, even in the British Houses of Parliament and the United States Congress. There are many articles and analyses that prove that sanctions against Zimbabwe bite deeply into almost every aspect of the country's economic and cultural life. The present writer has encountered numerous examples in his own experience in the arts of the ways sanctions have disadvantaged and discriminated against Zimbabwean artists and arts organisations. For instance, a Zimbabwean organisation cannot operate or benefit from a Pay Pal facility on its or any other site. This is because, in the words of Pay Pal itself, Zimbabwe is 'a sanctioned country'.

7   Included in *African Theatre: Southern Africa*. [J.G. Ed.]

8   There are hopeful signs that changes can be made. Firstly, a National Theatre Association has been formed. Such an association has the potential to play an important part in advocating and educating. Secondly, a number of funders of theatre in Zimbabwe and the region that have hitherto almost funded festivals exclusively have come together and decided to change tack and invest in the 'proliferation' of theatre activity through support for performance outside festivals and outside large or capital cities. Investment will include the promotion of production, performance and touring , and of performance exchanges and collaborations. These will involve Zimbabwe and other countries in the region.

The Legacy of Festac '77
The challenge of the Nigerian National Theatre at Iganmu

AHMED YERIMA

'Nothing is more appropriate at this time in Black and African history than a re-discovery of those cultural and spiritual ties which bind together all Black and African peoples of the world over.' (Lt-General Olusegun Obasanjo, Head of State of Nigeria and Patron, 'Festac '77)

'This is indeed a moment when Black and African Peoples must intensify their efforts to posit their true identity in the contemporary world. This Festival represents an effort on our collective part to come together as a people so as to set in motion a new cultural awakening and cultural awareness in the Black and African world.' (Commander O.P. Fingesi, President of the International Festival Committee)

'My conclusion therefore, is as follows: if we wish the Second World Black and African Festival of Arts and Culture to be a success, as I do, we should consider its colloquium as the most important point which should define and illustrate black civilization and above all its spirit; that is, its culture, which is today the most powerful force in the universal civilization.' (H.E. President Leopold S. Senghor, President of Senegal)

The three statements quoted above were used to justify the organisation and the celebration of African culture and civilisation in a festival held in Nigeria during January/February 1977. The festival was known formally as 'The Second World Black and African Festival of Arts and Culture,' and informally as 'Festac '77'. Apart from the justifications given above, political reasons lay behind Nigeria's hosting of the festival. First, the 1970s was a decade of exploitation of resources that had resulted in Nigeria emerging as a major oil-producing nation. The government was benefitting from a huge increase in oil revenues at the time and the years were popularly referred to as the period of 'oil boom'. Second, Nigeria had recently emerged from a civil war, and had experienced a series of military coups and counter-coups which had shaken loyalties to Nigeria as a nation. Festac '77 gave the Military government, headed by Lt-General Olusegun Obasanjo, an opportunity to spend money on a cause that would make the country feel like a single political entity.

Third, Nigeria, having participated in the Dakar Festival of 1966, had observed the wider international benefits that could be derived from a cultural festival and was determined to live up to her reputation as the 'Giant of Africa'. The country wanted to celebrate through a festival that would be wider in scope, bigger, and reach deeper in terms of collective experience than the Dakar Festival. Since 1977, there has been no other festival of comparable size in Africa.

This chapter is concerned with one of the major legacies of Festac to the Nigerian people and the Nigerian nation – the National Theatre building. In 1977, Lagos was still the capital of Nigeria and because of this and its accessibility by air, sea and road, it was chosen as the venue for the Festival. A swampy area known as 'Iganmu' was selected as the site for the National Theatre because it was equidistant from Victoria Island and mainland Lagos.

The National Theatre building covers an area of 23,000 square metres and stands well over 31 metres high. Its shape has been compared to a saddle or, partly because of the Nigerian coat of arms over the main entrance, to a General's cap. Its design is based on a Bulgarian sports centre, but it is twice as big as the original. Rumour has it that the Minister of Information, Anthony Enahoro, saw the original on a visit to Bulgaria, liked the design, and requested that a much bigger version be built in Nigeria.

It must be made clear that at the time of the Festival, the building added to the grandeur of the event:

- It contained suitable public spaces, including the main Auditorium, which could seat 5,000, a large Conference/ Banquet Hall; two Cinemas, Exhibition Halls, and a variety of other rooms. In other words, it could accommodate several events and provide offices in the same building.
- There was space around the theatre for tents, and makeshift venues for outdoor programmes.
- The National Theatre also accommodated radio and television studios and recording facilities.
- The National Theatre car parks had space for 5,000 vehicles.
- There was an on-site police station to ensure a high level of security.
- There were rehearsal spaces.
- The whole building was embellished throughout with Nigerian artworks that transformed an architectural masterpiece into a museum and art gallery. The collection included works by some of Nigeria's foremost visual artists including Erhabor Emopkae, Yusuf Grillo, Lamidi Fakeye, and Bruce Onabrakpeya.

As a building, the National Theatre contributed to the success of Festac '77, but the real test was whether it would be a legacy of the festival. During Festac, the performances by the different nations reawakened old performance cultures and traditions among the Nigerian population, with their meanings and definitions of culture rediscovered. There was a new spirit abroad, a creative urge to perform, and the National Theatre became the ideal building for performances. This was clearly seen in relation to film-makers such as Ola Balogun, Ade Afolayan ('Ade Love'), Moses Olaiya ('Baba Sala') and Hubert Ogunde. The plush cinemas in the National Theatre proved ideal venues for premieres and short runs of the 35mm films they directed and produced

Stage performances also boomed. The Nigerian drama entry for Festac, *Langbodo*, drew on the skills and experience of a carefully marshalled team and was properly funded. Its example inspired both established playwrights such as Rasheed Gbadamosi, and Bode Osayin, and new ones, including Ben Tomoloju, Bassey Effiong, and Fred Agbeyegbe, all to set up their own drama groups and perform their works at the National Theatre. They were particularly encouraged by the National Theatre's Open Theatre Programme which ran from 1979 to 1990. For example Bode Osayin formed the Bode Osayin Arts Troupe and Akuro Theatre (which played *The Flood* and *Ogedengbe*); likewise, Ben Tomoloju, Kakaaki Production (*Jankariwo, Budiso* and *Mujemuje*); Fred Agbeyegbe, Ajo Productions (*The King Must Dance Naked*) and Bassey Effiong, Anansa Playhouse (*Things Fall Apart*).

The National Theatre was used as a venue for conferences, seminars and exhibitions, and it also provided office space for government parastatals that contributed to the cultural life of the nation. These included the National Gallery of Art (NGA), the National Council for Arts and Culture (NCAC) and the Centre for Black and African Arts and Civilization (CBAAC).

The significance of the National Theatre to the development of the art community was emphasised by Frank Aig-Imoukhuede, at one time the Federal Director of Culture, who wrote of the importance of the National Theatre to the development of creative and cultural activities in *A Handbook of Nigerian Culture* (1991). He pointed out that:

> Justification for this monumental undertaking by Nigeria (the National Theatre) goes beyond the immediate requirements of venues for FESTAC '77 to a long-felt need of providing a vigorous national base to the rich variety of artistic expressions both traditional and modern in Nigeria.

> The National Theatre now stands as an important rallying point for artists within Nigeria and a meeting point through bilateral exchange for artists from all parts of this globe to share and exchange experience with their Nigerian counterparts (119: 62).

Given this enthusiastic endorsement, it is necessary to examine why the position of the National Theatre as the main venue for theatrical activities in Nigeria was challenged in the years following Festac '77 and why it came to an end. There were, I think, five main reasons:

• Councils for Arts and Culture were established in each state and the National Festival for Arts and Culture (NAFEST) that rotated around the states was inaugurated. As a result, each state endeavoured to construct its own Cultural Centre and once these came into existence, less attention was paid to the National Theatre building in Lagos.

- The movement of the nation's capital from Lagos to Abuja meant that the attention of the government shifted. Because of this, funds voted for maintenance of and for activities at the National Theatre were drastically reduced.
- Other theatre venues were built or came back into use in Lagos. These included the MUSON Centre that was funded and constructed by the Music Society of Nigeria and the Glover Memorial Hall that was refurbished by the Lagos State Government. These venues offered alternatives to the National Theatre which suffered neglect.
- Fourthly, as the years passed, the sheer size and complexity of the National Theatre building created an increasing number of problems for both the users and administrators. A building that had been ideal for Festac could not be used to its full capacity in the period that followed. To tackle the situation the government set up a Management Committee headed by the Director-General of the Supervising Ministry, and including the Director of Culture and a Theatre Manager. The committee failed because the building could only function properly under the guidance of a group of professionals, theatre people who knew how to manage such a venture. They needed to plan programmes, maintain the building, prepare budgets, and attract potential investors. Without a team capable of performing all those tasks, the National Theatre as a venue lost its appeal and as a building started to decay.
- The fifth reason takes us back to Wole Soyinka's seminal thoughts on what constitutes a National Theatre and his observations about the mistakes made by African countries at the initial stage of wanting to build a National Theatre. Of the National Theatre in Kampala, in 1962, he wrote:

> The building itself is an embodiment of the general misconception of the word 'theatre'. Theatre, and especially a 'National Theatre', is never the lump of wood and mortar which architects splash on the landscape. We heard of the existence of a National Theatre (in Kampala) and ran to it full of joy and anticipation. We discovered that there was no theatre, there was nothing beyond a precious, attractive building in the town centre. But even within that narrow definition of the word, we had expected an architectural adventurousness - Kampala is, after all, a cosmopolis - so we felt justified in expecting from the theatre, not only a sense of local, but of international developments in the theatrical field. What we found was a doll's house, twin-brother to our own National Museum. There were cushioned spring-back seats - I approved this, having nothing against comfort - but it was disconcerting to find a miniature replica of a British provincial theatre... (Soyinka 1988: 3)

Despite this warning, Nigeria, like other African countries such as Ghana, made the mistake of replicating foreign monuments without thought to the African environment, the testing climate and the fallible maintenance culture.

Not sure how to run the National Theatre as a theatre, the Ministry of

Culture and Social Welfare – between 1975 and 1990 – moved in and used it as an administrative office block. At one point, the office of the minister, Mamman Anka, was actually in the building! The movement through the its spaces of large numbers of people who had no sense of the cultural and historical significance of the place soon took its toll on the fabric.

By 1991, fourteen years after it had come into use, no routine maintenance had been carried out on the building by the Bulgarians responsible or by anyone else – and it gradually ceased to function. The roof of the main auditorium was the first to crack, literally: water began to seep into the hall, and began to destroy the stage, the seats, the lighting equipment and the amplification system, even the priceless art works. Soon the crack in the auditorium roof spread to the other wings. The floor of the National Theatre became saturated, and a safety hazard. To prevent anyone being electrocuted, the mains supply lines were sealed off. Soon the central air-conditioning failed. This meant that the building – designed to operate in a temperate climate – became unbearably hot. Users described it as an 'oven', and there were no possibilities for adaptation: no openings could be made to allow for cross ventilation. The 'architectural masterpiece', the 'major legacy of Festac '77', was gradually becoming a structural nightmare, a millstone around the necks of theatre-lovers.

In 1991, in a bid to ameliorate the situation and 'save' the National Theatre, the Ministry of Culture, Youth and Social Welfare established the National Theatre and the National Troupe of Nigeria as separate parastatals. They were allocated distinct budgets and charged to run the National Theatre as a semi-professional state outfit. A management team of five was appointed, led by Jimmy Atte, a senior television producer, who became the first independent General Manager. However, the damage had been done and the theatre building was in a very sorry state.

In 1999, the return to power of Olusegun Obasanjo, who had opened the building and who I quoted at the beginning of this paper, was a turning point in the history of the National Theatre. When he had handed over to a civilian government in 1979, the Nigerian economy had been thriving and the infrastructure of the country was largely intact. For example, oil was flowing, the telephone system and the electricity generating system were operating, and the National Theatre was still 'new'. But by 1999 all had changed for the worse; the situation had deteriorated very seriously. In anger, Obasanjo adopted a 'privatisation' policy and put the National Theatre at the top of the 'For Sale' list – followed, it is interesting to note, by Tafawa Balewa Square, and the International Trade Fair Complex. To manage the sell-off Obasanjo set up the Bureau of Public Enterprises (BPE).

At about the same time, the relevant ministry appointed Femi Osofisan as the new General Manager of the National Theatre. The constraints on Osofisan were very limiting: he inherited Atte's management team, and a run-down theatre building filled with obsolete and broken equipment. There were no funds for repairs, and the frequent changes of ministers prevented Osofisan from taking decisive action. He was not even able to remove the National Theatre from the list in the hands of the Bureau of Public Enlightenment (BPE) – who lined up interested buyers. At the end of his four-year tenure of office, Osofisan returned to the University of Ibadan.

That the National Theatre of Nigeria exists today as a government building is due to two positive interventions. One was the singular effort of the Honourable Minister of Culture and Tourism, Frank Nchita Ogbuewu who broke protocol and challenged the decision to sell off the National Theatre. He refused to sign off the Power of Attorney that would have given BPE the power to 'concession' the National Theatre to the highest bidder. Instead, he demanded funds to make immediate repairs to the roof, to the panelled walls, to electrical fittings and equipment, and he undertook to recruit a new management team that would run the theatre at a profit. With the approval of the President in Council, he merged the National Theatre with the National Troupe of Nigeria, and, in 2006, he appointed the present writer Director-General of both companies.

The second positive intervention followed the coming to power of Umaru Yar'adua in 2007. His accession to the presidency coincided with a clamour for the cancellation of Obasanjo's privatisation policy. When he found that the National Theatre had been 'concessioned' to a company for the sum of N35 billion naira, he promptly stopped the process, had the circumstances investigated and found that the documentation was improper. Although the process has been stalled for some time, the National Theatre has not been delisted from the Federal Government list of properties to be 'concessioned by BPE.'

This action gave the relevant authorities in the Ministry of Tourism, Culture and National Orientation, the opportunity to further rehabilitate the building. Importantly, the Ministry and the Theatre management team won the confidence of the general artists' body, the stakeholders in the arts and culture sector, who were led by the veteran choir master Steve Rhodes. Other interested individuals included:

- Ejike Asiegbu of the Actors' Guild of Nigeria
- Greg Odutayo of the National Association of Nigerian Theatre Arts Practitioners (NANTAP)
- Husseini Shuaibu of the Dance Guild of Nigerian Dancers (GOND)
- Prince Jide Kosoko of the Association of Nigerian Theatre Arts Practitioners (ANTAP)
- Tolu Ajayi of the Society of Nigerian Artists (SNA)

Through anti-government marches, they called for a total cancellation of the concession order. The management then started on the repair and rehabilitation of the National Theatre building. The House of Assembly and Senate Committees on Culture and Tourism, then toured the National

Theatre and were persuaded that its rehabilitation required the provision of a larger budget and of funds to cover running costs. The present writer's management team was able to attract interested multi-nationals, including Coca Cola, Nigerian Breweries and Mr. Biggs (UTC) to identify with the efforts to restore the National Theatre and by 2009 most of the repair work required had been undertaken. Internally, within the merged structure of the National Theatre and National Troupe, the years between 2006 and 2009 were most productive in terms of theatrical productions for both organizations. Being a playwright/director, I was able to make facilities of the National Theatre available to the National Troupe. Staff worked together as a single production unit, and the new equipment and refurbished halls were made available for theatrical productions. Theatre groups were encouraged to show their productions at the National Theatre at reduced rental rates. Guest directors, such as Femi Osofisan (*Women of Owu*, 2007), Ben Tomoloju (2009) and Niji Akani (*A'etu*, 2008) were invited to direct plays.

At this point, I completed my tenure as Director-General and returned to university teaching. During his time as the relevant minister, Senator Jubril Bello Gada separated the National Theatre and National Troupe and appointed Mallam Kabir Yusuf and Martins Adaji to run the two organisations.

Conclusion

In looking back over the period covered here, the effect of the dilapidated state of what was once the 'pride of Nigeria' can, I think, be said to have affected the development of theatrical activities in Lagos and, more generally, of Nigeria in various ways. There were, however, other factors, including:

- The emergence of the Nollywood movie tradition in the late '80s, that served as a distraction and a source of income for artists who might have used the National Theatre for productions. The quick turn-around of shooting movies – often within two to four weeks - and the substantial payment to the artists offered advantages over the slower pace of theatrical productions, with auditions, casting, rehearsals, performances, and the lower financial rewards. Because of the challenge of Nollywood, there were fewer theatrical productions in Lagos.
- Insecurity in the country, especially in Lagos where armed robbery and kidnapping were on the increase, and contributed to the slowdown in the development of theatre during the late '70s and after. Because they felt threatened, prospective audiences stayed at home to watch television programmes or videos.
- Theatrical producers and drama groups were also inhibited by the escalating costs of putting on plays. The costs of renting rehearsal space, paying actors, making costumes and doing PR all increased dramatically

– partly, because of the levels set by Nollywood producers who were in competition for the same services.

- Venues such as the MUSON Center, Terrakulture, The Law School Hall, and the J.K. Randle Hall which emerged as alternatives to the National Theatre were purely commercial endeavours. Some did not have rehearsal spaces or facilities for technical run-throughs. Their rental rates were very high, and the producers could not guarantee breaking even after well-attended runs. The management teams at the National Theatre by contrast, and, as part of their responsibility to the society, had effectively subsidised theatre groups by charging less than the 'going-rate'. When the National Theatre was unavailable because it was in a dilapidated and unsafe state, groups incurred high costs or simply went out of business. There were fewer productions.

Outcomes

The National Theatre building constitutes an ambiguous part of our national heritage. First of all, it was a major legacy of Festac '77, it became an 'icon', 'a brand' and an 'inspiration' to generate creative development in the immediate post-Festac period. It became a symbol of excellence and pride.

Sadly, it is difficult to separate the later, 'dark' period of the National Theatre from the slow-down in the development of theatre in Lagos. The hope is that the government and the people of Nigeria will realise the need for the National Theatre and continue to restore it to full operation.

Every country must have a National Theatre, a house of culture, which celebrates the heritage of its owners and shares their national creative heritage with the new globalised world. It is then that African countries, who are always quick to build or replicate National Theatres, will know that maintenance and good administration of such structures will serve generations yet unborn.

BIBLIOGRAPHY

Akande, Victor (2010) *Hazy Pictures: The Arts, Business and Politics of The Nigerian Motion Picture Industry*, Ibadan: Kraft Books.

Aig-Imoukhuede, Frank. (1991) A *Handbook of Nigerian Culture*, Lagos: Dept of Culture.

Dasylva, Ademola. (2003) *Dapo Adelugba on Theatre Practice in Nigeria*, (interview) Ibadan: Ibadan Cultural Studies Group, University of Ibadan.

Festac '77 (1977) London: Africa Journal Limited.

Decree No. 47 National Theatre and the National Troupe Board Decree 1991 of The Federal Republic of Nigeria.

Soyinka, Wole. 'Towards A True Theatre' in *Art, Dialogue & Outrage: Essays on Literature and Culture*. (1988) (ed) by Biodun Jeyifo. Ibadan: New Horn Press.

Festac, Month by Month
& Soyinka's Involvement

JAMES GIBBS

One way in to appreciate the issues raised and impact of Festac '77 is through coverage in the Nigerian press, and the references that Wole Soyinka has subsequently made to the festival. In the paragraphs and pages below, significant elements are identified and relevant references are listed. From them it emerges that, in the run-up to Festac, there were delays and uncertainties. There was, for example, a concern about what Festac was celebrating, and how this related to ideas of, for example, progress and 'primitivity'. Beside this discussion there was a division that can be polarised in the positions taken by Leopold Senghor and Obafemi Awolowo, and into which can be read the influence of different experiences of colonialism and of the grounds on which the anti-colonial struggle was being waged. As the opening of Festival approached, rifts developed or widened. There were tensions between Nigeria and countries that had taken different political routes, such as Guinea, and there was concern about who should contribute under the banner of the 'Black and African World'. While international negotiations on these topics were taking place, anxiety was expressed about domestic issues such as the marginalisation of creative Nigerians. In the middle of this, and having just published a prison memoir in which he 'named names', Wole Soyinka returned to Nigeria from self-exile. An opponent of (most) military rulers and robustly critical of some of those involved in the Festival, Soyinka nonetheless became involved with the International Committee responsible for the event. Inevitably, in view of his Ogunian temperament, he contributed to controversies around it.

As frequently happens with big budget government projects, particularly but, of course, not exclusively, in Nigeria, there were some who pursued their own interests. In addition, there were also critics of various persuasions, including the profoundly cynical, who cast aspersions on the motives of anyone who became involved with the Festival.

The extent of Soyinka's involvement is not easy to measure. While he undertook a variety of tasks on behalf of those organising the Festival and delivered a public lecture at the colloquium on Black Civilisation and

22

Education, he also used the power of resignation to exert leverage and eventually distanced himself from the event. The newspaper articles itemised below make it clear that he travelled, liaised and negotiated in the weeks before the Festival, and that during it he relished welcoming Festivaliers to Nigeria and to his mother's table.

After the Festival ended, on 12 February 1977, he pondered the lessons to be learned from it and occasionally referred to them. The shortcomings he became aware of do not seem to have shaken his conviction that some good can come out of well organised festivals. His involvement with other Festivals, notably his commitment to the Lagos Black Heritage Festivals during April 2012, speaks of a continuing recognition of the value of festivals.

The partly annotated bibliography below lists key documents in chronological sequence and challenges readers to assess the significance of reports. The entries are from a variety of sources including the Nigerian press. The tone and political orientation of each publication is distinctive and positions can sometimes be deduced. The following Nigerian publications are referred to: *Daily Times* (*DT*), *Daily Sketch* (*DS*), *The Guardian*, *The Nigerian Tribune* (*NT*), *Punch, Sunday Concord* (*SC*) and *The Vanguard*.

Readers may be unfamiliar with those mentioned and the following 'key' may be of use. Reference is made to heads of state: Olusegun Obasanjo (Nigeria) and Leopold Senghor (Senegal); Yoruba political leaders: Obafemi Awolowo ('Awo'), and Anthony Enahoro, along with Awo's poet/ 'secretary' Odia Ofeimun, and to members of the Nigerian military regime: Promise Fingesi, Christopher Oluwole Rotimi and Paul C. Tarfa. The following were among the distinguished 'voices' in Nigeria's intellectual and creative community: Ayo Bankole, Hubert Ogunde, Kole Omotosho/ Omotoso, and Sonny Oti.

1973
'How are we preparing for (Festac)' *DT*, 22 2 73.
'Festac Theatre and Cultural Complex to cost N 24million – Festac village to house 1 mil visitors' *DT*, 16 5 73.

1975
'I beg to disagree. Sir.' *DT*, 21 2 75. (Advocates cutbacks to Festac's expenditure but supports the event. Awo, it seems, had said the Festival would look as if "we want to go backward simply because we don't know how to go forward." Regarding the opinion of European observers, Awo is quoted as saying: "They are interested in watching us demonstrate our primitivity … we should continue to improve in technology know how and not be showing the world how primitive we are."

'It's not too late to settle with musicians', Segun Adelugba. *DT*, 19 6 75. (Adelugba, who chronicled events relating to the Festival in some detail, refers to Festac's issues with Guinea and points out that local musicians had not been fully involved. The second point was taken up in 'Festac preparations … a one-man show – artists Sonny Oti, Ayo Bankole etc. object', *DT*, 3 7 75.)

DT, 5 7 75. (Kole Omotosho, back from Accra, reported that the claims of Swahili to be the *lingua franca* for Africa were being advanced there. Advised that Festac should note.)

'It's an ego trip', Odei Ofeimun, *DT*, 11 1 76. (This 'Anti Rotimi and pro Awolowo' piece by Awo's secretary asks: 'Do we need a Festival to achieve the aims of Festac?' Ofeimun's answer is that (only) a conference is needed.)

'Massive Boycott Threatens Festac', *DT* 5 12 75. (Refers to the threat of a Senegalese boycott 'should any non-black community be allowed to participate in the Colloquium'. Target seems to be 'Arab Africans'.)

'Soyinka returns', *DT*, 20 12 75. (Soyinka, returning home after some three years in self-exile, said he was convinced that Obasanjo's Government had popular support. He indicated his intention to make contact with Commander Promise Fingesi who was President of the International Festival Committee.)

1976
'Soyinka's Airport ordeal', *DT*, 10 5 76. (It seems that on 2 April Soyinka had been searched at Murtala Mohammed Airport and had run the risk of missing his plane. It transpired that, since returning to Nigeria, he had been in and out of the country three times. He was reported to have said: 'I have to travel because of Festac. … I am in addition engaged in a cultural survey involving most of West Africa over the next six months.' The projects, he maintained, were of more importance to others than to himself and he was quoted as saying: 'My professional geography does not embrace only Nigeria but the African continent and beyond.')

'2 bungled Festac funds', *DT*, 14 May 1976. (Chief Anthony Enahoro was 'found guilty of exploiting his connection with the Festival to his personal and financial advantage'.)

'Festac, a critical view', *DS* 1 10 76, pp. 5 and 20. (Segun Adelugba drew attention to confusion about the festival, and wrote about the exclusion of theatre legend Ogunde and others like him. Advocated full preparations.)

'Is Wole with Festac or Senghor', *Punch*, 2 11 76, p. 11. (Includes the following: 'It is now rumoured that Prof. Soyinka, who is a close friend of President Senghor, has resigned his appointment as he has been asked by the Senegalese Government to come over and direct a play…. A top official in the Festac Secretariat summed up: 'Don't mind the Prof. Instead of saying he wants to go and direct his play in Senegal, he was giving flimsy reasons for leaving the Festac.')

'Lagos motorists are warned: Horsewhip stays', *Punch*, 12 11 76, p. 1. (Paul C. Tarfa, Chairman of Operation Ease Traffic Committee, said 'Since the horse-whip appeared on the roads, drinking habits have been considerably more civilised.' 3. The whip was used to 'discipline motorists'.)

'Ogunde not in FESTAC', *Punch*, 2 12 76. (Apparently, having been side-lined by Festac, Ogunde planned an alternative 'Ogunde Festival' in '77.)

Omotos(h)o, Kole. 'The Question of Festac Colloquium', *DT*, 9 12 76. (Contributing to the discussion about race and representation at Festac, Omotoso, a student of Arabic, pointed out that Africans and Arabs had been brought close together by the Anti-Apartheid struggle and the oil crisis.)

Soyinka gave a Press Conference at the end of 1976. Coverage in the press included:

'UNWAP Press Conference at Ikoyi Hotel', *NT*, 30 12 76. (Reported that 'Dr Soyinka stressed that no government can be held to act honestly, loyally and responsibly to the people if it uses any tactics whatever to keep out of this gathering (Festac) artists and intellectuals who have anything of value to contribute to the black and African peoples in their continuing search for total liberation of creative fulfilment.' Soyinka regretted that the International Secretariat of Festac had become 'a strutting place for third rate diplomats whose main concern was to promote the specific outlook of individual leaders or to grind Festac to a halt'. It may be noted in passing that confrontational language of this kind has been a recurring feature of Soyinka's comportment as a controversialist from student days on and that it 'burns boats' as far as fruitful dialogue is concerned. On his position regarding the International Secretariat of Festac, he said: 'Demands are still made on me to which I respond wherever possible.' The following was among the reports of the Press Conference:

- 'Soyinka urges FMG', *DS*, 31 12 76, p. 4. (Reported that, at a special briefing, Soyinka appealed to Obasanjo to stop the bureaucracy of the 'International Secretariat of Festac'. Article includes the following statement: 'Nigeria will not buy any ideological cant which is all too often transparent guise for parochial power conflicts and … enmities.' Also quoted a reference to 'third rate diplomats and leaders blinded by their personal enmity with other African peoples'.)

22 January 1977

Soyinka delivered a paper entitled 'The Scholar in African Society' at the Festival Colloquium. With Soyinka described as 'Secretary-General' of the 'Union of Writers of the African People, Ile-Ife, Nigeria', this was reproduced in Volume 1 of the Colloquium Proceedings published by the Federal Military Government of Nigeria. Soyinka began by paying his 'sincere compliments to the Nigerian Government for the stand it has taken over the principles and aspirations of this Colloquium'. He then described that stand as being 'one of dynamic objectivity' and, in a manner that veered from the ironic to the genuine and invited comparison with various kinds of pyrotechnics, he addressed a number of issues relating to the organisation of the Festival. He mentioned, for example, the rejection of the paper submitted by Abdias do Nascimento, the recent death of the Pio Zimiru, Director of the Colloquium, and the historical-linguistic context in which the meeting was being held. Vivid language and bold positions ensured the contribution was given full attention and generated a response. For example, Soyinka defined a 'black scholar (as) a historicized machine for chewing up the carcass of knowledge to regenerate mortar for social reconstruction', and he shared his 'discovery' that 'a great deal of the ideological steam which erupts from time to time between scholars, writers, politicians but most especially heads of state on this continent is really not from this continent at all but from some very deep geysers, underground boiling pools located' in other continents and countries. Soyinka recycled trenchant observations from various documents, and rehearsed statements he had made about Negritude. In characteristically combative mode he responded to suggestions that he had 'sold out' on this matter. ('I have heard talk of a total sell-out of principles and beliefs.') This dimension draws attention to the value of recognising Soyinka as pugilist, or perhaps chess player, and the absolute necessity of placing his statements in context.

He has since made a number of comments that provide an indication of his activities during Festac '77 and of the lessons he learned from the event. They include the following:

1983
'Report on the funeral of Mrs Eniola Soyinka', *SC*, 01 05 83. ('EssBee' reported that during Festac Mrs Soyinka held open-house in Ebute Meta and that Soyinka sent 'droves' of foreign visitors to his mother's table for, according to him, 'an antidote to the disgusting taste which Festac was leaving in everybody's mouth'.)

1988
'The Wasted Generation The Real Wasters', *The Guardian* (Lagos), c.1520 August 1988. (Also in *DT*, August 18 and 19. This was a response to Bode Sowande's 'Open Letter to Soyinka', *Vanguard* (Lagos), 5 May. Soyinka picked up the title from an earlier article, and considered 'Wasters' to be those who destroy, kill, and condemn by spreading rumours. Soyinka referred to an episode at the time of Festac concerning an American's library. It was rumoured that Soyinka was trying to get a percentage on the purchase price. This I see as an example of 'wasting' by defaming, by always assuming that people are motived by self-interest.)

1991
'I'll Andrew if...,' *African Concord* (Lagos), 14 October 1991, 3748. (Introduced as follows: 'Soyinka, forthright as ever, speaks on Nigeria's problems', the article includes Soyinka's claim that he had 'saved Festac' for Obasanjo. This claim refers, I think, to the 'shuttle diplomacy' he was engaged in between Lagos and Dakar.)

1992
In Washington for an international conference on Culture and Development in Africa, Soyinka presented a paper entitled 'Culture, Memory and Development'. In it he referred to his experience during Festac of trying to organise a display of books and an architectural exhibition through which planners would be exposed to alternatives to 'perpendicularism ' (i.e. skyscrapers). Soyinka recommended that 'small was beautiful', and wanted architecture to be on the human scale. Clearly he felt that forces were mobilised to resist the alternatives he was trying to put forward.)

I referred above to the Lagos Black Heritage Festival that Soyinka has been involved with. While this event has been quite extensively covered by sources available on the internet, and has attracted some controversy, Soyinka's commitment to it indicates his recognition of the value of modest-scale festivals.

The Dakar Festivals of 1966 & 2010

YATMA DIEYE

It is not easy to compare the 1966 Festival held in Dakar with that held in 2011, but a glance at the programmes offered and of the people involved immediately shows the difference. Briefly, the organisers of the 2010 Festival were unable to find good actors to fill the programmes, and could not match the well-known artists and the great men of culture who had been involved in the 1966 edition.

This time the organisation was poor. During the second festival, people were often uncertain when and where events were going to take place. When you asked people about what was going on, the answer would invariably be: 'Nothing new is happening.'

Some say that the confusion was created because those in charge of the organisation of the event had nothing to do with culture. Dissatisfaction with the administration continues and up till now (May 2011) many of those employed during the festival have still not been paid and are running after their money.

Very sadly, the population as a whole did not feel involved in the recent festival. The general opinion was that the scheduling was poor – since it was held at a time when people had other, more basic concerns, including food and electricity. As the Latin expression goes: 'Primum vivere' (live first ... philosophise later). All this makes me think that our people are worryingly and unconsciously sliding towards some kind of philistinism.

Incidentally, the role of Kwame Kwei Armah, who has been mentioned as being a staunch supporter of Fesman 2, has come in for criticism since some suspect him of conniving with the authorities in their desperate effort to suggest the festival was a success. It is true that many young people attended the street concerts, but they were there simply for lack of anything better to do. Cameroonian musician Manu Dibango was one of those who was disenchanted and expressed his opinion of the Festival by referring to it as 'Festival Mondial des Arts Maigres', which can be taken to suggest that he though the claims made for the festival were exaggerated (*maigre* – thin, lean, meagre. J.G. Ed.).

I conclude these comments with an anecdote showing the very great extent to which the population was involved in the first Dakar festival. Two months before the event, there were rumours that workers would get a salary advance in order to participate fully in the festival. However, the government denied these reports, and the disappointed workers started protesting with graffiti. The favourite slogan was: 'No advance, No festival.' Orders were then given to arrest anyone found defacing walls. One day, a policeman caught a young man preparing to do so and was about to take him to the police station when he paused and asked the young man what he was going to write. When the reply was 'No advance, No festival', the policemen released the young artist with the words: 'OK go ahead, you can write.'

WEBOGRAPHY

See Exprimant sa Deception sur Radio France Internationale: Manu Dibango dénonce l'inorganisation http://senegal.senego.com/exprimant-sa-deception-sur-radio-france-internationale-manu-dibango-dénonce-l'inorganisation/ Accessed 2 June 2011.

African Renaissance between Rhetoric & the Aesthetics of Extravagance

FESMAN 2010 – Entrapped in Textuality

AMY NIANG

The Third Festival of Black Arts (FESMAN) held between December 10 and 31, 2010, was announced as heralding a Renaissance of Africa and its Diaspora, through an aesthetic embrace and a celebration of its creativity and its diverse identity. It was a projective extension of a vast programme of revival and unity encompassed in the ambitious New Partnership for African Development (NEPAD) initiative. President Abdoulaye Wade, initiator of the festival, was one of the proponents of NEPAD, along with Olusegun Obasanjo (Nigeria), Thabo Mbeki (South Africa) and Abdelaziz Bouteflika (Algeria). However, Wade's brand of renaissance is a product of delirium. It is a one-man show ripped out of the temporal frame of the African revival movement that enjoins moderation, lucidity and self-restraint as a sign of and in the service of progress. Wade's brand of renaissance is a belaboured concept emptied of its essence, and laid bare in its superfluity: a form of renaissance as posture which departs in so many ways from African Renaissance as praxis.

But we have to look beyond Wade's tendencies and tastes for extravaganza, and his desperate, reductivist attempts to leave his name to posterity. We have to be able to look at the FESMAN not only as a depraved extension of his excessive quest for recognition. In many ways, the works displayed in Dakar, by their sheer quality and diversity, made the festival a unique artistic moment during which ordinary people had access to the greatest works of art produced in all four corners of the globe, and to a pool of scientific, artistic and intellectual creations.

At its best, the festival was a unique moment of pure art, of Pan-African communion, during which time was frozen to let African genius shine and radiate to the rest of the world. It was a combination of great performances, and, at times, fruitful intellectual discussions and original exhibitions. It is doubtful, however, that the festival achieved its stated aim which was, in the words of President Wade to 'convey a new vision of Africa as free, proud, creative and optimistic'.

Another aim of the festival was to stage Black art as defined not narrowly by skin colour but by universal sensibilities that speak to African experiences of the world and of self. It was a moment of dialogue between Africa and itself, Africa and its children in Brazil, in Asia, Europe and America, and finally, it was an encounter between Africa and the world in which art, in its multiple tones and forms, was the sole idiom of exchange.

Everyday life as comedy, the festival as a caricature

As the dust settled upon what was a brief but intense moment of pan-African celebration, a lingering moral question remained. The context of the Festival was Senegal, a nation in which over half the population is engaged in a daily struggle to survive, in which there are sporadic and prolonged power-cuts, in which over 30% of youths are unemployed and wander about dreaming of escape from a bleak future by travelling to distant places by sea, air or any other means. It is a land in which peasants despair of laying their hands on the precious seeds that will ensure food for their families, and in which ignorance has increased while knowledge has declined. The question is 'Can this nation, Senegal, afford to indulge in a grandiose and very expensive extravaganza the sole purpose of which – beyond the rhetoric of renaissance – is to inflate the overblown ego of a president?' The purpose of the FESMAN was that President Wade was desperate to create a legacy, to leave something, anything, to posterity. He was prepared to do this at the risk of jeopardizing the present.

During the three weeks it lasted, the FESMAN rocked the country across hundreds of venues in Dakar, St Louis, Tubab Dialao, Rufisque and many other places. Foreign visitors got a real treat of sights, sounds and vibrations. However, despite thousands of young people gathering in stadia and squares to have a chance to see and hear famous artists from all over the world, the general attitude towards the festival ranged from indifference to contempt. For many Senegalese, the festival was a metaphor for a comedy of a very peculiar kind, 'The Wade Show', in which they had been unwilling actors for many years.

On the one hand, as a symbolic moment, the festival-drama succeeded in joining together the fragments of a disintegrated entity, Africa, its scattered children, its diasporas. On the other hand, the element of desire, intended to motivate the audience's subscription to the dramatic account, was utterly absent. Thus, unlike in typical artistic representations, this particular kind of drama was a source of blunt and dissonant disengagement between actors and audience, meaning and form, government and governed.

Ordinary people felt alienated from the festival partly because it had been put off so many times. Initially it was announced that the festival would be held near the beginning of Wade's term of office but it was postponed and postponed, and people lost confidence that they would make any contribution to the unpopular, 'popular' event. Many came to consider it a case of vulgarity, extravagance and of misjudged priorities; they saw art or what was masquerading as art laying siege to an unwilling city.

During the years they had been waiting for the festival, ordinary people had become increasingly aware of the prevalence of injustices. These injustices have not simply been ignored by those who govern; they have actually been caused or exacerbated by the irresponsible conduct of those in authority. People have come to locate the causes of their wretched and debased lives in the gross disparity between poor and rich that characterises Senegalese society.

A legacy by all means: a man's obsession with posterity

The FESMAN was a vivid 'temporary space' in which a genuine passion for art underpinned a controversial endeavour. During the celebrations, artistic creativity and the lingering remnants of a Pan-African nationalism were structured in discourses, painted on canvases and expressed in a whole variety of formats. For the duration of the festival, people were dazzled, but the event lacked any commitment to bettering the conditions of ordinary Africans and simply embodied the politics of self-aggrandizement.

The personal dimension of the rationale behind the festival cannot be denied. The festival was the result of one man's unrelenting quest for recognition rather than about celebrating African Renaissance. Wade's particular obsession is a desire to outshine his predecessors and he is determined to do this by leaving a mark on history. For that reason, his government has constantly been mobilised to fulfil the many visions of a self-proclaimed prophet whose 'cultural projects' include the ambitious 'Seven Wonders', a 10-hectare (27-acre) zone that includes the National Theatre, a School of Architecture, a Museum of African History, a National Library, a Museum of Art, a School of Art and a Concert Hall. However, his legacy to posterity might be no more than a historic incongruity, in other words the pillaging of scarce resources to fund a number of trivial enterprises. As the Marquis de Sade ventures in *Histoire de Juliette ou les Prospérités du Vice* '[f]oolish would be the head of state who would not have his pleasures paid for by the state; and what does the misery of people matter to us, provided that our passions are satisfied?'

Wade's obsession finds a focus in the political, intellectual and cultural legacy of Leopold Sedar Senghor, first President of post-colonial Senegal. Wade has a chip on his shoulder since he has neither Senghor's record nor his eminence. Senghor was an accomplished man of letters, a poet, a philosopher and a cultural theorist who sometimes felt his political duties to be too burdensome. For him, African Renaissance was a multidimensional concept that encompassed intellectual pursuit and emotional maturity with regards to Africa's past and present tribulations; it rescued pride lost in a history of self-rejection and low self-esteem. It was a beautiful and a much desired concept. The poet-president's passion for culture was translated into institutions embodying the country's cultural life and reflecting its ethnic diversity: the Ensemble Instrumental, the Ballet National du Sénéga' and the Théâtre National du Sénégal. Senghor's commitment to, and his legacy in, the promotion of art has been described and analysed by Elizabeth Harney (2004), Tracy Snipe (2010), and Abdou Sylla (1998). Since Senghor, theatres and festivals have been promoted throughout the country. For example, the Daniel Sorano National Theatre, built in 1965, was the brainchild of Senghor, and has welcomed world famous performers including James Brown, Michael Jackson, Hugh Masekela, Miriam Makeba, Salif Keita and Fela Kuti. The building has recently been renovated with a $36 million Chinese investment, and is now a six-storey Grand Theatre, arguably the largest structure of its kind on the continent. However, President's Wade's appropriation of it has deprived Senghor's vision of an historical moment at which Africa met her scattered self and reported back to the world through the universal language of art.

In the work of Senghor, that was supplemented by the contributions of Aimé Césaire, Negritude was a meaningful construct that was intended to build upon the common identity of Africa's children across the world in order to showcase their creativity in diversity and complexity. It also revealed the universal dimension of African artistic forms. Senghor was the driving force behind the First World Festival of Negro Arts in Dakar in 1966 in a particular historical context. During the Sixties, much of Africa was emerging from colonial oppression, but there were still areas on the continent and throughout the world where oppression persisted. In South Africa, for example, the black majority was still being stifled by a racist system of government; in the Portuguese colonies of Mozambique, Guinea Bissau, Cape Verde and Angola, Africans were denied the most basic rights to human dignity and freedom, and in the United States the nascent civil rights movements was only beginning to confront racial discrimination and segregation.

For Senghor, the 1966 Dakar Festival was meant to celebrate 'freedom regained, and the dawn of a new time'; it was to usher in a 'new humanism', one that transcended race, language, culture, and the anguish of racism. Such a humanist vision was reflected in the cosmopolitan, interactive atmosphere that prevailed throughout the festival, and in the unique intellectual and cultural exchanges. These were fostered by participants such as Alvin Ailey, Josephine Baker, Aimé Césaire, Duke Ellington, Langston Hughes, and André Malraux. In 1977, Nigeria, the 'Guest of Honour' in Dakar, hosted FESTAC, which offered an amazing range of performances. Held during a time of oil-boom, FESTAC was seen by Andrew Apter (2005) and others as supporting Nigeria's claim to be a great continental power.

Almost fifty years after the first festival, it would seem quite fitting that Africa should celebrate its renaissance along with its diverse and in many ways more mature Diaspora: significantly, Brazil was the 'Guest of Honour' in the Dakar Festival, 2010. The celebration of African renaissance was to crown a year full of celebrations across the continent, the highlight of which was the Soccer World Cup held in South Africa. Artistically, and more so symbolically, the festival achieved a unique historical success: it brought together over 6,000 artists from Africa and the Diaspora representing a variety of disciplines, including theatre, traditional and visual arts, photography, dance, urban design, architecture, literature, music, craft, science and technology.

Ten years of a one-man show

However, the historical context for the third festival was particularly difficult. There had been the public uproar about the Monument de la Renaissance Africaine and this rumbled on. To many in Senegal, the monument is an expensive celebration of an abstract concept; ordinary people cannot relate to it; and as an investment in a particular signifier it is also a blatant instrument (Niang 2010). Firstly, the Senegalese economy has been stagnant for the past few years partly because of an extraordinary crisis in the energy sector. Small businesses have been particularly badly affected: for example, tailors, carpenters, mechanics, welders, small traders, and caterers have suffered from power cuts. The national economy has been sluggish and regressive, the national mood has been depressed and investors have not been attracted. In the 2009-2010 Report prepared by the World Economic Forum, Senegal was ranked 113th out of 133 countries! According to government statistics at this time, over a billion pounds (£1,000 million) had been injected into the energy sector over a ten-year period. The only sign of improvement came during the 2010 Festival when the electricity company managed to ensure a steady supply of power to the city centre and to the different venues.

Secondly, the agricultural sector has been severely neglected under the administration of President Wade. Peasants have come to dread the wet season when, emerging from a long lean period, they wait with extreme anguish for seeds that might not come because economic operators and other intermediaries struggle to get paid by the government. Agriculture, particularly the cultivation of groundnuts, remains the industrial base of the country, with over 60% of the population depending on it, either directly or indirectly. Farmers are engaged in an unending struggle for survival, when crucial payments and other funding are taken away, diverted towards what they perceive to be wasteful, inessential, and excessive expenditure. Inevitably, they see their lives as an unending drama and the very activity of farming an absolute inanity (Sy 2010).

Thirdly, the country has been experiencing profound 'social crises': key areas, namely health, education and employment, have been neglected and many live in raw misery. The University of Dakar, once a regional academic centre of excellence that produced numerous intellectuals and professionals, has become an overcrowded institution, attempting to cope with over 60,000 students. Some have resorted to burning buses and taking office workers hostage in order to get their monthly allowances. The educational system was one of the few areas where the country fared well after independence: it has been utterly destroyed, along with its reputation for quality training of valuable human resources. Long gone are the days when education and culture were the subject of serious national debates and developments. During the 1990s, the National Conventions of education instituted, as, Momar Coumba Diop and Mamadou Diouf have shown, a National Cultural Charter which was in many ways President Diouf's translation of Senghor's Negritude. Despite many shortcomings in their implementation, these reforms contributed to reviving a troubled sector. The Charter may have had more impact than the 40% of the national budget which President Wade claims to inject, annually, into education.

Finally, in the past four years, a politico-legal entanglement has undermined any meaningful public debate. It has to do, on the one hand, with the legality of President Wade's candidacy in the 2012 elections, and, on the other, with his widely criticised monarchical project in favour of his son. The dissolution of state by a family has struck a very sensitive cord in the imagination of ordinary Senegalese. The organisation of the festival itself was partially entrusted to the president's daughter. This nomination came after the scandal associated with the President's son, Karim Karim Wade, and the National Agency for the Organisation of the Islamic Conference (ANOCI) set up to improve the roads in preparation for the conference. Karim Karim Wade is a chip off the old block, and, at the time of writing, (see author's article, *Pambazuka News* June 2011), combines four different portfolios in one. He controls about 45% of the state budget and has been dubbed 'Minister of Land, Earth, Sea and Sky'.

Wade came to power in 2000 after 26 years in opposition. He arrived with considerable popular support and with the backing of a coalition of centre and left parties. There were tremendous expectations of the potential benefits of a new mode of governance in which development policies would figure prominently. Hopes have been dashed and the country has had to endure the 'Wade Formula' - a mixture of callous indifference to the plight of the destitute and a marked tendency for sensational announcements of new 'plans', 'programmes', 'protocols', 'technologies' and other 'revolutions'. These have not been translated into coherent policies. Within a couple of years of his election, Wade became a dictatorial, erratic, clanist leader. He had a million visions and dreams but did not put in place a single, coherent programme of social or economic governance. He made no effort to shore up democratic gains and he did not try to preserve a social contract based upon a balance between the requirements of the politico-legal apparatus of a republic and the contribution of traditional social forces. Money has been central to his style of governance, consistent with his view that everything, including votes and popular support for his son could be bought.

Then there's the thorny issue of the cost of the festival; according to some estimates, including those of Assane Mbaye in a newspaper article of December 2010, it ran to £52,000,000, most of which came from the Senegalese taxpayer. Following the ANOCI scandal in which it was alleged by investigative journalist Abdou L Coulibaly that the sum involved was over £330 million, the FESMAN fuelled constitutional, structural tensions within Senegalese society, and prompted critical engagement with the structures of authority of the Wade government. To many observers, the festival embodied the culmination of a series of gratuitous excesses during Wade's controversial tenure. It represented the lowest point reached in the tortured history of 'post-alternance' Senegal, that is to say of the period following 19 March 2000 when Abdoulaye Wade defeated Abdou Diouf in a popular movement to end the latter's twenty-year rule. It provided a metaphor for the hypnotic capacity of mega-events to breed a sense of achievement in a ruling elite resolutely turned outward and collectively obsessed with power and wealth.

Of art and injustices

In addition to the dubious basis of its organisation, the FESMAN prompts questions about the way it was delivered and how it was funded. Such facts have yet to be made public, but it is clear, that, contrary to what the government likes to claim, the festival was neither 'commissioned' by the African Union (AU), nor financed by it. It was mostly paid for by the Senegalese taxpayer – or through loans that will take years to repay.

Particular questions must be raised about the participation of artists from the Diaspora whose Pan-African commitment was seriously tested by the financial-legal imbroglio that led to their works being held by an arts handling company because of an invoice that had not been settled by the Senegalese authorities. Matters reached a new level on 4 August, 2011, when Cape Town-based artist Johann van der Schijff launched a petition against the President of Senegal, his daughter Sindiély Wade, Deputy Director of the Festival, and ten other administrators and organisers of the FESMAN. The petition asked for the return of works by over a hundred artists and designers that were being held uninsured by LP Art, the Paris-based fine art transporters. Many diasporian artists had been deeply moved by Wade's vision of a Black cultural revival. They had been galvanised into action and responded to his call for 'Africans, all the sons and daughters of the Diaspora, all my fellow citizens, all the partners that are ready to walk by our side, all States, all international organizations, foundations, firms.... to make.... a shining success of this Festival, and for the rise of a new Africa.' They had sent their work to be displayed at a landmark Exhibition of Contemporary African and Diaspora Art, then found that property had been impounded in a dispute over a payment for which they had no responsibility. The economic loss and distress to the artists was enormous and pushed some to consider extreme measures. For example, Yinka Shonibare threatened to relinquish the National Order of the Lion medal given him by President Wade if the works were not returned at once. The artists' bitter dissatisfaction about their treatment centred particularly on the unfulfilled promises that they regarded as reflecting a disrespectful attitude towards them. Their petition included the following: 'The current unresolved situation does lasting harm to the aspirations of the spirit of African Revival and Black Pride the festival claimed to promote – not only amongst the participating designers and artists but also to the wider creative and artistic community.'

At the time of writing (2011), this latest episode in the FESMAN saga threatens to drag on for many years. It merely confirms that original complaints and criticisms were well-founded. The Festival was inadequately planned and costed; it demonstrably failed to present an Africa that is conscious, alive and not in a woeful condition.

Conclusion

Given the relatively negative record of President Wade's tenure many Senegalese are not surprised about what has happened and regard the FESMAN extravaganza as a synecdoche for the wasteful ways of the Wade's 10-year administration.

I readily acknowledge that the FESMAN offered moments of pure artistic insight; it was rich in variety and wide in scope. The opening ceremony, for example, welcomed over a thousand artists, including Baaba Maal, Toumani Diabaté, Wyclef Jean, Carlinhos Brown, Youssou N'Dour, and Angélique Kidjo, who performed before 40,000 amazed and delighted people.

The FESMAN meant that I was able to see the bones of Lucy, the three million year-old fossil hominid discovered in Ethiopia, which was brought to Senegal and exhibited at the National Museum. This exhibit showed that there were organisers who intended that the Festival would offer the public rare opportunities, wonderful experiences and access to the hidden artistic, cultural, scientific and intellectual gems of Africa.

However, on balance, and recognising the grave socio-economic situation, the FESMAN caused more frustration than jubilation. As a colleague of mine, A. Diop, reflected in May 2011: '[W]e have once again been at the mercy of the whims of our eccentric president, in the form of a "fête-ssivalé" [it was] painfully experienced in our very flesh; and we were mostly served with "tanebeer"' – night dancing sessions to the beat of drums. This was a way of saying that the festival was merely a noisy carnival.

BIBLIOGRAPHY

Apter, Andrew (2005) *The Pan-African Nation: Oil and the Spectacle of Culture in Nigeria*, Chicago: University of Chicago Press.

Coulibaly, A. L. (2009) *Contes et Mécomptes de l'Anoc: Le Scandale du Siècle*, Dakar and Paris: Harmattan and Sentinelles.

De Jong, Ferdinand and Foucher, Vincent (2010) 'La Tragédie du Roi Abdoulaye? Néo-modernisme et Renaissance Africaine dans le Sénégal Contemporain', *Politique Africaine*, 108: 187-204.

Diop, Momar Coumba and Diouf, Mamadou (1990) *Le Sénégal sous Abdou Diouf. État et société*, Paris: Karthala.

Harney, Elizabeth (2004) *In Senghor's Shadow: Art, Politics, and the Avant-Garde in Senegal, 1960-1995*, Durham: Duke University Press.

Mbaye, Assane, 'Sénégal: Fesman – L'Opposition et la Diaspora Même Combat', *Sud Quotidien*, 21 December 2010. http ://.seneweb.com/news/Contribution/quot-patrie-autisme-quot_n_46033.html

Niang, Amy (2010) 'African Renaissance, Reloaded: the old man, the behemoth and the impossible legacy', *Pambazuka News* 25 March 2010, Issue 475. http://pambazuka.org/en/category/features/63289

Niang, Amy (2011) 'Senegal: the Coming of Age of a Heir Apparent', *Pambazuka News*, 23 June 2011. http://pambazuka.org/en/category/features/74283

Sall, Amadou Lamine (2009). 'Il y a 43 ans, le Premier Festival Mondial des Arts Nègres!' *Africultures*, 29 July 2009.

Snipe, Tracy D. (1998). *Art and Politics in Senegal, 1960-1996*, Trenton: Africa World Press.

Snipe, Tracy D. (2010) 'La Tragédie du Roi Abdoulaye? Néomodernisme et Renaissance Africaine dans le Sénégal Contemporain' *Politique Africaine*, 108 : 187-204.

Sy, Samba (2010) 'Crise sociale, régime aux abois et contestation grandissante: l'onde de choc des révolutions arabes peut-elle toucher le Sénégal?' Conference paper, Fondation Gabriel Péri, March 2011. http://www.gabrielperi.fr/Conference-de-Samba-Sy

Sylla, Abdou (1998). *Arts Plastiques et Etat au Sénégal: Trente Cinq Ans de Mécénat au Sénégal*, Dakar: IFAN.

NOTE

See also, 30 March 2010, following elections in Senegal, Amy Niang's article entitled 'Macky's election restores hope to Senegal' http://africanarguments.org/2012/03/30/macky [J.G. Ed.]

Theatre Programme for FESMAN
& Commentary

JAMES GIBBS

Baaba Maal's recommendation seems to have been crucial in the appointment of Kwame Kwei Armah as FESMAN's artistic director. This emerges from a newspaper article by Hannah Pool that incorporated extensive quotations from a Skype interview conducted while Armah was in Senegal for the Festival. Armah told Pool about the opportunities and challenges offered by his role in the Festival and hinted at some of the issues that confronted him. The appointment meant that he was working on a very much larger scale than he was used to and in a very different context. His participation led to some criticism – see above – and gave him – see below – considerable satisfaction.

Armah brought out the 'large scale' quality of the challenge he had taken up when he told Pool: 'The last thing I directed (2008 *Let There Be Love*) had seven actors, and here I am directing a stadium, with 1,000 performers and with 40,000 people cheering'. He drew attention to the quality of the performers, listed in Niang's article, who took part in the opening ceremony.

He responded with enthusiasm to the Festival's theme of Renaissance. It was his view, as quoted by Pool, that, even in Britain, 'there is a black British renaissance – whether it's fashion with Ozwald Boateng, in architecture with David Adjaye, or in the visual arts with Yinka Shonibare or Chris Ofili. That new energy sweeping across Africa and its children is what this festival wanted to celebrate.'

While Armah's London points of reference might have been regarded as a limiting his input into Fesman, he saw his diasporian, indeed double diasporian – Armah was born in London to parents from Grenada – heritage as an advantage. And it certainly seems to have worked in his favour, as the African Diaspora was becoming increasingly central in the thinking about the Festival. From the quotation that follows, it is apparent that Armah saw his background and experience as positive – though it is not clear who he meant by 'everyone'. He said: 'The diaspora identity gives me the added dimension. Right at the core of this festival is that it's not an African festival, but a world festival. So everyone was invited, from the Jamaicans to the

Haitians to the African-Americans.' Of course, the groups he picks out have never been contentious in World Black and African Festival terms. Problems were, as has been registered, caused by the participation of Arabs in the Lagos Festac Colloquium.

In speaking of the stress he had been under, Armah referred to the difficulties caused by the postponement of the festival and about the political dimensions that came into consideration. By political, and in contrast to Dieye and Niang, Armah refers to pressure from ambassadors.

On the sensitive matter of funding, Pool reported, as Niang suggested, that the Festival cost £52 million, but thought that it had been paid for 'by the African Union, the government of Brazil (this year's guest of honour) and several corporate sponsors.' On the vexed question of finance, Armah was able to point out that 'most of the events were free to enter'.

He reflected on the intention, daunting indeed, to have every African country represented at the Festival and the need to challenge European preconceptions. He said: the Festival is 'about being holistic and defining African art not solely as exotica or seeing black theatre as only being about crime and corruption.'

Armah acknowledged there had been some problems. With understatement that might be called 'typically British', he conceded that 'Organisationally, there were some dramas' and explained 'philosophically', that they were inevitable – in view of the length of time that had elapsed since the last major festival in Dakar. He summed up his position by saying: 'Given it was the first time for 30 years that the festival (has taken) place, it was bound to have some administrative problems, but most were ironed out.'[1]

Armah showed some awareness of Senegalese politics and a disconcerting willingness to dismiss criticism of the Festival. Worryingly, he distanced himself from the rigorous scrutiny of issues by saying that he was aware 'of the opposition in Senegal talking about the cost of the festival' and wrote this off by adding: 'that's an opposition's job'. He went on to point out that he had 'been completely removed from the politics of the country, mainly because I had so much else to do.' By talking in this way, he brushed aside issues that, in the context of this volume, have to be held up for inspection. An enquiry into the finances of the Festival might begin with the funder Pool listed first: the African Union. From there it would be a small step to Muammar Gaddafi, whose creature the African Union had become and who some said attempted to annex Fesman through the supply of petrodollars. It will be recalled that in 2008, in a bid to usurp authority in Africa, Gaddafi had himself hailed as 'King of Kings' by two hundred holders of traditional African titles. Pictures were flashed around the world of Gaddafi enthroned among men weighed down with gold and wearing rich *kente* or heavily-embroidered *agbadas*.

Armah had found much to respond to in the life of the festival itself. He described the artists' village as being 'like the UN', and clarified what he meant by this unlikely comparison by saying: 'You sit in the cafeteria and

Mauritians are jamming, the Guadeloupeans are giving impromptu readings – it's artistic heaven. Being able to take in the great art, and then being able to chill out with world-class artists with my children has probably been the highlight of my life so far.'

Seeking a post-script to this, and before laying out for critical inspection the extensive theatre programme for the Festival, it is useful to juggle with the Kwei-Armah name and follow through the dialogue that the British-born, 'Ian Roberts', initiated when he changed his name to Kwame and added two names that had already become familiar to readers of novels by Ghanaian-born Ayi Kwei Armah. Ayi Kwei Armah, now operating a publishing house in Senegal, has a very different view of Festivals to that expressed by Kwame Kwei-Armah and encountering them helpfully extends the range of opinions contained in this volume.

In 1985, Ayi Kwei Armah, contributed an article entitled 'The Festival Syndrome' to *West Africa*. In it he reflected on the news that 'preparations (were) afoot for another festival of African culture, (intended to be a follow up to Festac-Lagos, itself a sequel to Dakar) scheduled for June 1986.' (See above for references to the repeated postponement of the second Dakar Festival.) Ayi Kwei Armah ruminated:

> This is the kind of news that raises the wry hope the some day Africa's creative and productive artists will see through the festival game and leave the parasites alias bureaucrats to organize, to participate in, and finally to make their petty personal profits from such wasteful demonstrations of intellectual bankruptcy – on their own. In short, such news is bad news. (Armah 2010, 133)

Ayi Kwei Armah's conviction that festivals in the Dakar – Lagos mould were 'a waste of time, money and human energy' proceeded from an awareness, akin to that expressed by Niang, of how inappropriate it was to celebrate on a large scale when many were 'agonizing'.

He was also convinced that 'Culture is a process, not an event.' Moving through different fields of artistic and creative endeavour – publishing, creating 'matchless music', film-making – and, ever a Pan-Africanist, bemoaning the hindrance of 'microstate frontiers, taxes, customs, and postal barriers', he wrote of the need for 'institutions supportive of creative cultural work on a steady yearly, monthly, weekly, daily, hourly, minute-to-minute basis' (136). He called for 'cerebration not celebration', and for constant commitment to cultural industries. Seeking an appropriate image, he spelt out the contrast between gentle, life-giving, daily rain, and destructive tropical storms in the course of which the heavens open and fertile top-soil is swept away by raging torrents. 'Sporadic festivals' were like, he indicated, the latter.

NOTE

1   One of the administrative problem that had not been 'ironed out' was that referred to by Niang. See The Art Newspaper of 22 November 2011 for a report on the saga of the impounded art works: http://edition.pagesuite-professional.co.uk/launch.aspx?re ferral=other&pnum=1&refresh=B1a7y90XT0q2&EID=42b46c7b-196b-46d0-8cc8-50f1f54cdf3a&skip=&p=1 Accessed 06 April 2012.

BIBLIOGRAPHY

Armah, Ayi Kwei, 'The Festival Syndrome'. First published *West Africa* (London) 15 April 1985, 726–727. Rpt in *Remembering the Dismembered Continent: Seedtime essays*, Popenguine: Per Ankh, 133–8.
Pool, Hannah. 'World Festival of Black Arts: a once in a decade event'. *Guardian*, 3 January 2011. http://www.guardian.co.uk/stage/2011/jan/03/world-festival-of-black-arts-kwei-armah; accessed o6 April 2012
Wambu, Onyekachi. 'Breach of Trust and the Festival Syndrome.' *New African* (London.), 512 (1978). See http://www.wipo.int/wipo_magazine/en/2011/01/article_0008.html Accessed 05 April 2012.

FESMAN THEATRE PROGRAMME

The following list of theatrical activities at FESMAN 2010 is based on the published programme for the Festival and on an article posted by Oumar Ndao. These sources did not always have the same details and it has not always been possible to assemble all the relevant information.

It is clear that the theatre programme included a range of activities such as productions, story-telling, 'tributes', puppet plays and Forum Theatre. The large number of groups with French links is notable, as is the lack of input from Anglophone Africa (see however reference to work by Soyinka and Ngugi). The participating theatre groups may be compared with, for example, those involved in the Benin International Theatre Festival. There is little or no overlap.

Please note that the sources do not always specify precise roles take by the named individuals. [J.G.]

Productions at FESMAN included

- *Kylek/A People's Cry from the Heart*, National Company of the Sudan, (text by Walid El-Amir El-Alfi)
- *Pas de Prison pour le Vent*, Quai des Arts Company, Guadeloupe/France, (text by Alain Foix)
- *Black Bazaar*, Polychrome Theatre Company, CAR/France (text by Alain Mabanckou)
- *Salina*, co-production by La Voix du Griot, France, Umané Culture,

Burkina Faso, and Arac National Guimba, Mali. (Note the involvement in the feminist play by the late Sotigui Kouyaté, see *African Theatre: Histories 1850-1950*, ix-x)

- *Verre Cassé/Broken Glass*, Musée DAPPER, France/Guadeloupe, (originally a comic novel text by Mabanckou, translated into English 2009)
- *The End*, Théâtre El Hamra, Tunisia ('sous la baguette d'Ezzedine Guenoun')
- *Petite fleur*, N'Zassa Company, Côte d'Ivoire/Burkina Faso (text by Fargass Assandé)
- *La Mort et le Cavalier du roi* (title translated on programme as 'Death and the King's Rider' [sic], Les Geueles Tapées, Senegal, (text by Wole Soyinka)
- *Badadroum* ('conte théâtralisé'/played tale), Compagnie Koykoyo, Niger
- *Fatma, the Voices of the Chameleon*, France/Senegal
- *Tribute to Souleymane Koly Navétanes*, Le Kotéba, Côte d'Ivoire
- *From Servitude to Freedom – Song of Freedom to Equality, to brotherhood of all the peoples, Melting Pots*. This may be *Le Chemin de la Liberté/The Way to Freedom*, official entry by Senegal, National Drama Group, (composed by several hands and directed by a collective)
- *Vérité de soldat/Truth of the Soldier*, BionBa Company, Mali, (based on an account by Songolo Samaké, group led by Jean Louis Sagot- Duvauroux)
- *Le combat de Mbombi/The Combat of Mbombi*, Les 'Renaissants' Company, Gabon (text, published 1977, by Vincent De Paul Nyonda, 1918–1995)
- *La Malice des Hommes/The Malice of Men*, Palais de la Culture d'Abidjan, Côte d'Ivoire, (tribute to Sidiki Bakabe)
- *Cia Dos Comuns*/Dos Comuns Company, Brazil
- *Bloody Niggers* (to say No to massacres), Belgium/Africa (text by Younouss Diallo)
- *The Pot of Koko Mballa*, National Theatre of Congo, Brazzaville
- *La Cruche cassée*, La Compagnie F'ÂME Senegal, (in Wolof based on *The Broken Pitcher* by Bernd Heinrich Wilhelm von Kleist (1777 –1811). Produced by Ibrahima Mbaye Sopé
- *Silent Voice, South Africa*. (Title may be short for *Silent Voice of Protest*)

Programmes marked as 'theatre' included

- *'Saina'* Tribute to Sotigui Kouyaté, La Voix du Griot (Burkina Faso/ Mali/France)
- *'Monk'/Life of Thelonius Monk*, Laurence Holder's Company, (USA)
- *Stories in Colour*, Mbinda/Ngazolo/Manfrei Obin/Ousmane Bangoura
- Forum Theatre, programme in Ziguinchor-Bignona, etc. (Text by Barbara Santos)
- *Theatre Caravan*, an itinerant event involving actors from Brazil, Guinée Bissau, Spain, Portugal, Mauritania, Burkina Faso, Gambia and Sénégal. Stops included Bignona, Kaolack, Kaffrine, Rufisque, and Pikine.

- Performance by Giant Puppets / Les Grandes personnes de Boromo, *The Dream of the Grand-parents*, Burkina Faso (Text by Idrissa Zongo)
- *Folk-tales from Côte d'Ivoire*, (Manfrei Obin)
- Equestrian spectacle by the Eye of the Cyclone, Burkina Faso
- *Quintet de l'Improvisation /Quintet of Improvisation*, French Diaspora
- *Ayiti (Haiti)*, tribute to Gérard Chenel and the Haitians of the 1966 Festival, Daniel Marcellin and Philippe Laurent
- *L'Echo des Pas de l'Homme/The Echo of Man's Steps* (Monologue by Diariéto Keïta)
- *The Voices of the Chameleon*, Senegal/France. (Second piece may have been Fatma de Mohamed Benguettaf)
- *Nuit caribéenne/Caribbean Night*, Les Berticks, Martinique (Text by Alioune Cissé).
- *The Unknown Soldiers*, tribute to Senegalese infantrymen, France/Mali/ Morocco/ Senegal (Khalid Tamer and Julien Favart).
- *Le Cœur des Enfants Léopards*, Cie Hipothésarts, Senegal/Belgium (Monologue by Ansou Diédhiou)
- *Country night*, included drama with music, dance, fashion
- *Champs de sons/Fields of Sounds* (Monologue by Emile Abossolo) Cameroon/Cameroun
- *Stories from Senegal and elsewhere ('Christmas presents for the children')* told by Mimi Barthélémy (Haïti), Manfreï Obin (Côte d'Ivoire), Mbinda Ngazolo (Cameroun), Ousmane Bangoura (Guinée), Taxi Suzy Ronel (Guadeloupe) who works with Massamba Guèye and Babacar Mbaye Ndack (Sénégal).
- The Master Classes/Workshops included a session to devoted to Ngugi wa Thiong'o's *I Will Marry When I want to* conducted by Baityr Ka.

WEBOGRAPHY

FESMAN programme, 12 April 2012, was accessible at http://www.slideshare.net/AbdouJeng/ black-festival-programme
http://www.gouv.sn/IMG/pdf/programme_201210.pdf
http://www.car-rapide.com/?p=1859
Benin International Theatre Festival, April 2012, See 'Benin International Theater Festival draws crowds', http://english.cntv.cn/program/cultureexpress/20120412/113172.shtml
Hortence, D. Batoumaï, '*Sénégal/Théâtre/ La mort et l'écuyer du Roi: Les Gueules Tapées* tiennent en haleine leur public'. Publié le 16 mai 2008 http://www.agn.netis-senegal.com/index. php?page=article&id_article=4403 accessed 2011 02 10
Mabanckou, Alain. See official site: http://www.alainmabanckou.net/
Ndao, Oumar, 'On Theatre at Fesman' http://blackworldfestival.com/wp/wp-content/ uploads/2010/09/programme-public-festival101230.pdf
Sopey, Ibrahima Mbeye, see 'Entrepreneurs in Africa', http://www.dw.de/popups/popup_ pdf/012197237,00.pdf

The Pan-African Historical Theatre Festival (PANAFEST) in Ghana 1992–2010
The vision and the reality

VICTOR K. YANKAH

'...*If people are to endear themselves to the Pan-African dream, then due acknowledgement must be given to the reality that, even though politics does influence the thinking of people, the people are first and foremost influenced by their culture.*' (Amma Darko 2006: 34)

Theatre history provides evidence of the evolution of theatre from rituals and festivals. The controversies surrounding the ceremonies relating to the life and death of Osiris in ancient Egypt notwithstanding, it is evident that some such celebration did exist, and the issue in contention, as far as theatre historians are concerned, is the impenetrable nature of the performances (Brocket 1995: 10). The Osiris celebrations, together with festivals of the Greeks celebrated in honour of the Dionysus, are only two illustrations of a substantial connection between festival and drama.

In spite of this evident link between festivals and theatre, some critics of African theatre downplay the significant dramatic elements that undergird African festivals. Ruth Finnegan, for instance, has described such enactments as 'quasi drama' (Finnegan 1970). My interest in drawing attention to her opinion is to make the point that the sometimes unrecognised seedlings of a strong dramatic tradition grow from the nursery of ritual and festival. Watered by creativity and by positive critical attitudes, they can flourish, but caustic criticism can nip them in the bud. The Greeks nurtured the dramatic elements and left behind a major theatrical tradition.

Efua Sutherland adopted a positive position in the promotion of Ghanaian drama. She advocated the evolution of modern Ghanaian drama from within the heterogeneous Ghanaian cultural milieu, encouraging a fusion of indigenous and imported theatrical elements. She had a vision of the development of Ghanaian drama to very significant heights. *Anansegoro*, a unique dramatic form she created, is a remarkable demonstration of her interest in setting a particular theatrical agenda for contemporary Ghanaian dramatists, and the influence of this theatrical innovation is evident in the plays of, for example, Asiedu Yirenkyi, Martin Owusu, and Yaw Asare.

Sutherland also played a vital role in the National Theatre Movement in Ghana, and she must be given credit for much that was achieved by those

45

involved in that movement. She also advocated a 'Historical Drama Festival' which later became known as the 'Pan-African Historical Theatre Festival' (PANAFEST). Her contribution to the birth of the Festival is described by Anyidoho thus:

> It was … in this final phase of her work that she gave to Ghana and the African world probably her grandest artistic vision for uplifting and reuniting African peoples through the arts – an original proposal for the Pan-African Historical Theatre Festival, the Panafest Movement. (Anyidoho 2000: 79)

The proposal in question was presented by the Drama Unit of the Institute of African Studies, University of Ghana in 1980, 'under the unit's schedule of Creative Development projects for the Theatre Movement' (Sutherland 1980). Although reference has often been made to this document as the source of the PANAFEST movement, it is my contention here that such references are often opportunistic and cosmetic. This is because what eventually emerged as PANAFEST differed in many significant respects from what Sutherland envisaged. The predicament in which PANAFEST finds itself in 2011 is in part traceable to the failure to consider aspects of Sutherland's original proposal.

PANAFEST is a biennial event that takes place in Cape Coast with related activities in Elmina, Accra, Assin Manso and Kumasi. To quote from the 1997 Souvenir Brochure, the event is aimed at

> …establishing the truth about the history of Africa and the experiences of its peoples using the vehicle of African arts and culture; providing a forum to promote unity between Africans on the continent and in the diaspora; and affirming the common heritage of African peoples the world over and defining Africa's contribution to world civilization.

The festival has three main objectives:

- to develop a framework for the identification and analysis of issues and needs, central to Africa's development and to the improvement of the quality of life of her people;
- to encourage regular reviews of Africa's developmental objectives, strategies and policies;
- to mobilize consensus on ends for the formulation of possible alternative options for development (PANAFEST '97 Souvenir Programme, 17).

The first PANAFEST was held from 12 to 19 December, 1992, in Cape Coast and Accra under the theme 'The Re-emergence of African Civilization'. This subsequently became the running theme of the festival, with sub-themes identified for each edition. The Festival has an intellectual component in the form of a two-day colloquium that runs parallel to its creative dimension. The colloquium is held at the University of Cape Coast.

Some brief comments on the aims and objectives listed above are essential because they provide a framework for the discussion of the deviations from

Sutherland's proposal that follows. First, the aims and objectives fail to address the theatrical dimension. This dimension is subsumed under 'arts and culture' but, given the name of the festival, it should have been more adequately expressed. Second, none of the three objectives has a basis in the arts; they are all political rather than cultural.

In 2011 PANAFEST was held from 23 July to 1 August, and the 2012 edition is planned to be a celebratory event that will appropriately mark the twentieth anniversary of the Festival. Significantly, the accompanying colloquium in 2011 was intended to provide a forum for stock-taking. The two-day event, with the theme 'Re-uniting the African Family: Challenges and Prospects', listed the following sub-themes for contemplation by participants:

• Whence have we come?
• Where are we now? Challenges and Successes
•' Rejuvenating PANAFEST: Our way and Our Will'
• PANAFEST: Our People, Our Soul and Our Future

Most of the panellists were Ghanaians who have been involved with the organisation of the Festival in one way or the other. They included Kohain Halevi, the Executive Secretary of PANAFEST, Professor Kofi Anyidoho, Dr Mohammed ben-Abdallah, and Nana Kobina Nketsiah V. Among those invited to provide perspectives from the diaspora were Drs Garland Hill and Reggie Jackson (PANAFEST 2011, Colloquium Programme).

My description of the programme of the last PANAFEST in the previous paragraph is not intended to suggest that it was a success. Quite the reverse: I think that PANAFEST has failed in large measure to achieve its founding objectives and has degenerated into what Nkrabea Effa-Dartey describes, in a 2006 article by John Owoo, as 'disco sessions, slave walks and musical extravaganza'.

In the first place the organisation of the 2011 edition as a deliberately low-key event on the grounds that the 2012 Festival was intended to be a major, twentieth anniversary celebration betrays an acknowledgement of a significant slump in the momentum of the festival. The sub-themes itemised are also revealing in this respect. 'Whence have we come?' suggests a return to the umbilicus of the festival, and 'Where are we now?' an assessment of contemporary realities. The third sub-theme, 'Rejuvenating PANAFEST: Our Way and Our Will', is a particularly clear admission of a decline in the fortunes of the Festival, a recognition that it craves rejuvenation. The last sub-theme, 'PANAFEST: Our people, Our Soul, Our Future', echoes an expression of the resolve of a people to reinvent a festival that appears to have lost its lustre.

A revitalisation of the festival could be achieved by returning to the principles laid down by Sutherland, those on which the festival was supposed to have been founded. I think it is owing to a digression from the initial artistic principles as envisaged by Sutherland and as laid down in her proposal that PANAFEST has failed to make a meaningful impact on the artistic landscape. The festival has also failed, and for the same reasons, to make a significant contribution to the tourist sector of the Ghanaian economy. In the paragraphs that follow, I intend to set the provisions made in Sutherland's proposal beside the framework that has evolved for the festival. The juxtaposition will draw attention to the challenges that have bedevilled the event and the extent to which its current structure has deviated from Sutherland's conception, which was, it will be recalled, of a theatre festival that was intended to transform the practice of theatre in Ghana.

Sutherland's proposal was made available to me by courtesy of Dr Esi Sutherland-Addy; I have based my description of the framework for the festival on what I learned from my participation in it and from analysis of its programme. The programme, incidentally, has seen little variation from edition to edition.

Nomenclature is an important identity marker, and the name given to an event is often a reflection of its content or intent. In her proposal, Sutherland advocated the establishment of an 'Historical Drama Festival in the Cape Coast Castle' with the primary focus on drama. However, as is apparent, the name of the festival was altered to read 'Pan-African Historical Theatre Festival'. Sutherland's proposal was indefinite and open, and the term 'Pan-African' was not included in the wording of the title of her proposal. The festival planners, however, introduced a revision which spelt out the festival's geographical coverage: Africa and the African diaspora. They also expanded its artistic scope from drama to theatre, thus paving the way for the inclusion of, for example, musical theatre, dance theatre, and puppetry. It is relevant to note that while intimating international dimensions, Sutherland's proposal was, first and foremost, to locate the drama festival within the context of the Ghana National Theatre Movement.

Attached to the copy of the Proposal I am working from are some rough notes confirming that the drama festival was conceived within the larger framework of the overall development of drama in Ghana. It was supposed to be an integrated, not a stand-alone event. Sutherland outlined four main activities that were to be carried out with the aim of promoting drama mostly for education and development. First, there was a rural development project focused on Atwia, the village in the Central Region where a 'story house' had been built and a tradition of story-telling nurtured. Then she proposed what she referred to in the notes as a 'Pan African Drama Festival'. This is the first and only mention of the Pan-African dimension to the event. The third activity in her rough outline is the twenty-fifth anniversary of the Ghana Drama Studio, and the fourth and final one is a children's drama project.

The implementation of ideas in these rough notes can be seen in the various projects executed and proposals presented by Sutherland that underscore the importance she attached to cultural transmission and social development through the arts.

The drama festival and development

Sutherland's proposal was made 'with Ghana's local and international interest in the context of her cultural policy' in view (Sutherland 1980: 1). To this end, her proposal called for 'catalyst programmes' directed towards development: the drama festival was proposed as one such catalyst. She wrote:

> The Historical drama festival is seen as a major catalyst programme providing a focus for artistic creation towards the goal of adding an important dimension to the Theatre Movement: (a) in the form of a substantial stock of dramas deriving from Ghanaian and African history, and (b) in the form of another tradition of theatre practice. (Sutherland 1980: 1)

From this passage, the position of theatre as the focal point of the Festival is incontestable. The evolution of theatrical varieties, the building of a stock of historical dramas as well as the cross-fertilisation of Ghanaian drama and drama from elsewhere in Africa emphasise Sutherland's interest in original ways of promoting national development through the arts. Other benefits to be derived from such an enterprise include the possible role of international bodies, such as UNESCO, especially in funding the project and employing it as a vehicle for its own programmes. Sutherland anticipated the possibility of tapping into artistic inspiration and talent from other countries, and the opportunity to attract resources in cash and in kind from internal and external sources to support theatre and other media.

Sutherland prepared her proposal in 1980 and presented it to a forum at the Institute of African Studies. However, its provisions were not adopted until 1992, when the first PANAFEST was organised. Paradoxically, the establishment of PANAFEST coincided with a period of decline in dramatic output in Ghana, a decline which to date has not been reversed. Pietro Deandrea provides a glimpse of the situation during the 1990s in the following observation: 'The Ghanaian situation is especially dreadful: during my second research stay in Ghana in 1997, I realized with amazement that not a single play had been published since my first visit in 1993! A four-year-long void is certainly something to think about' Deandrea (2002: 185).

The first PANAFEST took place with a great deal of fanfare. The festival theme, as we have seen, was 'The Re-emergence of African Civilization', greeted with enthusiasm by local artists, playwrights, actors, and directors who were all hopeful for a resurgence of the arts, especially drama. They welcomed what they anticipated would be an opportunity to exhibit talent and to attract funding. The optimism of these artists gave way to disillusionment when the programmes offered no indications of sponsorship for new creative artists.

In this respect, the neglect of the thoughtful provisions in Sutherland's proposal was particularly damaging. The proposal had recognised the importance of unearthing new dramatic talent and had laid down a programme that might achieve that end. In the section entitled 'Take-off Measures', Sutherland meticulously spelt out the format to be followed and the plan deserves to be reproduced here:

TAKE-OFF MEASURES (over a period of one year)

PART ONE

The professional committee will initiate the work for the development of dramas by the following measures:-

a. Announcement of the project to playwrights, potential playwrights and to poet-musicians.

b. A consultative seminar with members of the Ghana Historical Society.

c. An exercise to (i) enrol participants (ii) recruit tutors for the orientation workshops.

d. Launching of the first competition for historical dramas.

PART TWO

a. Implementation of a preliminary orientation workshop programme.

b. Call-in of scripts for assessment and conclusion of the first competition exercise.

c. Follow-up workshops for a selection of contestants, editorial consultants and production consultants.

PART THREE

a. Planning of the Festival event by a festival committee.

b. Announcement of winning dramas and commencement of production.

PARTICIPATION IN FESTIVAL PRODUCTIONS

It will be a principle to give different drama groups a chance to participate in the productions for the festival. (Sutherland 1980: 3-4)

Sutherland's detailed format, the fruit of many years spent fostering playwrights, was only marginally considered by the festival planners. It is evident from the proposal that Sutherland envisaged that 'the professional committee (the PANAFEST Committee in this case) would initiate a playwriting contest which would involve potential playwrights, poets and musicians. She suggested that orientation workshops would assist the writers to produce well-crafted scripts. In the second phase, she asked for a 'call-in of scripts' and assessment. The successful plays would, she anticipated, be produced at the festival. To ensure variety, other plays would surely be produced alongside these dramas and, in addition, there would be music and dance. Participants would come from not only Ghana, but also from other parts of Africa and from the African Diaspora.

The programme of the first PANAFEST in 1992 made some provision for the playwriting competition that Sutherland had proposed, and which was open to authors of historical dramas. However, little has been heard of the winning scripts. Indeed, had due recognition been accorded them as suggested in Sutherland's proposal, there would have been an explosion in dramatic writing. The idea of a contest to unearth new talents appears to have been abandoned after the first attempt, and with its abandonment the opportunity to unearth new Ghanaian dramas was lost. PANAFEST's loss was, incidentally, STUDRAFEST's gain, since the hunt for new dramatic talent was taken up by the organisers of the Student Drama Festivals that were also held in Cape Coast (Asiedu and Dorgbadzi 2006: 16-22).

PANAFEST and tourism

At the colloquium of the 2011 PANAFEST held from 27-28 July that year, Kofi Anyidoho, one of the panellists, lamented the fact that the festival was currently perceived as a touristic event rather than an artistic occasion. His submission drew a response from the Minister for Tourism, Sena Dansua, who indicated that her ministry was involved in PANAFEST as a supporting ministry because the festival was indeed of immense importance for the tourism sector. It needs to be said that Anyidoho's comments were well founded – as Dansua's response indicated. Leadership of the festival has, in fact, devolved from creative artists onto the shoulders of those involved in tourism. An examination of the composition of the planning committee for PANAFEST 2011 illustrates this trend: thirteen of the eighteen members on the committee were from either the Ministry of Tourism (including the Minister), the Ghana Tourist Board, or the Tour Operators' Association. Of the remaining six members of the committee, two were representatives of the PANAFEST Board, and two were academics - who were also dramatists and theatre researchers. The others were a traditional Chief and the Executive Secretary of the PANAFEST Foundation. The overwhelming influence of the tourism sector was confirmed by the fact that the Minister of Tourism was Chair and her deputy co-chair.

The perception of the festival as a tourist event has long been flagged up by the press. *The Spectator* of 11 August 2001 carried an article headed 'PANAFEST – A Global Fraternity of Culture and the Past' and linked the festival with tourism by reporting that 'The recent Pan-African festival (PANAFEST) and Emancipation Day went a long way to relive the painful yet eventful historical past of Ghana while making it possible for the country's rich tourism potential to be exposed to the world.' I suggest that the desire to shore up the country's tourism credentials was the driving motivation for the introduction, in 1998, of Emancipation Day alongside PANAFEST.

Tourism is an unavoidable accompaniment to any cultural, historical or artistic event of international dimension like a theatre festival. Examples of festivals that have drawn tourists include the World Festival of Black Arts, FESMAN in Senegal, and the Edinburgh Festival, the largest in the world. Participants and visitors at such events find time to look around places of historical or cultural interest. Inherent in Sutherland's proposal was an opportunity for exploiting touristic potential. Indeed, her proposal that the West African Museums Council should be involved implies an incorporation of places of historical and cultural significance in the planning for the festival. The venue, as she envisaged it, was Cape Coast Castle which, with Elmina Castle and other forts, has been recognised by UNESCO as a World Heritage Site. The choice of venue resonates with the interest in tourism promotion. Furthermore, the Pan-African dimension of the festival, as she conceived it, offers an invitation to all peoples of African origin to attend. For those whose ancestors were taken across the Atlantic, the historical, and spiritual, significance of the castles is very clear. Cape Coast Castle was one of the points of departure, or 'gates of exit', for captives and, in various ways, it provides a portal for those 'returning'. While the venues for the festival provide an impetus for tourism, the festival organisers must present artistic and cultural components that will draw people to the festival year after year after year.

Ownership

At the colloquium of the 2011 PANAFEST, a participant raised a very pertinent issue by asking: 'Who owns PANAFEST?' This question broached an important issue which appears to have been overlooked - or taken for granted – in the organisation of the festival. Non-Ghanaians see PANAFEST as a Ghanaian festival that they have been invited to. Indeed, PANAFEST provides a convenient opportunity for many in the African diaspora to attempt to reconnect with the motherland. There is no gainsaying that the festival is a Ghanaian affair, as the events are planned and executed by Ghanaians.

At this point it is enlightening to revisit Sutherland's proposal to familiarise ourselves with her thoughts about the ownership of the festival as she conceived it. Under 'Points of Organization', she wrote that:

> Several objectives of Ghana's cultural policy considered, it is most appropriate for this festival to occur in the context of a traditional festival. The Oguaa Fetu Afahye provides that context. Its organizing committee should be requested therefore, to accommodate the Historical Festival as an extension of the customary programmes.

I read this to imply that she suggests that the festival be held 'under the aegis' of the Oguaa Fetu Afahye, an affirmation of the importance of patterning the new after something that has already been time tested. Making the 'Historical Festival' an extension of a traditional festival has considerable merit. First, it is an invitation to the people of Cape Coast to appropriate the festival as their own and give it their support. This would ensure the involvement of the people in the festival and it would also guarantee continuity, because the people would have sufficient stake in it to want to see it successfully staged every two years. Secondly, as far as Africans in the diaspora are concerned, what could be more welcoming than a festival that not only seeks to link them to their mother continent and reunite them, but also has its roots firmly anchored in a traditional event that strongly manifests their culture of origin?

It would appear, however, that the indigenes do not completely embrace the festival. This is evident in the low patronage of the festival by the people of Cape Coast. Although further research is necessary to establish the pattern of patronage, a cursory survey of the audience at PANAFEST 2009 revealed that many of the patrons were those involved in the arts who had travelled from outside Cape Coast; those involved with Centres for National Culture; craftsmen who exhibit at the crafts bazaar; and visitors from the diaspora. Local participation is limited to attending musical events featuring popular artists.

Paucity of drama

Although the festival has its roots in a proposal for an 'Historical Theatre' festival, not much drama has featured. A survey of the souvenir programme of PANAFEST 97, one of the best patronised festivals, reveals that while there were over one hundred and fifty performances by groups, only six were plays.

Elolo Gharbin, who was on the programmes committee for PANAFEST 2009, explained to me that dramatic performances are poorly attended, and that locals do not patronise straight drama, particularly when it is in English. Examining the theatrical offerings, I would have expected that Concert Party, Ghana's most distinctive theatrical form, would be a major feature of PANAFEST programmes. However, although the two most popular Concert Party comedians of the time, Nkomode and Bob Okala, were given performance slots, there was not a single Concert Party performance listed. Popular West African theatre was, instead, represented by a Yoruba Travelling Theatre production.

In order to identify with PANAFEST, Ghanaians might expect to see their popular arts forms featured. Indeed, although the event is a 'Pan African' one, due recognition of local arts and cultural forms is important, as extreme internationalisation of the event stifles local creativity. At this point and in the context of PANAFEST, the quotation from Amma Darko at the beginning of this paper and addressed to the African Literature Association becomes very relevant.

Conclusion

From the foregoing discussion, it is evident that the implementation of PANAFEST has departed in several important respects from the proposal originally put forward by Sutherland for a festival to promote theatre in

Ghana. Some of the reasons for the deviation have been political: during the nineties, the government saw the festival as an opportunity to enhance its international image and to promote Ghana as the preferred destination for Africans in the Diaspora, and much emphasis was placed on attracting people of African descent from all over the world. Initially, the festival received both state and corporate support. In an interview he gave to Kojo T. Vieta, (1994), Akunu Darkey drew attention to the importance of the July 1985 declaration of Heads of State and Government about the 'need for an African Cultural Forum'. PANAFEST was partly a response to the aspirations expressed in that declaration, and, with support from Unesco, the International Theatre Institute and the Organisation of African Unity (OAU), PANAFEST was set up (see Idollor 1997). Other sponsors include the African Development Bank, and corporate bodies including Coca Cola and local breweries (see *Spectator* , 11 August 2001). However, there was a gradual reduction in this stream of funding for the event over the years, so that by 2007 PANAFEST was in danger of extinction. The situation was not helped by the failure – despite the colloquia that were part of all editions of PANAFEST – to produce a single publication.

I suggest that the history of the festival repays study as an example of how an artistic vision can be derailed under the impact of conflicting interests. PANAFEST has lost its focus, and, as Anyidoho contends above, appears to be a tourism event. Historical theatre does not feature on the programmes of the festival; the drama contest and the pre-production workshops proposed by Sutherland in order to nurture new writers have not been held. The festival organisers have departed from the concepts and practical arrangements proposed by Sutherland. They have also been unable to provide opportunities for the development of Ghana's most distinctive art forms such as the Concert Party, or created variety by the inclusion of other arts forms. Had these activities been undertaken, PANAFEST might, perhaps, have emerged as the finest Pan- African cultural event in the world. As it stands, it has become a lacklustre, biennial charade. Ghana runs the risk of losing a festival that had the potential to unearth fresh dramatic talents, and provide opportunities for both local and international artists. The benefits this cultural cross-fertilisation might have afforded artists and the impact it might have had on Ghanaian drama cannot be overemphasised.

BIBLIOGRAPHY

Anyidoho, Kofi (2002) 'Dr. Efua Sutherland: A Biographical Sketch,' in *Fontomfrom: Contemporary Ghanaian Literature, Theatre and Film* (eds) Kofi Anyidoho and James Gibbs Amsterdam and Atlanta: Rodopi

Asiedu, Awo and Sarah Dorgbadzi (2006) 'Competitive Youth Theatre Festivals in Ghana: Stage Motion and Studrafest' in Martin Banham, James Gibbs, and Femi Osofisan *African Theatre: Youth*, Oxford and Hollywood: James Currey and African Academic Press, 16-22.

Brocket, Oscar G. (1995) *History of the Theatre,* Boston: Allyn and Bacon.

Darko, Amma (2006) 'Rethinking Pan-Africanism', *ALA Bulletin*, 31, 2 Winter 2005/ No.2 Spring 2006.

Deandrea, Pietro (2002) *Fertile Crossings: Metamorphosis of Genre in Anglophone West African Literature*, Amsterdam and New York: Rodopi.

Finnegan, Ruth (1970) *Oral Literature in Africa*, Oxford: Clarendon Press.

Idollor, Danny 'From Panaflop to Pageant' *West Africa*, 13-19 October 1997, 1651

Sutherland, Efua T. (1980) 'Proposal for a Historical Drama Festival in Cape Coast Castle', Drama Research Unit, Institute of African Studies, University of Ghana. (The rights to that document are held by the Efua Sutherland Estate and it is quoted here by kind permission.)

Vieta, Kojo T. 'Uniting the African Family', *West Africa*, 5-11 December 1994, 2074.

Owoo, John. (2006) 'Nkrabea, The Man of Destiny Promises a Political Shock.' *Graphic Ghana* http://www.graphicghana.info/article.asp?artid=14293

PANAFEST 1997 Souvenir Brochure

PANAFEST 2011 Colloquium Brochure

The Spectator 11 August 2001, 14

http://www.graphicghana.info/article.asp?artid=14293

www.panafest.org On 15 March 2012 the opening sentence on this site read 'Welcome to what was once the Panafest - Ghana website. To satisfy your curiosity, I am the former webmaster and I have removed the website from the internet for non-payment of fees by the principal organisers of the event.' [J.G. Ed.]

PANAFEST through the Headlines
An annotated bibliography

JAMES GIBBS

Introduction

The following annotated list of entries about the Festival offers an approach to preparing a history of PANAFEST that complements and extends Victor Yankah's analysis. By way of pre-amble, the dates of the editions of the festival may be noted:

1.   2-19 December 1992
2.   9-18 December 1994
3.   29 August - 7 September 1997
4.   30 July - 8 August 1999
5.   27 July - 3 August 2001
6.   24 July - 1 August 2003
7.   21 July - 1 August 2005
8.   22 July - 1 August 2007
9.   16 July 2009
10.   23 July - 1 August 2011

The earlier part of the bibliography from which these entries have been extracted is available on-line from the Jahn Library for African Literatures at the Department of Anthropology and African Studies at the Johannes Gutenberg University Mainz (JGU) I am grateful to Dr Anja Oed who has made on-line access possible. See http://www.jahn-bibliothek.ifeas.uni-mainz.de

[1980]
Sutherland, Efua. 'A Proposal for an Historical Drama Festival in Cape Coast', paper presented to the Institute of African Studies, University of Ghana. In 1991, this was expanded into plans for PANAFEST, a Pan-African Historical Theatre Festival, first held 1992.

1992
PANAFEST '92 was held 12-19 December. This festival was tied in to a playwriting competition which was open to authors of historical dramas. Gocking (2005: 230) places PANAFEST in the context of raising income from tourism and 'roots' visitors. It is relevant to note that Ghana attracted 50,000 visitors per year during the early 80s, and 300,000 by 1995, in which year $237 million was earned from the tourist sector.

1994
Anon. 'Panafest', *New African* (London), October 1994, 29. (Looks forward to the festival, indicates its theme, carries the latest news about Stevie Wonder's participation, and mentions 'reverential ceremonies' at castles.)

Anon. 'Panafest '94', *Spectator*, 12 November 1994. (Reports that Winnie Mandela was expected, live TV coverage for South Africa was being arranged and that South African Breweries were involved in funding the participation of Brenda Fassi and Yvonne Chaka Chaka. Sarafina was also expected. Note the impact of 'Beer Wars' on funding for the arts.)

Anon. 'The moving force', *West Africa*, 5-11 December 1994, 2076-7. (A profile of John Darkey that draws attention to his performances in primary school, his use of the African Heritage Library, and his move to Legon to read English and Theatre Arts in 1978. In 1982, Asiedu Yirenkyi, then Secretary for Culture and Tourism, appointed him to be his Special Assistant. From there he moved to the National Youth Organising Commission where he became involved in planning the 12th World Festival of Youth and Students. He took Kwesi Adu-Amankwa's play *The African Experience* to Moscow where it won a Gold Award. In 1989, at the 13th World Festival of Youth and Students, held at Pyongyang, North Korea, he assisted in the production of *Rays of a New Dawn*. He then did an M. Phil. at Legon, conducting research on Popular Theatre in Ghana. He was subsequently asked to develop the Community Youth Cultural Programme of the National Commission on Culture, and then to coordinate and organise PANAFEST '92.)

Anon. 'Panafest', *New African Life* (London), December 1994, 3. (Build-up to the festival, (9th-18th); refers to Sutherland as 'the moving spirit' behind the event, and lists the stars expected: Dionne Warwick, Fela Kuti, Miriam Makeba, 'Alpha Blondy, Lucky Dube, Rita and Ziggy Marley and dozens of other top names'.)

Anyidoho, Kofi. 'PANAFEST '94 Colloquium', A report in the *African Literature Association Bulletin*, 21, 1, 1995, 6-7.

Maayang, L D. 'PANAFEST 1994, Black Renaissance. Tidal Waves', *Uhuru*, 6, 11, 1994, 12-14.

Ogunwa, Denrele. 'The tireless crusader', *West Africa*, 5-11 December 1994, 2080-81. (Portrait of Stevie Wonder indicating his commitment to PANAFEST: described as 'the medium to lead the Black and African race into the next Millennium'.)

Vieta, Kojo T. 'Uniting the African Family', *West Africa*, 5-11 December 1994, 2074. (An interview with John Akunu Darkey on the December Festival. Starts off with an account of the history of PANAFEST and draws attention to the importance of the July 1985 declaration of Heads of State and Government about the 'need for an African cultural forum...' Describes the role of Unesco and the ITI. Darkey quoted on the context of PANAFEST, i.e. its relation to the Dakar Festival and to Festac. Notes the success of the 1992 event and the decision to make PANAFEST biennial. Reports that an International Advisory Board and a PANAFEST Secretariat had been set up. Indicates that the programme for 1994 would include more than 90 different performances, a colloquium and a children's festival.)

1995
Anon. 'New Robes for the African', *Guardian* (Lagos), 9 December 1995, 18. (On PANAFEST Colloquium.)

Anon. 'Total facts of a Fiesta', *Guardian* (Lagos), 9 December 1995, 18 and 21. (Interview with Nana Brefoh-Boateng, Chief Director of the National Commission for Culture, on PANAFEST.)

Anon. 'Panafest: Singing but not Swinging', *New African* (London), February 1995, 8f. (Lists some of the problems connected with the festival: planes late, Stevie Wonder 'refused to leave his hotel room for a jig [sic] until a technical problem with his piano was put right'... [even then he had to play with the piano out of tune]. Comments on high prices [C25,000 to hear Stevie Wonder], poor local publicity, absence of big names [Dionne Warwick there in 1992, but not in 1994; Fela absent], and problems with transport.)

Hall, Ian. 'Panafest Dissected', *West Africa*, 6-12 February 1995, 176-7. (Hall, formerly a music teacher at Achimota School, provides background to the establishment of the festival, with references to Sutherland and Rawlings, the December 1991 'national phase festival', and the 'wider participation' in the festival of 1992. Hall comments on the quality of a paper that Kofi Awoonor delivered, and refers to the 'free for all' nature of the programme. Mentions difficulties experienced by 'ordinary' visitors; poor attendance; cancellation of some events; high gate fees for final performance, and absence of Stevie Wonder. Asks for candid discussion, and wonders why Britain was exporting 'groups reproducing Ghanaian music and dance'. Calls for a return to the spirit of 'the initial Black Arts Festival [Senegal 1965]' (sic), and avoidance of Carifesta and Festac problems. Refers to *Ghanaian Times*, 14 December 1994: 'President Unhappy with Panafest's Organisation' and to problems created by scheduling PANAFEST 1996 during August, when it would clash with the Notting Hill Carnival and come into conflict with then Oguaa Fetu Festival!)

1997
Anon. 'Master drummers from Ghana', *West Africa*, 21- 27 April 1997, 651. (Report on Kakatsitsi, a Ga group, who took part in PANAFEST.)

Anon. 'IRE FM and Panafest '97', *The Ghanaian Chronicle*, 24 August 1997, 8. (Reports that Jamaican FM station IRE 'is all set to partake in the Panafest '97 excitement'.)

Hall, Ian. 'Ghana's glory: Jerry's joy (i)', *West Africa*, 5-11 May 1997, 730-1. (iii), *West Africa*, 19-25 May 1997, 810-11. (In Part i, Hall reports on his visit to Ghana for the 40th Independence celebrations. Refers to the response to the reception of Rawlings at the Commonwealth Institute as 'highly reminiscent of 1960s Beatle mania' and mentions performances by musical and drama groups, including Abibigromma. Describes the 31st December Women's Movement ensemble present at 6 March as 'vibrant'. Writes that Rawlings' demeanour was 'avuncular' and records that he had himself been commissioned to compose 'Floreat Ghana' to launch PANAFEST '97. In Part iii, Hall expands on his search for singers and instrumentalists to take part in 'Floreat Ghana', and traces the career of Miriam Makeba. Looks ahead to 'exclusively [revealing Rawlings'] views on the life of the nation' in part iv.)

Idollor, Danny. 'From Panaflop to pageant', *West Africa*, 13-19 October 1997, 1651. (Severe critic of PANAFEST '94, Idollor found the '97 edition 'more modest but better focused'; referred to 'thousands of tourists'; noted pledge of OAU's continuing support, and enjoyed option of attending the 'local Fetu Afahye' festival. Idollor listed as highlights the performance of the Nigerian troupe and a ritual in which 400 'diasporians' took new names – and local organiser 'John Darkey' became 'Akuno Dake'. Only low point was the decision of Jewel Ackah to play 'ancient reggae tunes all night long'. Regarded the link with the local festival as very advantageous, and expressed high expectations for 1999.)

Williams, Radha. 'Panafest '97 arrives', *West Africa*, 25-31 August 1997, 1390. (Partly a reworking of publicity material in which Williams describes the 1997 Festival as the Third, and indicates that '4,000 world-class participants from more than 40 countries' are expected. Williams is the wife of Ian Hall, see above.)

1999
August 1999. Note: Agoro Theatre Company took part in PANAFEST; also put on a concert party and a play about the slave trade in Cape Coast Castle.

Anon. 'Panafest '99 opens tomorrow with an expected attendance of more than 5,000 participants', GNA item carried in *Daily Graphic* 23 July 1999, 16.

Abayateye, Felix. 'PANAFEST Soccer at Oguaa: can Dwarfs hold sway over Hearts today?' *Daily Graphic*, Friday, 6th August, 1999. (Soccer had become part of the PANAFEST programme.)

Ahinful, Kwamena. 'Whither PANAFEST? A critical analysis', *The Mirror*, 24 July 1999, 18. (PANAFEST is seen as Pan Africanist in thrust and unlikely to survive long. Ahinful sees forces acting against Ghana's leadership of the OAU also working against acceptance of Ghana having role as cultural leader. Considers Dakar 1966 a precursor of PANAFEST.)

Atafori, Ayuureyisisya Kapini. 'Interview with S. S. Annobil', 'Core message of Panafest is Development', *Business Watch* (Accra), 3, 6 July 1999, 12-15. (Annobil predicted a minimum of 3,000 participants and a maximum of 5,000. The emphasis was on 'Youth: the Agenda for the Next Millennium'. He recorded that eighty attended a Youth Camp in Adisadel College and that the festival was hoping for sponsorship but experiencing donor fatigue. 'People will appreciate if the festival is small but well organised.' Expressed disappointment with fund-raising activities in the US. Spoke of proposal for a PANAFEST Village, and shared a funding idea: every person of African descent all over the world should donate a dollar a year. Claims PANAFEST has been heard of and accepted world-wide as Africa's 'biggest cultural event'. Questioned about whether it was a 'mere tourism promotion package', and wrote of orders 'for the supply of different products in commercial quantities, especially our craft products, beads, etc.' Commented on overlapping of PANAFEST with Emancipation Day events: it was undoubtedly significant, he felt, that when the 2nd Annual Emancipation Day celebration was held at Assin Manso, the event was, according to *The Graphic*, 23 July 1999, 16, organised by the Ministry of Tourism and that the gathering was addressed by the Deputy Minister of Tourism, Owuraku Amofa.)

Davis, Desmond. 'Huge Turn Out for PANAFEST Expected in Ghana', *Panafrican News Agency*, 14 May 1999. (This is a report from London that 10,000 [!] were expected to attend the festival. Comments that it was 'too big for the Ghanaian government alone to fund it' so an international committee had been formed. Quotes Kojo Yankah extensively on, for example, Emancipation Day. Refers to a PANAFEST Village to be built near Elmina that would become 'a home for intellectuals, artists and cultural performers'.)

Nkrabeah, Kwame. 'Emancipation – Panafest', *The Independent*, 5 August 1999, 10. (Argues that 'throughout the history of Ghana, there is no such date in our records' as Emancipation Day. PANAFEST, he asserts, is for those from abroad. Considers 'Uniting the African family' a mystifying title.)

Tuurosong, Damascus. 'Cape Coast Braces for Panafest', *Business Watch* (Accra), 3, 6, July 1999, 10.

Panafest Official Souvenir Brochure 1999 (This publication indicated that the events had been 'organised under the auspices of the Organisation of African Unity and the Government of Ghana'. Aware of shortcomings in the '92 and '94 editions, Kojo Yankah, Chairman of the PANAFEST Foundation, observed that PANAFEST '97 'was adjudged a grand success'. Mike Afedi Gizo, Minister of Tourism, drew attention to the targeting of the 'peoples of African descent in the Diaspora'. The Chairman of the National Commission on Culture plugged a new element: the Slave Route experience with a reference to Assin Manso, and concluded his contribution to the brochure 'Long live Pan-African culture, long live Ghana!' The Executive Secretary, Sammy S. Annobil, provided escape clauses by referring to the brief period since his appointment (9 months), and the need to build a 'new working team to service the Secretariat'. He indicated that inexperienced National Service Personnel had been given responsibilities, and ended by indicating the challenge being taken up by what he called 'the Panafest Movement'. This was to 'move beyond rhetoric to unite the African family to ensure our total emancipation'. [NB: This was a statement that employed rhetoric in the same breath that it stressed the limitations of rhetoric.] The roots of the festival are traced, for example in 'The History of Panafest,' to Efua Sutherland's 1980 'Proposal for a Historical Drama Festival in Cape Coast'. The popular elements, represented by the visit of the Jamaican national soccer team and the International Music Concert at the Trade Fair Site [Saturday 7 August to Sunday 8] were also, it was pointed out, radical departures from Sutherland's vision.)

Okoku, Baffour. 'Fake OAU Official Convicted by Court', *Ghanaian Times*, 10 August. (Okoku reported that 'Ben Zongo Chirek Omar … a journalist with a TV station' had been tried, judged and fined. He had been found guilty of falsely pretending to be a public officer, being in possession of forged documents, and altering faked documents – under section 237.166 and 167 of Act 29/60 of the Criminal Code. A fine of Cedis 1.4 million was imposed, of which Cedis 900,000 were due to the Panafest Foundation to offset costs incurred in transportation, accommodation and lodging for two days. Failure to pay would mean 24 months imprisonment followed by deportation. Note: Omar passed himself as an AU delegate and had been royally entertained by PANAFEST officials, much to their subsequent embarrassment. J.G.)

2001

Anon. 'Panafest adopts Yaa Asantewa documentary', *The Mirror*, 16 June 2001, 21. (Refers to a film written and directed by Ivor Agyeman-Duah. The film had been shown at the African Studies Conference and at Leeds where Duah was working with Adzido as 'a consultant for the Arts Council'.)

Anon. 'Panafest 2001 and Emancipation Day', *The Mirror*, 4 August 2001, 22. (Includes the following quote: 'PANAFEST as you would know is the largest and most prestigious event of Africans in the world. It is a very high profile event that has set standards for itself the world over.... It will be celebrated annually.')

Anon. 'PANAFEST– a global fraternity of Culture and the Past', *The Spectator*, 11 August 2001, 5. (Report includes the following: 'The Recent Pan African Festival (PANAFEST) and Emancipation Day went a long way to relive the painful, yet eventful historical past of Ghana while making it also possible for the country's rich tourism potential to be exposed to the whole...'.)

Anon. 'Sponsors of Panafest and Emancipation Day Celebrations', *Spectator*, 11 August 2001, 14. (Sponsors included the African Development Bank, Western Union, Coca Cola, Kasapreko, and Ghana Breweries Limited. All were given certificates.)

Anon. 'Panafest in Pictures', *The Mirror*, 14 August 2001, 13. (Refers to involvement of the Hon. Hawa Yakubu, Minister of Tourism.)

Gibbs, James. 'Noticeboard', in *African Theatre: Playwrights and Politics*, eds, Martin Banham, James Gibbs, Femi Osofisan. Oxford: James Currey, 2001, 191-203. (Carries an account of PANAFEST 1999.)

Tetteh, Dudley. 'Panafest launched', *Spectator*, 21 July 2001, 5. (Reports that the Festival was launched by Vice-President, Alhaji Aliu Mahama, and was on the theme, 'Re-emergence of African Civilisation'. The dates given as 21 July to 1 August and the programme was to include a pilgrimage to Paga (far North), an IT forum at UCC, and wreath-laying at tombs of returnees 'Crystal and Carson' at Assin Manso. Kojo Yankah was still Chair of International Board of PANAFEST and 'Cook Art' was part of the festival.)

2003

At this time the PANAFEST 2003 website www.ghanaweb.com was live, drew attention to the support being received from the African Union, and listed the objectives of the festival. These stressed establishing links with the Diaspora and contributions to development. No reference was made to 'historical' drama, though history and drama were mentioned. The programme included a Durbar, rites of passage, re-enacting a slave march, a candle-lit vigil, and Emancipation Day commemoration. PANAFEST was held 23-26 July. (See www.pefghana.org, 'Press release 30 May 2003': 'Press launch of Panafest 2003'. Board members included Esi Sutherland and Rabbi Kohain Halevi. See Gyan-Apenteng: 2003.)

Anon. 'Inflation – PANAFEST to create forum for seeking reparation for Africa.' (Posting 18 Jun 2003 . Headline expanded: 'This year's edition of the Pan-African-Historical-Theatre-Festival, PANAFEST 2003, would be used to press for reparation for Africa. The Executive Director of the PANAFEST Foundation, Rabbi Kohain Halevi, told the Ghana News Agency [GNA] in an interview at Cape Coast that the 'pillage, plunder and exploitation meted out to Africans by their colonial masters are evidence of the injustices that the continent suffered'. Theme: 'Uniting the African Family – Dialogue on African Tradition and Culture in the 21st Century Globalization'. www.pefghana.org accessed 29/06/2004.)

Anon. 'Profanous lyrics and the Youth.' ? 2 August 2003. (The Youth Day celebration at PANAFEST was, it seems, used to draw the attention of young minds to the corrupting lyrics of popular songs.)

Anon. 2003. 'First Lady urges African women to uphold traditions and values.' (Article reported on the 'women's day forum' on 'Traditional and cultural values of the African woman in the 21st century' that 'brought together about 500 women from Ghana, the United States and Nigeria'. Includes: 'The First Lady, Mrs Theresa Kufuor on Tuesday called on African women to use the celebration of Panafest/Emancipation Day to rededicate themselves to the traditions and values around them over the last 500 years and more. She regretted that the "distortion of a number of these values, particularly with the invasion of European culture and economic exploitation, has marginalized women's knowledge and agency". Mrs Kufuor made the call in an address read for her'... Note also that 'Mrs Kufuor paid tribute to Madam Efua Sutherland, whose original ideas sowed the seed for Panafest, focusing "our minds on our past, present and future through our powerfully moving artistic traditions".' See http://www.ghana. co.uk/news/content.asp?articleID=9493)

Bubuama, MacDonald. 'PANAFEST, Emancipation will unite Africans' *Daily Graphic*, 28 July 2003, 17. (Reports that Kojo Yankah spoke at the Emancipation event at Assin Praso Heritage Village. There were tributes to Efua Sutherland and to Rawlings 'who [we read] also put forward the idea of Emancipation Day in 1998 after attending a similar event in the Caribbean in 1998'.)

Gyan-Apenteng, Kwadwo 'Sankofa'. 'Panafest set to thrill!' *Michigan Citizen*, 2 August 2003. (A board member has an article published in the US. Refers to over 5,000 artists participating from some 40 countries being represented.)

Moffatt, Nii Addokwei. 'PANAFEST kicks off', *The Mirror*, 26 July 2003, 28. (Reports that PANAFEST opened at National Theatre, i.e. in Accra, on 24 July. Announces that a play by Owusu (*The Twins*) would be performed on the 29th, and that there would be a Vigil for Emancipation Day (31st). There was to be a concert to round things off. Note: Many sets of twins had been collected for the production. JG.)

Nutor, Nutor Bibini. 'Panafest Launch Spells Hope for Continent', *Ghanaian Times*, 2 August 2003, 14. (Reports on the launch of 'Organization of African Development Initiative Systems' by Nkrabea Effah-Darteh, held at Adisadel during PANAFEST. This was linked with the Black Lineage Reality Research Centre (BLRRC). *Pan African Post* (a newspaper), 'Arise and Shine Africa' (a patriotic cassette), and Effah-Dartey's *The Pan African Renaissance and the hidden prophecy* (book) were also launched. Note: My impression is that the BLRRC was a short-lived initiative of Narrow Way Gospel. (website down, April 2012.)

Quaicoe, Shirley. 'Panellists from Cape Coast express views on PANAFEST and Emancipation', *The Mirror*, 2 August 2003, 20. (Includes comments from Esi Sutherland.)

2005
Anon. 'Panafest will remain the bona fide property of Ghana - Yankah', www.ghanaweb.com source GNA. (Quotes Yankah at inauguration of a 25-member national executive committee (NEC) given responsibility for planning PANAFEST 2005.)

Anon. 'All is set for the 7th PANAFEST, says Yankah', www.ghanahomepage. com 11 February 2005. (Report of a Press Conference given by Yankah at which he reported on preliminary work undertaken by the PANAFEST Foundation. He announced that the edition would be held from 21 July to 1 August and the theme was: 'The Re-emergence of African Civilization'. He indicated that he had requested that airlines make discount fares available for those attending the festival.)

Bonney, Emmanuel. 'Panafest kicks off July 24', 13 July 2005. Accessed 18/7/2005: (Kojo Yankah spoke about the programme that would include a

Durbar, carnival, emancipation day events, and bazaar. The article stressed that the festival was a developmental, educational and spiritual occasion, not a tourism event. Reported that no Ghana government agency had offered to support any Ghanaian artists – as yet. Looked forward to the launching of the Joseph Project that involved welcoming returnees from the African diaspora, in 2007.)

Giomanni, Francesca. 'Panafest 2005: The Re-Emergence of African Civilization', See *afriche e orienti* - the journal (Bologna), issue 4, 2005.

Gocking, Roger. *The History of Ghana*, Waterford, CT: Greenwood, 2005. (Includes relevant background on the arts and tourism.)

Kemp, Renee. 'An Apology in Ghana', www.pbs.org/wonders/Episodes/ Epi3/3_rete4d.htm, 14 01 2005. (Kemp describes paying a visit to Cape Coast 'last year' for PANAFEST, and watching a ritual apology from chiefs. She says the event was held 'just outside Accra' and suggests it removes any justification of action by predatory young African-Americans. She describes the occasion as 400 years in coming and the atmosphere as 'joyous'.)

Morosetti, Tiziana. 'Panfest 2005: Review of ben-Abdallah's *The Slaves Revisited*', *Research in African Literatures*, 39, 2 (Summer 2007), 227-232. (Review of a new version of the play put on in Cape Coast Castle.)

Owoo, John. 'Nkrabea, The Man Of Destiny Promises A Political Shock', *Graphic Ghana*, http://www.graphicghana.info/article.asp?artid=14293. (Includes: 'Theatre man, Nkrabea Effah-Dartey, has retreated into backstage and [is] gearing up to strike what he describes as the biggest shock on the world of politics.' Indicates that Nkrabea intends to run for President on the New Patriotic Party ticket. Nkrabea is described as having 'over 100 scripts to his credit', and as leading a theatre group, Theatre Mirrors, that 'has put up over 1,000 public performances'. His policies include support for the arts – 'there are (he is quoted as saying) 93 jobs for every single production', and he talks of upgrading PANAFEST that has 'degenerated into disco sessions, slave walks and musical extravaganza'.)

2007
Paintsil, David Allan. 'Ghana: Citizens Urged to Participate in Panafest', http://allafrica.com/stories/200706260945.html, *Ghanaian Chronicle* (Accra), 26 June 2007 (Posted to the web 26 June 2007. Reports that the Co-Chairman of the Pan-African Historical Theatre Festival (PANAFEST) and Omanhene of Oguaa Traditional Area, Osabarima Kwesi Atta II, had called on Ghanaians to participate in PANAFEST, Emancipation Day, and the Joseph Project 'slated from July 22 to August 2'.)

2009
Anon. 'Tourism Minister promises grand Panafest, Emancipation 2011', *Travel and Tourism*, 3 August 2009. See http://www.modernghana.com/ news/230723/1/tourism-minister-promises-grand-panafest-emancipat. html. 'The Minister of Travel and Tourism, Mrs Juliana Azumah-Mensah, has promised Ghanaians and Africans in the Diaspora a grand Pan African Festival (Panafest) and Emancipation Day in the year 2011, following the not too impressive one this year.'

Anny, Josh. 'Poorly organized Panafest ends, but last concert was good', *Daily Express* (Accra), 8 August, 2009. (Final paragraph contains a reference to need for government involvement.)

Paintsil , David Alan. 'Panafest 2009 Opens in Cape Coast', http://allafrica. com/stories/200907271717.html, and http://www.modernghana.com/ news/229869/1/panafest-2009-opens-in-cape-coast.html 28 July 2009. (Included a call by President John Evans Atta Mills for 'the African Union [AU] to renew its commitment to the celebration of the Pan African Historical Theatre Festival (Panafest), [in order] to accelerate the unification of Africans in the Diaspora, and those on the continent'. The speech, that was read on the President's behalf by Mike Alex Hammah, Minister of Transportation, 'also appealed to the AU to give Africans in the Diaspora a forum at AU summits …'. The Central Regional Minister, Ama Benyiwa Doe, spoke about the slave routes.

Zaney, G D. 'Ghana Prepares to celebrate Panafest / Emancipation and World Tourism Days', See www.modernghana.com. (Refers to forthcoming events: e.g. PANAFEST to be held 16 July – 1 August. Zaney dates Emancipation Day celebration from 1998; and PANAFEST from 1992 as a biennial event linked to telling 'the truth about the history of Africa'. Mrs Azumah-Mensah , Minister of Tourism, spoke about these events.)

2010
Adrover, Lauren, David Donkor and Christina S. McMahon. 'The Ethics and Pragmatics of Making Heritage a Commodity: Ghana's PANAFEST 2009', *The Drama Review* (New York), 54 (Summer 2010), 155-161. (The three contributors describe and reflect on experiences at PANAFEST events and raise pertinent questions. Illustrations include pictures of Centre Resurgent performing *The PlainTruth* in the courtyard of Cape Coast Castle. The research benefits from interviews with Kohain Haleyi conducted on 20 November and 11 October 2009.)

2011
Daabu, Malik Abass Daabu. 'PANAFEST launched but diasporians unhappy', *My Joy on Line*, http://news.myjoyonline.com/travel/201106/68286.asp,

accessed 2011/06/27. (Daabu gave particular prominence to the concern expressed by 'A member of the diasporian community in Ghana, KOFI EL SHABAZZ, [who...] accused successive governments of systematically undermining the objectives of the Pan-African Festival [PANAFEST], and Emancipation Day'. Shabazz spoke emotionally at the Accra opening of the event as did the Minister of Tourism, Akua Sena Dansua. Dansua 'admonished EL SHABAZZ and the others to help the government make the programme a success by inviting as many Diasporians as possible'. The theme was 'Re-Uniting the African Family: Challenges and Prospects' and the programme included wreath laying, an international concert, a Grand Durbar of Chiefs and People of Cape Coast, visits to historical sites in Cape Coast and Elmina, the symbolic crossing of the River Pra, a Redemption March, and a Reverential Night with a candle light procession through Cape Coast Castle, and Emancipation Day Celebration at Assin Manso. See: http://news.myjoyonline.com/travel/201106/68286.asp)

2012
Ayim-Aboagye, Desmond. 2012 PANAFEST and Emancipation Day celebration launched', 14 April 2012, http://www.modernghana.com/ news/389020/1/2012-panafest-and-emancipation-day-celebration-lau. html. This is an account of an event looking forward to the festival. It was held in Accra and the Minister of Tourism dwelt on promoting 'Ghana as the gateway to Africa'.

International Festivals & Transnational Theatre Circuits in Egypt
Ambassadors of no nation

SONALI PAHWA

Egypt's former Minister of Culture, Farouk Hosni, inaugurated the Cairo International Festival for Experimental Theatre (CIFTET) in 1988, when Hosni Mubarak's regime had launched a wave of reforms aimed at globalising the national economy in accordance with International Monetary Fund guidelines. As imported commodities began to pour into Egypt in greater volume, and as satellite television channels brought in foreign genres, state officials sought pre-emptively to define the future of national culture in an era of economic globalisation. The word *al-thaqafa* (culture) had connoted high culture in Arabic, and the Ministry of Culture had traditionally subsidised literature and art as well as the theatre, that, in the European sense, had gained prestige as a result of Ottoman and British rule. Together with other Western art forms, it had entered the Egyptian cultural canon, and during the 20th century, Egyptian theatre grew robustly. It prospered particularly during periods when state theatres fostered playwriting and subsidised ticket prices. During the 1960s and 70s, state cultural institutions also sponsored playwrights and directors to study abroad, and commissioned a significant number of translations. Intellectual exchange with Eastern Europe, the Soviet Union, and Britain made for a varied theatre that conducted a dialogue with international trends. However, according to Farouk Hosni, appointed by a regime initiating neo-liberal reforms, the new period of globalisation called for a new style of international theatre.

The culture minister contributed a mission statement to the brochure for the first edition of CIFET that began: 'The idea of the Cairo International Festival for Experimental Theatre emerged from my faith that creative expression in all its forms finds a surprising vibrancy in the moment of crossing from one society to another' (quoted in Awad 1989: 1). While the benefits of transnational cultural exchange were well known in Egypt, Hosni's initiative that brought in performances rather than texts, caused a stir, and CIFET opened a welcome window onto the world of theatre outside the nation's borders. Echoing the piecemeal liberalisation of the economy, however, international exchange in theatre was limited to imports, and

Farouk Hosni

An abstract painter who became a state cultural attaché early in his career, Hosni spent two decades in Paris and Rome before being appointed Minister of Culture in 1987. As a loyal functionary and a European-style avant-gardist, Hosni was the regime's ideal choice for formulating cultural policy for a new era of economic globalisation. In an effort to create more visibility for the work of Egyptian artists and dramatists internationally, Hosni instituted in Egypt the festivals and art biennales he had seen in Europe. He also inaugurated new venues in Cairo, such as the Hanager Arts Centre and Modern Dance School, specialising in European-style avant-garde arts. He came in for some criticism from artists involved in both independent and state institutions who thought he was detached from the rich local arts scene and too interested in bringing foreign artists to Egypt.

Hosni's nepotistic administrative style, and his failure to defend artists' freedom when they came under attack for criticising the religious establishment, led to unpopularity. In 2005, after a fatal fire at the Beni Suef Cultural Palace brought to national attention the neglect of small theatres by a ministry that invested its resources in large-scale festivals, he resigned his post briefly.

In 2009, his bid to lead UNESCO was defeated because of the revelation that he had responded to criticism of Hebrew books in the Bibliotheca Alexandrina with a rhetorical statement that these books should be burnt. This nationalist gesture, at a time when Hebrew language and literature continued to be taught at Cairo University, epitomised the defensive stance of Mubarak's Ministry of Culture, which tempered top-down globalisation and unpopular geopolitical alliances with doses of populist rhetoric.

controlled by the state. The invitations sent out by the Ministry of Culture were addressed to government bodies in other countries and official entries were expected. However, despite the rigid control of who participated, CIFET was established as a diverse and exciting ten-day extravaganza. The festival encouraged a large number of fringe performances, several by the independent troupes that had grown out of Egypt's lively university and amateur theatre scene. Officially a venue for viewing world theatre, CIFET became valuable as a site for encounters between dramatists and critics. Many of these took place under the official radar.

Spectatorship, performance and the politics of international exchange

When I attended CIFET from 2002 to 2004, the festival was a major event. Forty-three nations, including sixteen Arab countries, took part and 73 groups participated. The productions were among the most highly anticipated and the best attended performances on Cairo's theatrical calendar. I remember, for example, the excitement with which members of a Cairo puppet theatre troupe watched the Teatro del Carretto's 2002 production of *Biancaneve* (*Snow White*) that featured both puppets and human performers. A number of trans-Arab collaborations blossomed at the festival, and one between Iraqi playwright, Qasim Mohamed, and Egyptian director Hany el-Metennawy resulted in a stirring dance-theatre performance, *Masks, Fabrics and Destinies*, that won the jury's ensemble award in 2003. The festival was a welcome space for exchanging ideas and techniques, particularly for Egyptian dramatists in their twenties and thirties who had few resources for travel. In an earlier generation, they might have taken up permanent jobs in state theatres, and participated in official programmes for foreign travel and study abroad. But in the 21st century overstaffed state institutions were not recruiting and the Ministry of Culture concentrated its budget on a handful of flagship programmes. In this context, younger dramatists relied on training workshops and festivals for exposure to different theatre styles and techniques. Sometimes they delved into CIFET-sponsored translations to find new texts to dramatise. Inasmuch as Egyptian dramatists, like their counterparts elsewhere, were in search of new ways of making theatre, the Cairo International Festival was their main opportunity for discovery.

At each edition of CIFET, young Egyptian directors and troupes marshalled their resources to put on performances that mattered. Even if they had already staged a play once, the prospect of a large 'CIFET audience' and the chance that a famous critic might be present meant that it was worth polishing up the production and putting it on again. Groups knew that a production that succeeded at CIFET, as *Masks, Fabrics, and Destinies* had, might win invitations to participate in other international theatre festivals. However, despite the opportunities it created, some of Egypt's independent dramatists were critical of the festival. Starved of funds for their productions, they resented the vast amounts of taxpayers' money spent on accommodating foreign visitors in five-star hotels during the festival.

These dramatists were working to establish a sustained, continuing theatre in Egypt, a creative life that lasted longer than the ten whirlwind days of CIFET. They were aware that, out of its substantial resources, the Ministry of Culture had built just one new institution in Cairo – the Hanager Experimental Theatre – as a home for new plays by younger dramatists unaffiliated with state theatres. While independent troupes embraced the Hanager and considered it their 'home', they felt that its ten or twelve annual productions fell far short of their needs. For them, CIFET was a blessing, since it was a space for visibility and exposure, and a frustrating, expensive, half-measure in terms of state investment in a national theatre. In 1990, when CIFET was cancelled due to the Gulf War, a group of ten theatre troupes founded the Free Theatre Movement with its own annual festival and a manifesto claiming artistic independence as a right – even when artists applied for production money from state funds. The Free Theatre Movement had its share of crises, but its festival became a fixture in Cairo's theatrical calendar, and even made occasional 'outings' to Minya and Alexandria.

Finding style in translation

On a typical September day at CIFET, the morning and afternoon sessions consisted of paper presentations and roundtable discussion by critics and were poorly attended. Academics who had travelled from afar and were curious to learn more about Arab and Egyptian theatre history, found themselves stymied by linguistic differences and inadequate translation facilities. At the same time, dramatists and critics from Tunisia, Syria or Palestine were pleased to meet up with old friends from the Arab festival circuit. They were often senior members of their theatre communities and their visits were sponsored by their respective Ministries of Culture, or by other state bodies. Younger theatre people were sidelined, and upcoming Egyptian dramatists steered clear of the academic sessions. However, in the evenings, the festival venues were quite different: they buzzed with the pre-theatre chatter of younger Egyptians and of adventurous foreign visitors. Plays in various languages were performed with little or no translation facilities before overflow audiences who had waited eagerly at theatre doors and box-offices. Cultural and linguistic difference proved as attractive in performances as they were counter-productive in the exchange of academic ideas.

For my Egyptian friends, the kinetics and images of physical theatre performances were often the most appealing aspect of CIFET performances.

They spoke enthusiastically of the lyrical dance-and-spoken word perfor-mance, *Neverland*, by Dutch director Kris Niklison at CIFET 2002,[1] and of the South Korean company, Yohangza, that incorporated ritual into its avant-garde play, *Karma*, an award-winner at CIFET 2003. In the absence of surtitle technology at most of Cairo's theatres, CIFET's selection committee sensibly favoured plays that made minimal linguistic demands.

The effect of this (unofficial) policy on Egypt's independent theatre troupes was significant. The Shrapnel Theatre Troupe, a festival veteran, incorporated striking visual images into socially aware productions that included an adaptation of Phaedra centred on a young man struggling against an authoritarian father and unable to marry.

CIFET had the effect of granting legitimacy to dance theatre in Egypt. Mohamed Shafik, Karima Mansour, Mirette Mechail, and Reem Hegab were among the gifted dancers welcomed by theatre troupes as directors and performers, and sometimes as movement trainers for physical theatre productions.

Increasingly, video screens were fitted into Cairo's state theatres and these made multimedia performances possible. While often used to provide backdrops, such as rain for the storm scene in *King Lear*, some independent troupes used them to critique Egyptian and Arab media. For example, the 2004 multimedia productions, *Messing with the Mind* (by Khaled el-Sawy's Haraka troupe) and *Mother I want to be a millionaire* (by Ahmed el-Attar's Ma'bad), used television footage in order to stage satires of, respectively, Arab satellite television during the Iraq war and of the Pop Idol/ X Factor talent show format.

CIFET also strengthened the quest for a distinctively Egyptian theatre among troupes specialising in popular culture. This movement was familiar from the work of the Warsha troupe, whose stunning adaptations of the Hilaliya epic and the ballad of Hassan and Naima had won wide acclaim during the 1980s. CIFET legitimised their preoccupation and encouraged a growing enthusiasm for *shaabi* (popular) theatre in avant-garde circles. The results were seen in the 1998 award-winner *Kohl Pillow* in which the musician-director Intissar Abdel Fattah incorporated rhythm and ritual, and in the perceptive, folksy comedies put on in Cairo by the Misahharati troupe and in Alexandria by Hala. Some dramatists complained that this trend signalled the 'folklorisation' of Egyptian theatre, the preoccupation with folksy genres based on traditional forms that had disappeared from the lives of the urban, middle-class Egyptians who made up the bulk of the theatre-going community. But others welcomed the return of folk culture to the theatrical mainstream, arguing that for decades Egypt's theatre academy had upheld passé, European, literary drama as a model, and had failed to respond to the anti-literary movements of the 20th-century European avant-garde. CIFET consolidated the respectability of folk-style theatre among contemporary Egyptian theatre people.

Globalisation and trans-nationalism in the festival economy

In Egypt's era of neo-liberal globalisation, beginning in the 1990s, state officials re-imagined transnational cultural exchange as a one-way street, importing foreign styles and genres into Egypt. This policy included facilitating the entry of foreign art gallery owners who imposed their own vision of the avant-garde art on local artists, and the paying of foreign dramatists to teach Egyptians playwriting techniques through workshops. However, trans-national exchange through and around CIFET exceeded the space circumscribed by the Ministry of Culture. The annual festivals fostered exchange on its fringe no less than within the official competition among the productions nominated by state cultural bodies. As Egyptian dramatists chatted with visitors over coffee, and shared scripts and techniques, they gained a broader knowledge than was possible within teaching workshops or at Cairo's Academy of Arts. CIFET became a staging ground for the eclectic styles that independent Egyptian dramatists developed. In their own annual, free theatre festivals, and in year-round performances in spaces across Cairo, these troupes presented plays that defied the ossified genre divisions between tragedy and comedy and between modern and folk theatre that were considered important in Egypt's state theatres.

Genre and social space had been linked programmatically in the policies of successive Egyptian ministries of culture. Separate theatres specialised in different genres and were intended to appeal to distinct audiences. The flagship National Theatre showcased classic European dramas and new plays by Egypt's established playwrights for the cosmopolitan literati. Meanwhile, less prestigious and, by comparison, poorly-equipped theatres hosted popular comedies for broader-based audiences. In this way, the theatre landscape of the Egyptian capital reflected a class-based vision of social aesthetics that was fundamentally at odds with the vision of international theatre and the concept of dramatic genres as products of different national cultures that had given birth to CIFET.

The eclectic Egyptian theatre which blossomed in the wake of CIFET made it clear that Egyptians recognised varieties of their experience across dramatic genres. This had political implications, since audiences accustomed to experiencing disparity within a politically repressive, economically liberal, and vastly unequal society, responded to the shock of aesthetic difference within a performance. Furthermore, the internationalism of CIFET prompted local dramatists to explore the diversity of culture within Egypt. Rapid social changes produced generational differences in the capital, while uneven developments in metropolitan and provincial Egypt often accentuated regional differences. While the idea of a national theatre was undone by widening disparities within the nation, the small scale and idiosyncratic styles of plays at the international experimental festival appealed to those Egyptian dramatists grappling with social change.

After the Revolution of 25 January 2011, Farouk Hosni lost his position, and the former regime's policies of globalisation were discredited in both economic and cultural terms. CIFET 2011 has been cancelled, with the official explanation that at a time of upheaval the transitional Egyptian government cannot ensure the security of visiting theatre troupes.

At the time of writing (in the middle of 2011), it seems quite possible that CIFET will not return: it was too closely linked with an unpopular minister and his policies. However, other international festivals may well emerge in its place. There are indications of what form this might take since Cairo's emerging free theatre dramatists have joined forces with musicians and artists to organise a monthly open-air arts festival called Art is a Square (*al-fann midan*). These practitioners have left behind the bureaucratic institutions of the Ministry of Culture and embraced a free festival mode of organisation that encourages participation by new artists and emphasises collaboration. Transnational exchange is part of the independent theatre world in many different ways, from dramatists' use of translated texts to their participation in technical workshops organised by visiting artists.

It can be argued that CIFET prepared for this development, that it put Egypt on the world theatre map, and that it opened avenues for exchange between Egyptian and foreign dramatists. The 2011 uprising and anticipated loosening of restrictions on cultural production promise to redraw the map of theatrical networks and make transnationalism serve Egyptian dramatists more richly.

NOTE

1   For more details on this and other plays at CIFET 2002, see Nehad Selaiha, 2002. 'Intersections, Transpositions'. *Al-Ahram Weekly* 19–25 September 2002. http://weekly. ahram.org.eg/2002/604/cul.htm

REFERENCE

Samir Awad, ed., 1989. *Mahrajan al-qahira al-dawli li-l-masrah al-tajribi* 1-10 September 1988 *al-kitab al-watha'iqi*, p. 1

The Jos Theatre Festival 2004–2011
A theatre festival in a divided community

PATRICK-JUDE OTEH

Introduction

In an article jointly written with Victor S. Dugga that appeared in *African Theatre: Companies* (2008), I told part of the story of the Jos Repertory Theatre (JRT). Here I will draw out a single strand from our experience – the organisation of a series of theatre festivals – and explore what lessons can be learnt from trying to foster an elaborate theatre event in a city being swept into a self-destructive spiral. Since background erupts into the foreground in this study, it is important to sketch in something of the geographical, social, cultural and political context of the city of Jos in which JRT has endeavoured to establish and maintain an annual Festival.

Capital of the appropriately named Plateau State, the city of Jos enjoys a pleasant climate and boasts beautiful rock formations. For many decades, it was regarded as a rich melting pot of communities and performance traditions. With the arrival of television in Nigeria, Jos became the setting for soap operas, such as *Cockcrow at Dawn* and *Behind the Clouds,* and so came to represent the republic to itself. In 2000, it was a thriving commercial centre, its prosperity and vitality epitomised by the huge market in the Terminus area. However, an eruption of religious intolerance on 7 September, 2001, in which hundreds died, proved the terrifying harbinger of an unsettled decade. The casualty figures have always been a source of dispute. For example, the official figure for the 2001 crisis was 165 civilians and one soldier but CNN reported that over 1,000 had been killed.[1] In the following year, the market went up in flames in circumstances that have never been explained. This scattered the traders throughout the urban area, and subsequently shops sprang up in all nooks and corners of the city. The loss of revenue to the government resulting from the hiatus in commercial life has been just one of a series of challenges that has confronted successive governments.

The tensions that erupted in 2001 have led to the solidification of the divisions in the city that has moved apart into religious, ethnic and linguistic

75

enclaves. Levels of violence have fluctuated with peaks of terrifyingly naked aggression and brutal destruction, and the years covered by the Jos Festivals, from 2004 onwards, have seen the arts struggle to exist against this bloody backcloth. In this context, to complain about curfews or to use their existence to explain decisions may seem to suggest a turning away from social engagement. The curfews are just part of the difficult situation that has confronted us.

While acknowledging difficulties and failures, I nevertheless hold out hope, based on the evidence of the support received in the dark days of March 2009, that the festival can offer a space where the different segments of the community can, however briefly, come together. I am convinced that the festival, that the theatre, can free people from self-imposed imprisonment, from living isolated lives behind locked doors in defended ghettos. That, however, is the light at the end of the tunnel. My contribution to this book is plodding rather than inspirational, drawing attention to policies and personalities, hopes and fears, highs and lows of six years as a festival organiser – or a would-be festival organiser.

The Jos Theatre Festivals: an overview

In 2004, the Jos Repertory Theatre received support from the West African office of the Ford Foundation.[2] The arrangement included support for a Festival of Theatre and since then JRT has tried to organise annual festivals. For reasons that have been suggested and will become clearer, we have succeeded in mounting only five festivals, in 2004, 2006, 2007, 2008, and 2009. The arrangements, including the venue for events, the month for performances, together with the source of the performing groups and the kind of plays selected have varied in response to various pressures. Lessons have been learned, opportunities have offered themselves and constraints have altered. Over the years, the festivals have had an impact that I have found hard to measure, but that I will attempt to suggest.

The first festival was held over five weekends during March and April 2004 with all performances at the state Arts Centre. Subsequently programmes have been more intensive, typically lasting seven to ten days, and we have moved from the Arts Centre to a hotel and, more recently, to the Cultural Centre established in Jos by the Alliance Française. The starting times of performances have been affected both by the level of violence in the city, and by the imposition of curfews. Transport problems, such as the closing of the airport, and perceptions (real or exaggerated) of the level of danger in the State have had an impact on the participation of groups from outside the city. Inevitably the size of our budget has affected what we have been able to offer and achieve. In the brief report that follows it can be seen that what reaches the stage is clearly affected by those who have supported us. The influence of the Ford Foundation, the British Council, and the

Alliance Française can be detected in various decisions that I refer to.

In trying to assess the achievements of the Jos Theatre Festivals, we are particularly proud of our success in providing opportunities for local performers and in exposing them to a range of challenges. We are happy that we have attracted and collaborated with groups from outside Jos and outside Nigeria. While we have been wounded by the violence in the city in the most tragic way – performers have been killed! – and while we concede that the violence has been followed by the 'death' – or at least the falling into a coma for a period from 2009 – of the festival itself, I am, I insist, confident that the festival was missed and it will be repeatedly revived.

With the help of an Appendix in which basic facts about the festival programmes are laid out, I will tell the story of the first five festivals highlighting the evolution of a tradition and drawing attention to some of the factors that have affected work for the stage. [Drawing on material available after this paper was submitted, information has been added about the 6th, the 2012 edition of the festival. J.G. Ed.]

The format of the 2004 Jos Festival of Theatre

In planning the first Jos Festival of Theatre, the organisers were certain that they wanted to arrange a varied and appropriate programme, and to create a meeting ground where locals could interact with those prominent in the national and international theatre. We hoped, within quite narrow budgetary constraints, to establish a breeding ground for a new generation of men and women of the Nigerian stage.

The initial programme was arrived at through discussions between the artistic director and the production coordinator of JRT, Patrick-Jude Oteh and Austin Efe Okonkwo, and reflected interest in the national heritage and in productions that might point to the future of the theatre in the country. This initial two-man team later metamorphosed into a six-man national play selection committee which was tasked not only to decide on the works for the festival but also with choosing directors for the new initiative. Leaders of this committee over the years have included a playwright, Professor Sam Kafewo of the Ahmadu Bello University, and a poet, Denja Abdullahi.

In the event, five productions were scheduled in 2004: two were Nigerian classics, *Death and the King's Horseman* and an adaptation of *Things Fall Apart*. Two others had roots in Jos: a new play, *Our House*, developed as part of a collaborative venture with a theatre group in Glasgow (see *African Theatre: Companies*) and a dance drama, *My Pride* by Joe Fom (presented by The Black Heritage Group) explored the repercussions of polygamy and early marriage. The fifth production was a revival of Yahaya Dangana's *The Royal Chamber* by a group made up of performers from Abuja, Lagos, Minna, Kaduna and Jos that had initially been brought together to put on the production at the All Africa Games, Abuja in 2003.

We chose the 3,000-seat Professor Luka Bentu Arts Centre for the festival venue. The foundation stone for this state-supported facility had been laid during the heady 1970s, but the building was still uncompleted more than thirty years later. We had thought that using the Centre would draw attention to its poor state of repair and we hoped that the N50,000 we paid each weekend, a total of N250,000 (US$1,650), would be used for essential work and maintenance. (We were wildly optimistic: this did not happen and the Centre remains a sorry sight, one among several uncompleted projects in Plateau State.)

The First Festival was spread over five week-ends with each play running Thursday-Friday-Saturday. This arrangement, accommodating perceptions that theatre-going was an end-of-week activity, had major implications for the advertising budget. In order to try to attract audiences, we set in motion a prolonged, sustained and expensive publicity campaign. We printed one poster listing all the shows and then had flyers for each play distributed around the city during the week of performance. Knowing the power of the electronic media, we recorded radio and television jingles that ran throughout the festival. Although we were given discounts from the two dominant stations in Jos – the federal government-owned Nigerian Television Authority (NTA) and the state government-owned Plateau Radio and Television Corporation (PRTVC), the publicity costs were very high and, it must be admitted, unsuccessful. Even though the 'five weekends' arrangement allowed news of the festival to spread by word of mouth, audiences were disappointing. There were perhaps 125 people each night in the 3,000-seat auditorium.

Providing accommodation for the performers was a major budgetary item. In JRT we had learned to make use of small, versatile, hard-working casts – and this was reflected in demands made on the five actors who put on *Our House*. Other groups had not learned that lesson. This was particularly the case with the production of *The Royal Chamber* that involved a company that numbered twenty-five! As will be apparent from a glance at the plays put on at subsequent festivals, programmes have included several two-handers, namely the hugely successful South African plays *Woza Albert!* and *Sizwe Bansi is Dead*. My own work as a facilitator, including *Chariot without Riders*, put on at the Second Festival, reflects my experience of working with Collective Artistes and with the Performance Studio Workshop under the direction of Chuck Mike. I was particularly impressed when working with him on Biyi Bandele's adaptation of Chinua Achebe's *Things Fall Apart*. Other influential works include the plays created by Mbongeni Ngema, Barney Simon and John Kani.

The drawing out of the festival meant that there was, sadly, little or no interaction between different groups. When the festival was over, we looked back on it with some satisfaction, but we also recognised that it had been a logistical nightmare and a tremendous drain on our financial resources.

The Second Jos Theatre Festival 2006

We initially anticipated that the Second Festival would be in 2005, but when we set to work we soon recognised that it would take time to absorb the lessons of 2004. One of these was that preparations could not be rushed; another that sourcing scripts was a slow process. The success of *Our House* showed us both the value of creating opportunities for new writers and new directors and that these things could not be rushed.

We reconciled ourselves to missing a year and recognised the need to make some radical changes in planning the Second Festival and holding it in 2006. For example, having noted that no improvements had been made to the Professor Luka Bentu Arts Centre, we resolved to move performances to the much smaller (250-seater) hall of the Crest Hotel and Gardens in the up-marked Rayfield area of the city. The move worked and we attracted members of the government who would never have attended performances in the run-down Arts Centre. We received great encouragement from the proprietor of the hotel who showed his appreciation in practical ways. For example, performers staying at the hotel were offered discounted rates and the hall was renamed 'Festival Hall'.

With groups staying and performing on a single site, transport costs and stress levels were reduced, and there was the added benefit that a festival atmosphere was created: in and around the hotel, there was rewarding interaction between members of different companies

I have already mentioned *Chariot without Riders*, an economical piece that drew forth exceptional performances from the two actors involved: Seyi Lovingkindness Babalola and Rotimi Oladapo. The Festival programme also included *Ajarat,* a new script for that year's festival, and some imported innovative work – the result of the link we had cultivated with members of the Clyde Unity Theatre. We continued the 'tradition' of including a dance drama, this time by Ebony Theatre from Benue State, and a classic text from the Nigerian repertoire – this time *The Lion and the Jewel.*

Happily, there was space in the Festival programme for the participation of Project Phakama and for the acting workshops they conducted. International presences, partly made possible by the British Council, included Mari Binnie from the Clyde Unity Theatre in Glasgow, and Paul Brett and Tabitha Neal, part of the London International Festival of Theatre.

The change of venue altered the atmosphere of the Festival and the composition of the audiences, since, as we anticipated, those who found their way to the Hotel tended to include the affluent and holders of important government posts. For better or worse, the festival became a function to be seen at. To illustrate how our partnership with the Crest Hotel worked it should be recorded that we hired the hall at half the usual rate and paid N500,000 (US$3,290) for the ten-day festival. No doubt glad to be full and enjoying the extra business that the festival brought, cast and crew members were able to stay at the hotel at less than half the advertised rates. A room normally costing N7,500 (US$50) was available to us for N3,000 (US$20).

Segun Ajayi summarised the impact of the festival in an article that appeared 6 March 2006 in the following terms: '...for a long time, residents of the rock city will relive the excitements of a fiesta that was not only organised to foster a theatre-going culture in the capital city but (to) test virgin scripts and discover fresh talents.'

Third, Fourth and Fifth Festivals, 2007, 2008, 2009

The Third Jos Theatre Festival was also centred on the Crest Hotel but, anxious to spread its impact, we also made use of some facilities at what was then the French Cultural Centre and is now the French Institute (FCC), operated by the Alliance Française. While we cherished our collaboration with the Ford Foundation, the input from the British Council, and the partnership established with the Crest Hotel, we became deeply involved over the years with the Alliance Française who provided the venue for all the events within the festival. We were very grateful for this support and reciprocated by putting on a French play as part of the event.

Between 16 and 25 February 2007, the third festival offered a programme of six plays that remained true in some respects to the 'tradition' established in the earlier years. The productions offered included a dance drama, in this case *Yaga Simi – for the sake of love,* and a classic of African drama, not Nigerian this time: *Sizwe Bansi is Dead.* In addition to some new work, including *Beyond the Sunset,* brought up from Lagos, and *Bara* by Folorunsho Moshood, there was, for the first time, a production of a European classic, Anouilh's *Antigone.* The choice and the production, on which I collaborated with the Deputy Director of the Alliance Française in Jos, Pierre Marques Alfarroba, indicated the exploration of collaborative possibilities with the French cultural body.

For the Fourth Festival, held in May 2008, all productions were mounted at the FCC where the facilities were ideal. The Centre has both an open-air performance space that can accommodate 600, and an indoor theatre that can hold 160. The 'front of house' is more than adequate with surrounding walls that offer opportunities to display posters of previous productions and on which our sponsors can advertise. In a corner of the site, there is an attractive bar.

The move to the FCC was facilitated by the interest in the theatre of influential figures in the French expatriate community, notably Jean Louis Reborra, the Director of the Alliance Française, and his colleague, Pierre Marques Alfarroba. Following the involvement with *Antigone* mentioned above, Alfarroba directed Reborra's play, *Mots,* and emerged as an actor in the role of the District Commissioner in *Things Fall Apart.* This informed and creative input was coupled with valuable support from the French Embassy that came with the condition that a play by a French dramatist be included in the programme. From the Appendix it can be seen that in addition to the plays mentioned, the festival programmes have included work by Eugène Ionesco (2008) – Rumanian but Francophone and Francophile – and Jean-Paul Sartre (2009). This inclusion of European work reflects our openness to influence and the realities of running a theatre festival.

In other respects, the selection continued along familiar lines; indeed it even included a revival of *Things Fall Apart* that had opened the first festival. Room was also found for another classic African theatre text, Joe de Graft's *Sons and Daughters*. Soyinka was represented by his difficult *Madmen and Specialists* that gained from being seen in the same programme as a quintessential Absurdist text, *The Lesson*. New work was present in the form of CIDA'S *No More Mistakes* that formed a bridge to the didactic productions about HIV/AIDS that JRT had put on with funding from the Ford Foundation.

Since we were still accommodating performers in the Crest Hotel, the use of the FCC meant that we incurred transport costs. However, our difficulties were set against the advantage of making things easier for others, and we were aware that it was more convenient for patrons using public transport to get to the FCC than to the Hotel. The conditions attached to our original grant from the Ford Foundation required that we hold the festival during February and March of each year but, because of the level of tension in Jos at the beginning of 2008, we had to negotiate for a later date. As we did so, we began to receive calls from regular patrons suggesting that we move the festival to Abuja. Responding to these requests, we fixed a date in March when the Jos Festival would be held in the federal capital. We even decided on a title that reflected the transfer and called it 'Jos Festival of Theatre (in Abuja)!' with the strap line: 'Sharing the talents of the city of Jos with the city of Abuja!' As can be imagined, this anticipated migration raised huge issues of organisation and increased expenditure. At this point, however, the Dusk to Dawn (6pm to 6am) curfew was altered to 9pm to 6am, and this gave us the option of scheduling performances in Jos in the early evening. We calculated that workers who left their offices at 3.00 pm would be able to attend performances at the FCC that started at 5.00 and, when shows finished at 6.30, they could reach home before 9.00 pm.

In shifting the venue for performances, we were careful not to alienate the proprietor of the Crest: links were maintained and visiting performers were still accommodated there. In the event, the idea of moving to Abuja was shelved, but has never been lost sight of. Continuing disruptions to life in Jos have meant that we have repeatedly considered the possibility of holding the Festival in Abuja.

The November 2008 crisis led to the loss of many lives. As before the number is disputed, but the formula 'more than 500 people' is frequently encountered. By February 2009, Jos was a divided city with areas 'set aside' for the indigenes, for incoming Christians and also incoming Moslems. This separation was not established by government fiat but was the result of the crisis and of internal migrations: each group felt more secure within its own zone, with people of like minds and beliefs.

Planning for the Fourth and Fifth Jos Theatre Festivals was undertaken in tense situations of either a stampede or an actual crisis. The stampede takes the form of people running all over the town with no one knowing what the real challenge is or where the danger is coming from.

In planning the Fifth Festival (2009), we lined up the wonderful South African two-hander *Woza Albert!* We also found a dance drama in Bose Ayeni-Tsevende's *Morning yet on Judgement Day*, accommodated Jean-Paul Sartre's existentialist *No Exit*, and promoted local works by Philip Begho and Adinoyi Ojo Onukaba that showed our success in sourcing a wide range of material. Both Begho's *Smallie* and Adinoyi Ojo Onukaba's *A Resting Place* had been submitted in response to JRT's call for scripts. The festival was rounded off with Soyinka's *The Trials of Brother Jero* – a really challenging call to the faithful to be alert to the wiles of those who set themselves up as religious leaders.

We are acutely aware that our audiences are adept at detecting local resonances in the plays put on – they draw out, or read in, relevant messages. On 6 April 2009, blogger Sumaila Isah Umaisha posted the following in response to the festival productions:

> The choice of the plays for the festival was equally influenced by the crisis and its aftermath. From Athol Fugard's *Woza Albert!* [sic] directed by Tunde Awosanmi, to Wole Soyinka's *The Trials of Brother Jero* directed by Austin Efe Okonkwo, the plays focus on the need for tolerance and peaceful co-existence irrespective of religious, ethnic or political differences. Even the new plays – Spencer Okoroafor's *Visa to Nowhere* and Phillip Begho's *Smallie* – are loud statements on the Jos experience. The festival was a dedication to the Jos crisis and at the same time a celebration of the Nigerian theatre and theatre practitioners.

The mood of the 2009 Festival was significantly different from the other festivals. We had thought that because of the tension in the city, attendances would be down but we were very wrong. Patrons turned out in their hundreds, and one night of the final play, *Brother Jero*, attracted an audience of 615! It was immensely gratifying, almost as if, after being trapped in their houses by the crisis, people were released by and for the production. We felt that the festival was contributing to healing the rifts in the community.

Looking back and forward

In retrospect, we can see that the troubles in Jos have cost us dear in financial terms. Since 2006 the income from the festival has plummeted, and we have 'lost' some N4,000,000 (US$26,316) that we might have expected from gate fees, sponsorship and advertising. Our hotel partners and the other organisations that were beginning to identify with the festival as an annual event have also suffered.

Because the crisis has continued the festival was not held in 2010 or 2011. The city has become deeply segregated along Moslem, Christian, Indigene and Non-Indigene lines. There are 'no-go' areas and, as a result local people, our audiences, are uncertain about where the festival, almost literally, stands. Invited performers have often remarked that they can't imagine how people still live in this town. Now even those of us who live here are perplexed. Violence escalates, family life has become difficult, commercial – and artistic life – is almost impossible.

With groups inside Nigeria but beyond the borders of Plateau State we have often found it difficult to get a quick response to an invitation. This is due to the fact that a lot of us are incurable optimists who believe that things will always happen at the last minute in our favour. We must always understand that once 'a crisis' starts, the airport in Plateau State shuts down and the daily flight that comes in from Lagos is disrupted until the situation improves. For the Nigerian groups coming in by air, we have to guarantee that they will be met at the airport. If it is not possible for them to fly directly to Jos, we have to meet them in Abuja and transport them to Jos, usually with a police escort.

At the 2009/Fifth edition of the Jos Festival of Theatre, it became clear that the festival could survive, and indeed thrive, without a regular grant from the Ford Foundation. This was due principally to the fact that we were able to fundraise a total of N615,000 (US$4,011) from internal sources and to this was added our income from tickets N400,000 (US$2,614). It is also pertinent at this point to note that the Ford Foundation had encouraged us to seek other partners and raise funds from them. The only limit that the Foundation set was that we could not spend more than N3,000,000 (US$19,607) of their grant to us on the event; it was clear that the festival was to be only a part of our output, and that the grant had to last us eighteen months.

We were aware that other festivals were held in Nigeria and these include the annual National Festival of Arts (NAFEST) that is supported by the Ministry of Tourism and Culture and the National Council for Arts and Culture. There is also the more recently established Abuja Carnival which is supported by the Federal Capital Territory and the Federal Ministry of Tourism and Culture. Because of their links with the federal government and because they encompass all the arts, we referred to the Jos Festival of Theatre as 'the only surviving independent theatre festival in Nigeria'.

Against the odds and despite challenges, the Jos Festival of Theatre has retained its independence and its commitment to the stage and has survived. Given the current situation in the city, we do not know what the future will hold. However, we are optimistic that once a solution has been found to the Jos crisis, the festival will be restored to robust life. The talents are ready and the promoters of the festival are willing.

Coda [J.G. Ed.]

After Patrick-Jude Oteh submitted this account and just before this volume went to press, reports came in of the 2012 edition of the Jos Theatre Festival. In an attempt to provide an update, I have extracted the following from a piece with the byline, 'From the live stage with Patrick-Jude Oteh' and other sources that were posted during February and March 2012. I have also added a summary of the programme to the Appendix.[3]

The Sixth edition of the JTF opened on 25 February 2012 at the Alliance Française, with the 'classic' contribution to the programme of a dramatisation of Achebe's *Arrow of God*, written by Emeka Nwabueze and entitled *When the Arrow Rebounds*. Sectarian violence erupted in Jos the next day when suicide bombers attacked the headquarters of the Church of Christ in Nigeria (COCIN). Despite the damage and disruption this caused, the festival, as in the past, defied the odds by continuing. Indeed, partly because American support meant gate fees could be waived, the turnout was 'unprecedented in the history of the festival'. The programme offered a closely-packed week of performances together with workshops in arts management, directing and salsa dancing.

The Achebe adaptation was repeated on the Sunday – the day of the explosion – and was followed by *Ceremonies in Dark Old Men* (Lonne Elder III), *Bargain Hunting* (Adinoyi Ojo Onukaba), *For One Night Only* (Dipo Agboluaje) and *The Man Who Never Died* (Barrie Stavis).

The plays by Elder and Stavis draw attention to the major American input to the 2012 Festival, and this emphasis was also found in the extent to which the example of the Kennedy Centre for the Performing Arts provided a model for the arts management course that Jude-Oteh has helped establish. Set in Chicago, *Ceremonies* was written by an African American actor-playwright with impeccable credentials: he had been in the cast of the Broadway production of Lorraine Hansberry's *Raisin in the Sun*! His play, like *Raisin*, drew attention to the circumstances of Black family life in the US. More particularly, it explored family tensions and the limited options available for employment.

Stavis's play, presented on 1 and 2 March, told the story of Swedish-American folk-singer and labour activist Joe Hill (1879-1915). The script, published in 1954, is notable for is modest staging requirements, and is just one of the many tributes to Hill's integrity and creativity. Through his concern for the exploited and, more specifically in this context, through Paul Robeson who recorded 'I dreamed I saw Joe Hill last night', the Swedish-American has a place in African American history. This chimed with the interest of the US Mission in Nigeria and, as a result of US support for the Festival, entrance fees were removed.

While the first two productions on the programme can be described as 'family tragedies', the third was very different. In Oladipo Agboluaje's *For One Night Only,* that is significantly subtitled '*a migration fantasy*', the London-born, partly Nigerian-educated dramatist explores the aspirations and frustrations of two illegal immigrants in the UK who hope to find success in the entertainment industry. Produced at the Ovalhouse Theatre (London) in 2008, the play indicates that writing and talent fostered among the diasporian community in the UK, and by such bodies as the Ovalhouse, Tiata Fahodzi and Soho Theatre, is starting to provide material for adventurous Nigerian groups.

Finally, the festival programme also gave an opportunity for patrons to see *Bargain Hunting* by Adinoyi Ojo Onukaba, sometimes 'Onukaba Adinoyi-Ojo', the former managing director of the *Daily Times*. His play, *The Killing Swamp* that draws on the life and untimely death of Ken Saro-Wiwa came to attention when it was shortlisted for a major Nigerian prize in 2010, but *Bargain Hunting* is not nearly so well known. It is a family-focused drama raising the issues of euthanasia and inheritance and was directed by Emman Emeasealu of the University of Port Harcourt with a company from Rivers State.

As in previous years, possibilities of enabling the festival to make an impact in Abuja were explored, but transport costs were, as in previous years, a major limiting factor. As can be imagined, the cost of travelling particularly affected the prospect of incorporating the production from distant Port Harcourt in the programme

NOTES

1 See TELL Magazine, No 11, March 22, 2010, pg.28 and '300 bodies taken to mosque on 2nd day of Nigeria riots'. CNN. 2008-08-29. http://www.cnn.com/2008/WORLD/africa/11/29/nigeria.riots.ap/index.html?imw=Y&iref=mpstoryemail Retrieved 2008-11-30

2 Over the years, the JRT has gratefully received support from a variety of funders. In addition to the Ford Foundation, these have included the British Council, the French Cultural Centre, the Canadian International Development Agency (CIDA), the National Action Committee on Aids (NACA), the Plateau State Aids Control Agency (PLACA), United States Agency for International Development-International Foundation for Education and Self Help (USAID-IFESH), the International Committee for Artists' Freedom (ICAF) and the International Performers Aid Trust (IPAT). Our local partners and sponsors have included the Grand Cereal, Peejays Foods, Nigerian Film Corporation, Jos International Breweries, Coca Cola, 7Up, and SWAN Water.

3 Additional information http://allafrica.com/stories/201202260183.html 'Jos feast of theatre opens', Our Reporter 15/02/2012 http://www.thenationonlineng.net/2011/index.php/arts/life-midweek-magazine/36785-jos-feast-of-theatre-opens.html; 'Theatre defies security threat on the Plateau', Ozolua Uhakheme 14/03/2012 00:00:00 http://www.thenationonlineng.net/2011/index.php/arts/life-midweek-magazine/39631-theatre-defies-security-threat-on-the-plateau.html. All accessed 15/03/2012

BIBLIOGRAPHY

Ajayi, Segun. 'Ajarat's soul seeks justice for the girl-child', *Wednesday*, March 8, 2006
   http://64.182.81.172/webpages/features/arts/2006/mar/08/arts-08-03-2006-002.htm
Ajayi, Segun. 'Sweet Revenge flags off Jos drama fiesta', January 17, 2007. See http://
   64.182.81.172/webpages/features/arts/2007/jan/17/arts-17-01-2007-002.htm   Accessed
   2011.06.02.
Oteh, Patrick-Jude, Interview 4 April 2009. See http://everythinliterature.blogspot.com/
   2009/04 /jos-repertory-theatre-is-growing-oteh.html

APPENDIX OF PRODUCTIONS FEATURED IN THE FESTIVALS

The First Jos Festival of Theatre, 18 March – April 18 2004

Produced by Jos Repertory Theatre, featuring five plays spread into five weekends:

   Chinua Achebe's *Things Fall Apart* 18 – 21 March
   British Council's Connecting Futures *Our House* 25 – 28 March 28
   Black Heritage Troupe's Dance Drama *My Pride* 1 – 4 April
   Yahaya Dangana's *The Royal Chamber* 8 – 11 April
   Wole Soyinka's *Death and The King's Horseman* 15 – 18 April

The Second Jos Festival of Theatre: 24 February – 5 March 2006

Bunmi Obasa Julius-Adeoye's *Ajarat* directed by Gloria Ogunyemi-Okoh, 24 – 25 February

Workshop devised *Chariot Without Riders* facilitated by Patrick-Jude Oteh, 26 February

My Friend Matt scripted by Mari Binnie from Adam Zamenzad's novel, *My Friend Matt* and *Hena the Whore* – both directed by Mari Binnie, Patrick-Jude Oteh & John Binnie, 27 February

Dance Drama choreographed by Bose Tsevende *Meeme*, 28 February & 1 March

Othman Alsanus' *Oluaiye* directed by Makinde Adeniran, 2 & 3 March

Wole Soyinka's *The Lion and the Jewel* directed by Patrick-Jude Oteh, 4 & 5 March

Participation by the London International Festival of Theatre featuring Project Phakama & Acting Workshops and the Glasgow based Clyde Unity Theatre, UK, at the Crest Hotel, Jos

The Third Jos Festival of Theatre, 2007

Irene Salami's *Sweet Revenge* directed by Isreal Wekpe, 16 – 17 February
Lekan Balogun's *Beyond the Sunset* directed by Austin Okonkwo, 18 – 19

February

Jean Anouilh's *Antigone* directed by Patrick-Jude Oteh/Pierre Marques Alfarroba, 20 February

Athol Fugard's *Sizwe Bansi is Dead* directed by Patrick-Jude Oteh, 21 February

Folorunsho Moshood's *Bara* directed by Toyin Bifarin-Ogundeji, 22 – 23 February

Yakubu Nyango's *Yaga Simi – For the Sake of Love* – (dance drama) choreographed by Yakubu Nyango, 24 – 25 February

Venue: Crest Hotel and Gardens, Jos/Alliance Française, Jos

The Fourth Jos Festival Of Theatre, 16 – 22 May 2008

Chinua Achebe's *Things Fall Apart* directed by Patrick-Jude Oteh, 16 – 17 May

Cida's *No More Mistakes* directed by Austin Okonkwo, 18 May

Eugène Ionesco's *The Lesson* directed by Patrick-Jude Oteh/Pierre Marques Alfarroba's *Mots (Words)* directed by Jean-Louis Reborra, 19 May

J.C. De Graft's *Sons and Daughters* directed by Reuben Embu, 20 May

Wole Soyinka's *Madmen and Specialists* directed by Patrick-Jude Oteh, 21–22 May

Venue: Crest Hotel and Gardens, Old Airport Road, Jos

The Fifth Jos Festival of Theatre 2009, 20–29 March 2009

Mtwa, Simon & Ngema's *Woza Albert!* directed by Tunde Awosanmi, 20 – 21 March

Bose Ayeni-Tsevende's *Morning Yet On Judgement Day* based on the book *U Are A Poet* and choreographed by Bose Ayeni – Tsevende, 22 March

Spencer Okoroafor's *Visa to Nowhere* directed by Eucharia Egah, 23 March

Phillip Begho's *Smallie* directed by Wapi Barau, 24 March

Jean-Paul Sartre's *No Exit* directed by Patrick-Jude Oteh, 25 March

Adinoyi Ojo Onukaba's *A Resting Place* directed by Emmanuel Degri, 26 – 27 March

Wole Soyinka's *The Trials Of Brother Jero* directed by Austin Efe Okonkwo, 28 – 29 March

Venue: Alliance Française, Jos.

The Sixth Jos Festival of Theatre, 25 February – 2 March 2012

Saturday 25 February – Opening of the Sixth Jos Festival of Theatre with performance of Emeka Nwabueze's *When the Arrow Rebounds* – Stage Adaptation of Chinua Achebe's *Arrow of God*

Lonne Elder III's *Ceremonies in Dark Old Men*, 27 February

Adinoyi Ojo Onukaba's *Bargain Hunting* by Group from Port Harcourt / Rivers State led by Emman Emasealu, 28 February

Dipo Agboluaje's *For One Night Only – A Migration Fantasy,* Wednesday 29 February

Barrie Stavis' *The Man Who Never Died,* Thursday 1 March

Closing Ceremonies featuring modern dances and final performance of Barrie Stavis' *The Man Who Never Died* Friday 2 March
Time: 5.00 – 7.00 pm daily
Venue: Alliance Française, Opposite J.D. Gomwalk Building (Standard Building), by West of Mines, Jos, Plateau State
Gate: Free! Courtesy of the US Mission Nigeria

The Grahamstown Festival
& the Making of a Dramatist
An interview with Andrew Buckland

JAMES GIBBS

The following interview with Andrew Buckland was conducted by email in March 2012.

JG: *Andrew Buckland, thank you very much for agreeing to be interviewed. Since the early 1980s, you have produced work for the Grahamstown Festival. Could you give some idea what the festival was like in those days and how you approached the prospect of performing at it?*

AB: All responses to these questions need to be prefixed by the understanding that I feel unable to comment in any authentic way on how festivals contribute to the evolution of theatre in Africa. I have no real experiential knowledge of what the 'Grahamstown Festival', and later the 'National Arts Festival' has meant for the majority of theatre makers and artists in this country during the time that it has been running, except through anecdote and conversational discussions with other individual artists.

Growing up in Southern Africa between 1954 and 2012, a white person's experience of the country and the world is seriously tempered by a privileged position. I entered South Africa from Rhodesia in 1973 to escape conscription and, clutching a study permit denied to most citizens of South Africa at the time, I immediately absorbed, because of my colour, privileges and opportunities denied those same majority of citizens of this country. This dynamic might have been diminished in terms of legislation since 1994, but the effects, in terms of day to day existence in 2012, are still very much coloured by this reality. I was only vaguely aware of this privilege during my teens and early twenties in a 'middle of the road', 'liberal' catholic kind of way. Much of my maturing and political and cultural journey began from within this privileged frame. The experience of the festivals has been very different for the vast majority of artists in this country. And, for the most part, remains so.

I was a student when the festival was launched and from the perspective of a young, and for the most part pretty naive immigrant from Zimbabwe/

Rhodesia, it provided extraordinary possibilities for exposure and development of a 'career'. It was also a hotbed of new artistic and political creativity, albeit for a privileged and predominantly white audience. In fact during the eighties the townships were still patrolled by army vehicles, entry by a white person was by permit only and still the festival went on in the 'safe' side of town. It served by providing a kind of microcosm of the country and may perhaps have had a small influence on the minds of the audiences, but essentially the artists were preaching to the converted.

In April 1985, the 1820 Foundation that is responsible for the festival commissioned a work from me to be included in the main festival programme of that same year. The tenth anniversary festival was announced as having a Shakespearean theme. I then conceived, directed and performed a one-man mime show titled *Touchstones*. Drawing on several quotes from *King Lear*, *The Tempest*, *Antony and Cleopatra*, *Twelfth Night* and *Much Ado About Nothing*, I attempted to explore, through the medium of mime, some facets of contemporary South African life as reflected in the works of William Shakespeare. The fate of the unemployed, the passbook problem, the life of mineworkers, and the attitude of the police featured in the subjects covered in a comic, satirical, and non-verbal style.

In January 1986, I was the recipient of the Standard Bank Young Artists Award for Drama. This required me to create a production for the 1986 Festival. I had been working for some time on a study of the life of Vaslav Nijinsky, the legendary dancer of the Ballets Russes. In close collaboration with the actor Soli Philander, who agreed to direct the play, together with musician Shawn Naidoo and designer Lindy Roberts, we created *Pas de Deux*. Drawing extensively from Nijinsky's diaries, we produced a one-man performance as part of the main programme of the festival and in all the major centres of South Africa.

I was deeply affected by this show as it received a chorus of boos and bravos on the opening night because of its political content and aesthetic; the very same reaction which Nijinsky had received when his revolutionary work was first exposed to the public. It seemed clear to me at that time that, for artists, the choices had narrowed and unless one engaged with the struggle through the content and form of one's work, and the structures which determined access to audiences and where to perform, then the work would be, in real terms, worthless.

There were other festivals organised at the same time with a much more consciously political agenda such as the 'Towards a People's Culture' Festival in Cape Town in December 1986. For which, with Soli and Shawn and other collaborators, we created; 'Everything but the Shower Scene'; a political cabaret drawing its inspiration from the full spectrum of South African political life which aimed its vitriol at the complacent and mostly white middle class audience which did nothing to change the *status quo* in the country. The festival was unfortunately banned, but we did perform in Cape Town in the Jazzart Studios in Johannesburg at the

Market Theatre, and at the 1987 Grahamstown Arts Festival. The National Arts Festival provided an ideal opportunity to reach at least a section of its target audience.

During these years, for a young freelance theatre-maker and performer, the festival formed a central and pivotal point in the year's calendar both in terms of exposing work and perhaps economically surviving the year as long as one had been able to build up a festival audience. Also key to this survival was the participation in the National and Regional Schools Festivals, also run by what was the 1820 Settlers Foundation and which, after 1994, soon became the Grahamstown Foundation. These festivals were incredibly active in building audiences not only for particular artists but for theatre and art in general. They have had an incalculable impact on pupils from schools which would otherwise have had no contact with the quality and volume of performance work delivered by the carefully structured Schools' Festival programmes.

It also has to be noted that during this time there were many other opportunities for an artist who was interested in 'activist art'. Many of what one might call mini-festivals were organised around politically relevant dates or celebrations by the ANC, the End Conscription Campaign, the UDF, and other resistance organisations. These drew some of the most politically relevant and brilliantly crafted expressions of protest in cultural events which sometimes managed, because of their venue and organising body, to find access across the colour and economical barriers which marked life at that time.

The majority of work which was aimed at the audience to which I had the most access through venues such as the Market Theatre was being driven by works like *Woza Albert!* or *Bopha* and *Asinimali* and other derivatives of these major works. I was struck by the fact that the middle class, white, privileged audience was able to 'exoticise' this material, to rave about its artistic value and go home without any shift in behaviour. In April 1988, I was offered a late-night slot at the opening of a new venue in the Market Theatre Complex. Under the mentorship of a classically-trained percussionist, Maciek Schejbal, I focussed my attention on training and developing myself as a physical performer. At the same time I became aware of the phenomenon of a particular species of insect which thrives in the lush gardens of Johannesburg's more affluent suburbs and so was born a satirical allegory called *The Ugly Noo Noo*. This the Market Theatre co-funded in a 50/50 collaboration over many years and part of which included performances at the Grahamstown and other festivals including Edinburgh, which opened up a range of international performance opportunities.

The National Arts Festival quickly followed up with further support by agreeing to fund a work, *Thing?* in 1990. This was a collaboration with Jennie Reznek, Seputla Sepogodi and Maciek Schejbal based on research into quantum mechanics and the area of study known as The New Physics. We constructed a modern creation myth combining all the elements of theatre performance discovered in *No Easy Walk* and *The Ugly Noo Noo*.

Between 1992 and 1995, I presented two new theatre works through the National Arts Festival; *Bloodstream*, (originally co-produced by the Market Theatre) and *Feedback*, both of which cemented a solid audience base at the National Arts Festival.

In 1995, as a senior lecturer in the Drama Department at Rhodes University in Grahamstown, it was my responsibility to oversee the Department's entry into the National Student Drama Festival. The result was *Myth Phalluth*; a satirical study of mythology and the roles in which the feminine was cast in many creation mythologies from around the globe.

The next year, I was funded again by the National Arts Festival to create a collaboration between senior students of the drama department and performers from local Grahamstown community groups: *Human Race*. This was a work built around the narrative of the Comrades Marathon which dealt with political issues through the satirical frame of the world famous sporting event.

I was then commissioned to create a 'mime' work for the Klein Karroo Nasionale Kunstefees (KKNK) for which I created *Noisy Walk*; a development of the work *Between the Teeth* and responding to the title of Mandela's work *No Easy Walk to Freedom* which had been such a pivotal influence on my understanding of the country as a young man.

The experience of *Noisy Walk* in 1996 gave the KKNK confidence in my work and so funded the creation of a new work, the result of which was *The Water Juggler* in 1998. This played at the National Arts Festival, the Schools' Festivals and several other minor festivals which had by then emerged, including HIFA. That same year I received minor funding under the umbrella of the Studio Project in response to a proposal I had submitted to work as a consultant with local community theatre makers and performers, the Masande Players, on a work which celebrated one of the local chiefs who had formed part of the resistance to the English invasion in the 1820s. The result was *Sandilea*.

The financial support offered by being a part of the National Arts Festival Fringe made possible, along with the support of the Market Theatre, the creation of *The Well Being*: a collaboration with Lara Foot-Newton and Lionel Newton. Since playing *The Ugly Noo Noo* at the Traverse Theatre in Edinburgh, I had built up a relationship with them, aided by the three Fringe First Awards I had won for *The Ugly Noo Noo*, *Bloodstream* and *Feedback*, which I believe made them more open to accept my application for inclusion in their programme. This exposure opened up contact with international producers which facilitated the touring of the show to Canada, the USA and Sweden, Belgium, Zambia, Zimbabwe, and Namibia.

In 1999, I was supported in a funding application to the Studio Project to create a work called *A Dream of Rhini* (the isiXhosa name for Grahamstown). This was a project about the history of Grahamstown from the perspective of a local township inhabitant and was performed entirely by township actors.

In 2001, the National Arts Festival supported a proposal I put forward to create a play called *Makana,* which told the story of a major confrontation between the British army and the AmaXhosa resistance forces at Grahamstown in 1822. This featured on the main programme in 2001 and received a satisfyingly broad range of critical responses and a contract for a season in the Market Theatre later that year. It featured the performances by myself and one of the country's prominent and experienced black performers, Bheki Mkhwane, and two Grahamstown township performers, Ntomboxolo Donyeli and Nyebo Swartbooi, with whom I had over several years developed a relationship through workshops and community theatrical interactions with specific applied theatre themes. These two actors were supported by the budget through months of research into the history of the City of Grahamstown, and developmental and experiential work. *Makana* was performed also at the Market Theatre and the Nelson Mandela Gateway to Robben Island. None of this would have been possible without the considered financial support of NAF. Over the past few years, the festival has supported the development of local South African artistic endeavour while remaining a conduit for international acts.

JG: *Are challenges and opportunities still present at the Festival?*

AB: Obviously they differ as the years have created a very different environment in which people are making art. The challenges are probably greater from a financial point of view. The National Arts Festival is structured after the Edinburgh International Arts Festival having a Main Programme of commissioned or invited works and Fringe Programme . So if one is lucky enough to be commissioned to create work for the main Festival Programme, a budget is provided, but Fringe artists, especially theatre-makers, have the costs of transport and accommodation on top of actual production costs to deal with. The opportunities provided by the possibility of further seasons based on the show being seen by producers is more alive and more internationally active. The festival serves as a market for producers and more use it for this. The problem is that few local theatres have the funds to mount productions or keep companies so the seasons are invariably short-lived and this has limited financial rewards.

However, the work is produced and on a festival programme has the opportunity to be seen by an audience determined to enjoy itself ' and looking for potential. The possibility and fear of failure on the Fringe is less sharp as the exposure is contained, although the financial implications are much more serious.

The major challenge for this festival and most festivals in South Africa – and in fact most artistic activity in South Africa – is to make it accessible to a wider audience. The *status quo* is one in which most of the wealth still sits in the bank accounts of whites, or those of a relatively small, exclusive black elite. Most big business is white-owned, and, while there is a growing black middle class, it is not especially evident in poorer provinces such as the Eastern Cape. So the National Arts Festival (NAF) at Grahamstown, as it stands, still reflects an apartheid division. Most of the audience is white, middle class. Attendance at NAF is not seen as a way to spend disposable income by the majority of the black communities in South Africa.

JG: *You have won many prizes and awards at festivals over the years. How do you feel about what can be seen as a competitive element? Is that element an essential part of the festival format?*

AB: Awards were certainly useful in building the promotion packs and media releases sent to producers and other festival organisers e.g. Edinburgh, Adelaide etc. Like a microcosm of the industry, they serve to lift the head of your work out of the ocean of work available and consequently provide a better chance of having it seen. It is also a way of reflecting quality to peers.

JG: *Your work with mime has been singled out as both a characteristic and of an exceptional quality. Were there any particular mime artists or traditions of mime that you became aware of? Did the Festival affect the development of an emphasis on mime?*

AB: My career and life in theatre is based a good deal on inherited privilege. I was able to attend a tertiary institution and study – and to change courses mid-way because I had had the opportunity to discover that my strength lay in performance. Then I was further privileged to have teachers of exceptional quality who introduced the idea of theatre and performance training through physicality and a body-based pedagogy. Part of this included classical mime training based on Étienne Decroux's 'corporeal mime' and 'isolations'. I took to these and in the late seventies and early eighties, as I left university and began freelancing. I was one of a very few people with these performance skills. Consequently I got more work – besides enjoying it and finding it creatively fulfilling. The mime I was taught very much followed the French tradition made popular by Marcel Marceau; the white-faced illusion technique very much in the comic mode. Charlie Chaplin and Marceau were certainly powerful influences.

JG: *What were the other influences that affected your approach to drama, and the evolution of your style of production/performance?*

AB: As above, my teachers, specifically Professor Roy Sargeant, Jane Osborne and, especially Gary Gordon guided me and challenged me toward finding a unique performance mode. My awareness of the political power of performance, especially through non-verbal visual story-telling and characterisation, made me pursue the potential of mime even more. Added to this were the experiences I had had from my interactions with

Grahamstown and then Johannesburg township performers and groups. These exchanges obviously exposed me to township performance style exemplified by Gibson Kente and his protégés Mbongeni Ngema and Percy Mtwa. These highly stylised and physically precise styles provided a solid frame for the development of a new or hybrid performance technique which engaged with every aspect of performance; physical, vocal, scenic, aural, etc.

JG: *Looking back over the time you were freelance during the eighties, how did you survive? Were festivals a distraction or an encouragement to you?*

AB: Surviving in the eighties in Johannesburg as a freelance performer and teacher and theatre-maker meant the daily attempt to live a balanced life between doing 'sell-out' TV commercial auditions, corporate theatre gigs, politically active/reactive performance, spending time teaching and learning from different cultural groups. Clearly the apartheid structure was facing its demise. The only way was to engage in learning. The combination of acting and teaching is appropriate since one teaches in order, essentially, to learn and good learners make good teachers. The same for actors - good learners.

The festival provided a context in which to expose work and explore form etc, but the audience was essentially privileged, almost exclusively white and the laws were preventing any cross over of cultural activity into the township areas of any town – let alone a festival town. So most of the political theatre was protest theatre trying to wake up the white, middle and upper class audience to the fact that they had a responsibility which they needed to face, and, more so, that they had the power to change. The festival also provided a focussed time of networking interactions which gave one the opportunity to connect with black artists – but this always in a context and atmosphere of oppression. As a place to truly develop and explore a popular culture the festival did little more than make patently obvious and viscerally present the absurdity and horror of the separation and oppression founded on economic principles which lay at the heart of apartheid. The eighties were seeing walls coming crumbling down and the consequent rise in oppressive violence made the time very creatively vibrant.

JG: *You have taught in a variety of contexts. How has working with groups in, for example, Soweto and Cape Town, with dance as well as drama companies and with children as well as adults affected your practice?*

AB: It was my teachers at Rhodes who demonstrated and inculcated in me an understanding of the powerful link between learning, research, enquiry and creativity. I was encouraged to do a paper in education at honours level and from my post-grad years I was involved in teaching theatre at the local township schools. This made sense to me in political terms as well. At this time I was driven by a confused, politically adolescent feeling of white guilt and a simpler and more active sense of responsibility about the circumstances of people's lives and how, unless we engaged in changing the said circumstances, we had little right to live in the country.

In 1976 I was drafted into the Rhodesian army and fought with that uniform on for a year during which my understanding of this responsibility solidified. After my return, graduation and move to Johannesburg, the opportunities to engage with learners in township contexts was what I sought in order to give meaning to my work and my existence. I would never carry a gun again, yet the struggle demanded work to engage with the change. More effective than festivals at this time were cultural events organised by organisations such as the ANC, the End Conscription Campaign, the United Democratic Front and others at which performances with solid political content were exposed to a wider audience than that found at festivals. Working with these groups and interacting with these artists who had developed their craft through such a radically different context from mine impacted on me in a deeply significant way. I began to understand more fully the notion that no art, no creation is made without a context and if the creation ignores this context it lacks any real integrity. In this environment every work was political. Every action was political. Every choice had political consequences, and the choice of subject matter or context of learning determined the potential outcome.

JG: *Have you been aware of festivals shaping the work produced by the groups you have worked with?*

AB: I haven't been aware of this except that it might encourage the creation of work according to the festival format of relatively short shows. I suppose there might be a sense of developing work specifically for a festival audience in mind, but usually this includes a notion that this audience is fairly well-read, has a critical faculty and will be relatively discerning from an artistic point of view. In as much as festivals are, at the moment, the best means of having work exposed with the potential of it growing an audience, I would say that they are a positive influence. Albeit that the producers are interested in making work which has a life or 'has financial legs', rather than just having artistic 'credibility'.

JG: *Since 1992 you have worked from a base in Rhodes University Drama Department. While there you seem to have fought for different patterns of degree. What is wrong with the University's approach to theatre studies?*

AB: The idea that I have fought for different patterns of degree may well be an impression created by my habit of blogging uncensored during a year spent working for Cirque du Soleil in Las Vegas between 2008 and 2009. (That, incidentally, was facilitated through the National Arts Festival in that the Cirque talent scouts came to the National Arts Festival in order to source acts and performers in the early 2000's.)

There has been a good deal of debate with regard to the structuring of Drama degrees as four-year degrees instead of the three-year plus honours format which we now operate under. The University was keen for us to consider developing a four-year degree. Most of the other drama departments in South Africa now offer this type of degree. In answer to the question I would like to offer a two-pronged response:

a) As a department in the 'academy', the Rhodes Drama Department is a descendant, like many other drama departments in the country, of a project of English departments. Hence the name 'Drama Department' still rings with literary resonance and causes me to have to endure cringingly embarrassing encounters with other academics at this university who insist on making 'drama' type 'jokes' about our discipline. We are happier with the notion that we teach and research theatre studies. There is a still a vague sense of us being only tongue-in-cheekily serious in our scholarship, and the research and creative outputs are sometimes seen by colleagues as something slightly childish – to do with 'playing' rather than really serious academic endeavour. This is not a reflection of the 'official' view of the Dean of Humanities nor of the administration as a whole, who continue to be very supportive.

b) We do not, and cannot, offer a vocational degree which is designed and purports to prepare students for the 'profession'. We do not teach film studies, film acting or production; we do not teach radio or any of the other media except theatre and live performance. As a staff, we are also very sceptical about the reality of a 'profession' in the performing arts, especially in the Eastern Cape today. We are a small department with limited staff and so have created a carefully structured curriculum based on our capacity and a vision of theatre shared by the staff. Part of this vision includes the idea of theatre and performance created on the foundation of rigorous research, adventurous creativity, technical performance skill and detailed documentation and archiving. We are pitched, I suppose, in line with the university vision of itself as a centre of research. For this to work I have come to feel, and most of the staff agree... (not all and the subject is still in debate), that the three-year degree in which drama (theatre studies) is one major, or minor in the first two years provides the ideal environment for a wide range of students. Whether they are interested in entering the 'profession' or not, they will find the advantages of allowing theatre studies to have a positive impact on their development as human beings. It is our experience, and that of other creative arts departments at Rhodes, that the research outputs which the post-grad students who also majored in another subject, possibly philosophy or history or isiXhosa or whatever, are much richer than that produced by students studying theatre or drama exclusively over four years. So for now we work within the three-year Bachelor's degree, then an Honours and, hopefully, Master's and Doctorate after that. On the way, we are producing graduates who are also thinking, creative practitioners and participants in the field of live performance.

JG: *You have lived on a large map for many years and, for example, had early contact with the Edinburgh Festival. Are there lessons that South and Southern Africa can learn from gatherings of theatre people in other places?*

AB: The impression of the size of the map on which I have lived may seem large from my CV, but in fact it has been relatively limited compared to many other performing artists in the country. The last time I took one of my own works to Edinburgh was in 2004. The only lesson I feel anyone can learn from other festivals is how sublimely similar and how perfectly diverse we are as a species. I would articulate this lesson as 'the more festivals the better', for people, for art, for humanity. We may not be able to make theatre a part of everyone's everyday life, but the more festivals we make, small ones, big ones, middle sized, to celebrate this or that, the more chance we have of saving ourselves from the pit of mediocrity into which the bulk of television and the popular media product relentlessly pulls us.

JG: *What about the Festivals you have been part of in other parts of Africa – beyond Grahamstown? What sort of contributions are events such as the Klein Karroo and Harare Festivals making to theatre in the continent?*

AB: These are two of many. What contributions are they making to theatre on the continent...? I am not in a position to judge. Apart from providing a platform for new and emerging work to be seen, and the chance to network and meet face to face with fellow artists and theatre makers. There are also other festivals such as Bushfire in Swaziland and so on.

JG: *Do festivals provide value for money? I ask this because sometimes festivals absorb a substantial proportion of the funds available for the theatre (from government and/or commercial sponsorship); and the contributions they make to sustainable, year-round theatre are not always apparent.*

AB: Okay. Value to whom...? To the citizens whose tax-payer rands are being spent? To the festival goers who attend? The problem with festivals in South Africa is that we still live in a country which has not radically changed in real terms since the demise of apartheid. Laws have changed and there is a growing, new moneyed elite, however, essentially, the majority of poor people are black, the majority of white people are wealthy, (if not then 'comfortable') and the poor are only getting poorer. The geographical and economical structure of urban areas, in which most festivals are situated, remains the same. The poor still live in the townships and live a very difficult existence which is not sufficiently supported by the government or the commercial bodies which rely on the labour resources they control. This is reflected in the festivals, to a large degree, in that the majority of audiences are white middle and upper class and the majority of shows which do well, which are attended by a paying audience, are predominantly from a white middle class context. Much more interesting than the major festivals are the smaller ones that are politely termed 'community theatre' festivals in which emerging, disadvantaged artists with limited resources have opportunities to present new work, develop skills through creative interactions, and simply meet other artists face to face.

JG: *Looking back over your contact with Grahamstown, how would you summarise the impact on the national scene? (Has it just responded to changes or has it anticipated them?)*

AB: The festival, I think, has been the platform on which artists have been given the resources to make work. This work has variously anticipated changes, or has screamed in anger for changes; some have responded to these realities and some have consciously avoided considering them in order to create diversionary entertainment. The selection of material for the main programme has simply reflected the cultural and creative and artistic clemency of the make up of the selection committees.

JG: *Do you see a future for theatre festivals in Africa?*

AB: I believe the hope for festivals in Africa and the world lies not only in the model of the major international festival designed around the paradigm of providing more opportunities for artists to create work for the consumer-driven entertainment industry. The exchange which happens through the festivals on the continent, and especially the minor festivals – often termed community theatre festivals –actively provides support for artists who remain. The systems are still driven by the capitalist structure of the industry in the country and the world which relies on financial returns and consumable products with a high demand to a defined target market, and this is the major empowering force in allowing a work to find support and an audience.

It also needs to be said now that I have been the Head of the Drama Department here at Rhodes since July 2010, it is undeniable that the structure of the arts festival in our town provides an extraordinary relationship in which students of theatre and performance can have access to a challenging and stimulating range of performance experiences both as audience and participant. But then this has to be viewed in the light of the fact that the majority of students here are from relatively privileged backgrounds and social situations, and so the citizens who have access to tertiary education through funding, geographical and economical education are limited. During apartheid this access was defined and determined by legislation. In the South Africa of 2012 it is determined by economic and political structures.

JG: *Andrew Buckland, thank you very much.*

Prison Graduates

EFO KODJO MAWUGBE

Introduction: A review of a production of *APTS*, subsequently retitled *Prison Graduates*

The production of Efo Kodjo Mawugbe's *APTS, Acquired Prison Traumatic Syndrome*, given in the presence of the playwright at the Efua T. Sutherland Drama Studio, Legon, Ghana, on 27 August 2005, represented a major outing for a new play of national significance. Sadly, the production was not as bold as the text.

In the course of the fluid, wide-ranging drama, the audience was repeatedly reminded that there were parallels between events in the play and the history of the nation in which it was being performed. The challenge of independence was alluded to again and again, and the audience became aware that they were watching a drama addressed to the Ghanaian nation as an historic milestone approached.

There are those, Michael Etherton among them, who have pointed out that it has been the fate of African dramatists to have their multi-layered texts reduced to simple, or simplistic, statements on national debates. My impression is that, though his play is not simplistic, Mawugbe would not mind the national parallels being drawn. Indeed, he encourages spectators to contemplate the weaknesses that drive his characters, who are joyously released at the start of the play, so that all but one seek the protection of prison at the end. It is appropriate to recall that in 1957, Ghana kept her 'tryst with destiny', and to ponder, in the light of this trajectory, how resolute it is in its determination to remain independent as it approaches the big five zero.

Since Mawugbe has found a style that enables his characters to parade before the audience a variety of experiences, the play asks many questions. In the theatrical vocabulary he employs, I find traces of South African experiments, particularly those which saw the theatre liberated by the example of Jerzy Grotowski and reunited with indigenous traditions. In the process of growth in Johannesburg and Cape Town, the contribution of Barney Simon was crucial, and there were moments watching *APTS* when one felt in the presence of the sort of work that Simon produced in collaboration with Mbongeni Ngema and Percy Mtwa. One might also mention in this connection other South African texts, including *Sizwe Bansi is Dead* (Athol Fugard, John Kani and Winston Ntshona) and, particularly pertinently, *Asinamali!* by Mbongeni Ngema. Mawugbe, who returned to the School of Performing Arts as a mature student to study playwriting, has responded to cousins, brothers and uncles in South Africa.

Revelling in theatricality, delighting in African physical theatre, Mawugbe's released prisoners, Abutu (Ebenezer Osae-Aye), Gomido (Morgan Saviour Ashiagbor), Chaka (Fifi Coleman) and Basabasa (Kenneth Senyo Fiati) put us through the wringer. Some of the episodes were more weighty than others. There was, for example, telling social comment and astute political observation in the encounters at the hospital and at the British High Commission. By comparison with these, 'the visit to the Japanese restaurant' was flippant, thrown in for light relief. The first two were fuelled by anger and suffering, rounded and substantial. The third, on the other hand, lacked teeth, lacked flesh, didn't quite 'work hard enough'.

I think that even the stronger passages in this Theatre Arts Department's production could be revisited. For example, one scene would have been more telling if the rather odd detail about the man's wedding ring had been omitted, and I wondered about the very rude, final rejection of the visa application. I suspect an allusion to British hypocrisy, expressed by a smile as the application was disdainfully rejected would have been more telling. As far as the staging is concerned, I want to know why there was such a convenient 'visa window' available for the High Commission sequence. I would have much preferred evidence of improvisation – such as that relished by the South Africans mentioned.

I am not sure why the director, who also played Basabasa, felt it incumbent on him to present the play within a set and on the 'conventional stage' part of the Drama Studio. This is a text that thrives on theatricality, on actors creating effects with a few key props; it does not need carpentry. I am convinced that, with carefully controlled lighting and strong sound effects, *APTS* would make a very profound impact in the round. At the Drama Studio on August 27th, it received a treatment that was safer, tamer, more naturalistic than the text required. That the production succeeded as well as it did with the audience – they enjoyed it hugely – was, I think, because of the energy and commitment of the performances. I hope that actors will tour it and play it in a variety of spaces. They should have confidence in the text and take it to audiences.

It was very important that the playwright was able to see his play performed, and entirely appropriate that he was applauded enthusiastically when called to join the cast at the end. Those following events in the Ghanaian theatre have long been aware of Mawugbe's emergence as an important presence, and this play further consolidated his reputation as a writer. While some in the Legon audience participated vocally in time-honoured manner, it was quickly apparent that Mawugbe had got there before them, that he was in control. The lines he had put into his actors' mouths were much better than those offered by the would-be wits in the third row.

JAMES GIBBS

The play was produced by the Theatre Arts Department, in association with Mbaasem and the Morel Trust at the Efua T. Sutherland Drama Studio, Legon, in August 2005, directed by Kenneth Senyo Fiati.

CAST

Abuto	Ebenezer Osae-Aye
Gomidio	Morgan Saviour Ashiagbor
Chaka	Fifi Coleman
Basabasa	Kenneth Senyo Fiati
Prison Officer	Anthony Kofi Boakye
Prison Chaplain	Korshivi Edem Mawugbe

STAGE CREW

Lighting	Kwame Acheampong
Lights	Michael Tuffour-Ampem
Costumes	Joyce Asiedu

The play is reproduced here with kind permission of the author's literary executors who retain full copyright, moral and intellectual property rights.

CHARACTERS

Abutu	A very hot-tempered young man. Doubles as 'Nurse II' and 'Orderly'
Chaka	Leader of the group. Doubles as 'Nurse I' and Abusa Panyin.
Basabasa	Speaks Pidgin English with amazing fluency.
Gomido:	Highly temperamental and never sees eye to eye with Abutu.
Prison Officer	Doubles as Chaplain and Voice.

Author's synopsis: *Prison Graduates* is a satire that employs a state penitentiary and four of its inmates granted presidential amnesty as a metaphor and as a backdrop against which is projected the strides made by former African colonies towards the realization of the socio-economic and political aspirations of their citizens before, during and after the attainment of independence.

Note to the director: Apart from the Chaplain, all four major characters are ex-convicts just released from the local Maximum Security Prison. The Prison Officer who appears at the end can be played by Abutu. The success of the performance depends much on the improvisational skills of the actors supported by the different props and other paraphernalia that make up their individual *belongings* brought from prison.

FIRST LEG

(Early morning. Inside the prison yard. The prisoners are locked up in their cells. one can hear the pealing of a distant church bell. A distant lone voice is reciting what sounds like a remixed version of Psalm 23.)

Lone voice: The Lord is our shepherd, We shall not want. He maketh us to lie down on cold dungeon floors;… He locketh us behind the steel bars and says He restoreth our self esteem…
(Sound of heavy crunching footsteps as in military boots are heard coming from around the corner)
Two voices: He goes ahead of us to die on the gallows for our sake…
(Sound of clanging bunch of keys as heavy padlock is being opened)
More voices: Yea though we live through this valley of our prison sentences, we'll fear no prison officer, for thou art with us. Thy rod and thy staff…
(Sound of very heavy iron gates opening. Prisoners begin murmuring. Enter prison officers)
Prison Officer: Order… Order… Order! I say! (*There is instant silence.*) All inmates should back off the cell gates …Now!
(Sound of shuffling feet as prisoners move away from cell gates. There is absolute silence)
P. Officer: (*moves in with military precision, clears his throat and speaks with authority*) The following inmates have been granted presidential amnesty and are therefore to be released unconditionally. (*Pause. Clears throat*] Prisoner number… xyz24.
Abutu: Yes, Sir!
P. Officer: Prisoner number W W W 96.
Gomido: Yes, Sah!
P. Officer: (*talking very fast*) Prisoner number PT 007.

Chaka: (*excitedly*) Yes, Sir!

P. Officer: (*talking really fast*) Prisoner KW 66

Basabasa: (*excitedly*) Hallelujah!

All Inmates: AMEN!

P. Officer: (*sternly*) Who is that dozing prisoner? (*Pause*) Since when did *Hallelujah* and *Amen*, become the standard prison call and response?

Basabasa: I sorry Sah … Na slip of tongue Sah!

P. Officer: Slip of brain more likely. Never mind, you four are now free.

Prisoners: (*confused*) You mean…we… are… (*Pause*)

P. Officer: Believe me. You are no longer convicts… You are free to go out.

Prisoners: We are all free, you say?

P. Officer: Yes, you are all now free! (*Prisoners scream excitedly*)

Prisoners: (*over excitedly*) We are free… free…Freedom… Freedom!

P. Officer: Order…Order… Order!

Prisoners: Yes, Sah!

P. Officer: (*sternly*) As you go out, be good citizens. If by some strange fate, you should be either slow or fast-tracked in here, I promise you a real hard time. Do you copy?

Prisoners: (*confidently*) Yes, Suh!

P. Officer: Your discharge papers are ready for collection at the Chaplain's office. Pick them up on your way out. Good luck!

Prisoners: (*excitedly*) Thank you, Sah!

P. Officer: You are discharged! Get lost!

Prisoners: Yes, Sah!

P. Officer: (*authoritatively*) Orderly!

Orderly: Yes Sah!

P. Officer: Remove their shackles at once and take them to the Chaplain's office for their belongings and discharge papers.

Orderly: Yes Sah! Permission to carry on Sah!

Officer: Carry on.

Orderly: (*issuing orders*) Prisoners, about turn. By the left, quick march, left-right, left-right, left-right… left-right…left-right…

(*Prisoners march out*)

SECOND LEG

(*Office of the Prison Chaplain. A soft Christian hymn can be heard. Chaplain in his deep voice can be heard humming along as he goes through some sheets of papers in front of him. Standing around his desk are the four ex-convicts, Abutu, Chaka, Basabasa and Gomido.*)

Chaplain: In the name of the Father, the Son and the Holy Ghost. Amen!

Prisoners: Amen!

Chaplain: You are now free, liberated, in fact, emancipated!

Abutu: And emaciated!

Chaplain: Well, Number 24, you can't blame me. Mine was to feed you spiritually, which I believe, in the name of the Father, Son and Holy Ghost, I did, to the best of my ability. Here, take my hand... May the grace of our Lord... and the peace of God which passeth all understanding, be and abide with...

Gomido: (*in a sudden outburst of anger*) Blast your handshake Reverend... I'd rather shake hands with a leper than with a double-tongued charlatan like you.

Basabasa: Ma bruda, 96, wetin be de wahala? Beg your pardon.

Chaka: Those are very strong words to use against a Man of God inside a vestry.

Abutu: Such words could make it difficult for you to enter Heaven.

Gomido: You hypocrite, you Serpent!

Chaka: (*sternly*) Number 96, Stop it.

Gomido: (*throwing caution to the wind*) Reverend Father, do whatever you want, Go ahead. You mother f...

Chaka: (*more sternly*) 96, Stop it, I say!

Chaplain: (*not in the least ruffled, coolly sings along the hymn in the background*) May the good Lord of Heaven, have mercy on you my boy.

Gomido: (*angrily*) And may the same Lord delete your name from the register of His good shepherds. You deceiver of His innocent flock.

Basabasa: Oh No! 96, why you de block una chance to enter heaven?

Chaplain: Thank you, 66, my boy.

Gomido: (*aggressively*) Don't you worry, by the time we get to heaven... that is if there is any such place, this wolf in sheep's clothe would be nowhere there. I bet you, he is a dishonest...

Chaka: Folks, let's cease fire.

Gomido: And he calls himself a worker in the Lord's vineyard...

Chaka: (*authoritatively*) Cease fire, I said. (*silence*)

Chaplain: (softly) Well, I think you ought to be going now.

Abutu/Chaka/Basabasa: Yes, Chappie... Bye, Chappie.

Chaplain: Bye, and may the Good Lord be with you, 24, 007, and 66.... and the devil with that one over there... (*He bangs the door*)

Gomido: (*highly infuriated*) You heard him, didn't you? I tell you, folks, if that Chappie were God's tap-turner, he'll ensure water flows only to his mother-in-law's kitchen.

Chaka: We have our dispatch papers. Let us forget about him.

Gomido: You, can forget, but not I who bear the scar of his treachery.

Basabasa: Wetin at all him do you? Beg your pardon.

Abutu: Yes, why all this bitterness towards the Man of God?

Chaka: Can you tell us? (*pause*)

Gomido: (*heaves a sigh*) Let's first get away from here then I can tell you.

THIRD LEG

(*In Front of Prison Gates. Ex-convicts arrive with their few belongings to sit in front of the prison gates. Prominent among the items is an unfinished door mat in its frame.*)

Chaka: Now, brother, tell us why you are so bitter with Chappie.

Basa: Na so, we all want to sabey, abi I lie?

Gomido: Hmmmm… You see, I should have been out much earlier but I had to do a time-added on, all because of him.

Abutu: Something like an injury time, right?

Chaka: (*sternly*) Hey 24, be serious.

Abutu: I am very sorry. (*pause*)

Chaka: My brother, carry on.

Gomido: You know I was transferred here from Anomabo.

Chaka & Co: Yes.

Gomido: He was the Chaplain at Anomabo when I began to serve my sentence. By then I had become a born-again Christian.

Basa: Beg your pardon!

Chaka: Hold it there. (*pause*) 96, you say you had become what-again?

Gomido: Born-Again!

(*laughter from colleagues*)

Basa: Let us all pray… 'Our farda, which art in Heaven, make una forget our daily bread as we already de steal from bakers dat don't trespass against us'… Wonders never go end. A cockroach becoming born-again?

Gomido: Believe me, folks. During one of Chappie's powerful sermons, at Anomabo, I lifted up both hands in full surrender and accepted Jesus Christ as my Lord and personal Cellmate. (*Chaka and the rest break into laughter*) Chappie assured us… I mean all those who accepted the Lord that day, that the Lord, was ever faithful and just to forgive us all of our sins, transgressions and iniquities.

Abutu: Oh yes, '*He could turn your scarlet red sins into snow white bed sheets…*'.

Gomido: (*surprised*) Those were his exact words. 24, how did you know that? Did he play the same trick on you?

Abutu: Not me, but on Tsatsu, a very good friend of mine, at Nsawam.

Basa: Oh… I see. De Chappie ino be proper man of God.

Chaka: And what happened?

Gomido: Hmmm… I was so moved by Chappie's sermon that, I went up to him after the church service. (*sob*)

Basabasa: Beg your pardon…Why you go see am?

Gomido: I …I… (*sob*) I went to confess a robbery I was involved in … but had until then not been detected by the police. (*sob*)

Chaka & Co: (*shocked*) You did what?

Gomido: Yes

Chaka & Co: How could you? (*silence*)

Chaka: What happened after that?

Gomido: The following morning, I was re-interrogated. The dust-laden docket was retrieved, wiped clean and I was whisked to court…(*sob*)… tried…and sentenced to do three years of time – added – on. (*sob*)

Chaka & Co: (*shocked*) Jeeez!

Basabasa: Abi, you craze?... Beg your pardon.

Abutu: The Chappie outsmarted you.

Gomido: (*sob*) I never knew that every Prison Chappie worked for God above and the system below… (*sob*)

Basabasa: My brudas, if una look-look de matter proper-proper, I tink say, technically speaking, we no for put blame on Chappie.

Chaka & Co: Why?

Basabasa: De Chappie him never say if una confess una CRIME, de state or de law of de land go forgive una. Chappie say dat, de Lord which art in Heaven, hallowed be thy name … na him go forgive una SINS.

Abutu: (*seems to have realised the logic in Basabasa's statement*) You are right. Technically speaking, a sin may not necessarily be a crime in the eyes of the law of the land.

Basa: Na so!... Beg your pardon.

Chaka: In other words, whereas the Lord which art in Heaven shall always forgive us our sins, when we confess them, the law of the land shall punish us for the crimes we confess.

Basa: Na so.

Gomido: (*almost to himself*) So, there was a catch.

Abutu: That is why we say there are only two things that are given free of charge in any prison.

Chaka & Co: (*in unison*) The air you breathe and the number you wear in place of your name.

Abutu: You should have told me earlier and I would have made Chappie pay for it double.

Chaka: And he would have short-changed you double by getting you to do a time-added on in solitary for insubordination.

(*Gomido sobs*)

Chaka: Stop crying. All that belongs to the past now. My brother, wipe your tears. Let's talk about something else.

Abutu: Something else, such as…?

Basa: Such as Freedom, what else?

Chaka: I tell you folks, the only time you experience the beauty of democracy is when you step out of prison after a long sentence. No one understands freedom better than a prisoner

Basa: Like Kwame Nkrumah!

Gomido: Like Nelson Mandela! (*sings*) Free… Nelson Mandela, walking side by side with Winnie Mandela... on the crowded narrow streets of Soweto.

Abutu: Can you imagine you are in this prison for only God knows how many years. All your relations outside have long forgotten about you. You no longer exist in their memory. Then, one day, out of the blues, you have all the freedom in the world hurled at you…in fact, thrown at you, like a basketball. Hahahaha!

Gomido: A basketball can hurt your fingers if you don't know how to handle it.

Chaka: That may be true, my brother, but I feel freedom ought not be looked at as an abstract concept. It should be the concrete source and precondition of free will. The person who is not free has no choices and the person who can not choose is not a person but an animal – or worse still, a machine.

Basa: Na true! Dat person be like corn mill machine… Tu-tu-tu-tu-tu. Beg your pardon.

Gomido: I agree freedom is never more sharply focused than when it is denied to you. But it could equally be dangerous when thrown at you like a basketball and not handled with care.

Basa: For me, ino dey like basketball at all.

Abutu & Chaka: How do you see it then?

Basa: I feel say ibi like music wey for long time choke for inside throat for person wey be deaf and dumb. Den one day, Jesus perform him miracle and suddenly deaf and dumb person fit hear and talk. Abi wey tin him go do? He go scream! (*screams*) Freedom!
I feel say I for sing freedom!
I feel say make I cry freedom!

Chaka: (*to Gomido*) What about you, 24?

Gomido: (*as if reciting a poem*) I feel like sleeping and dreaming.
Dreaming unfettered dreams.
Yes, dreams of all prison inmates in solitary,
Joining hands in solidarity
Chanting songs of Asafo
And driving out all the prison officers
And taking over the prisons.
(*begins to chant a fiery asafo war song. ex-convicts join in the singing*)
Yes, that is the day when prisoners
Shall be accountable unto themselves
And not to some cheating Prison Officers.
I have a dream…
A dream of a prison without walls…
A dream of a prison where the unique and
Cherished principles of universal human rights
Are practised irrespective of…

Abutu: Hold it there! (*pause*) Inmate 96, you are under arrest!

Basa: Arrest…24,Wetin him do?

Gomido: Where is my crime?

Abutu: 96, in your head. You are attempting to sleep and dream. In fact, sleeping and dreaming and preaching anarchy in your dream. (*Gomido tries to explain*) You have every right to remain silent. Any thing you say here and now may be used against you in a court of law in dreamland, after you've served your prison sentence… (*pause*) Meanwhile, you are hereby sentenced to… (*pause*) Your freedom (*laughter*)

Chaka: (*to Abutu*) And you, 24, tell us how you feel right now.

Abutu: To tell you the truth, I feel like a nation just attained independence after centuries of colonial rule.

Basa: Na true. So make we change una names. Beg your pardon. (*pause*)

Gomido: 007, I think the brother is right. We need new names and a new freedom song. Something resembling a national anthem. (*He begins to sing 'Say It Loud, I am Black and Proud' a James Brown song.*)

Basa: Abi wey kine song be dat one?

Gomido: That is our new national anthem. Don't you like it?

Abutu: (*emphatically*) No!

Chaka: Why?

Abutu: We need to be original.
We need something of our own.
To reflect our new status…
Our independence…
Our freedom…
Our sovereignty…
Our emancipation!
Don't you see?
We need to create for ourselves a new identity…
A new flag…
A new image.

Gomido: Re-branding!

Basa: Na so, a new brand of freedom flag!

Gomido: Remember former Tanganyika…
former Northern and Southern Rhodesia…

Abutu: South West Africa…
The Gold Coast…
Dahomey…

Chaka: That is definitely better than referring to each other by the numbers given to us from our prison past.

Abutu & Co: Precisely.

Chaka: So, you, Number 24, what shall be your new name?

Abutu: I want to be known as AYITEY HEWALE. But I don't really mind being called Abutu…

Chaka: And you, my Bruda, Number 96?

Gomido: I wish to be called YAOVI NUNYA a.k.a. GOMIDO! All documents bearing my former name remain valid.

Chaka: (*to Basabasa*) What about you number 66?

Basabasa: (*as if he is a child reciting a nursery rhyme*) De title of my new name na 'Basa-into-Brackets-Squared'. (*Abutu bursts out laughing*) Wetin, my name no sweet? Beg your pardon

Abutu: (*trying with difficulty to control his laughter*) Come to think of it… an illiterate Primary School dropout, having for his name a mathematical equation. (*laughs*) Instead of sticking to his simple rural name of…

Basa: (*angrily*) Your morda be de Rural… Your farda be de rural… Your uncle wey him no get…

Chaka: Cease fire!

Basa: Your morda wey dey for your village na him be proper rural. … Your whole family be…

Chaka: I order you two to cease fire… Now! (*silence*)

Abutu: Well.

Gomido: Well, what?

Abutu: (*to Chaka*) 007, I think it is your turn to let us know your Independence name.

Chaka: Yes, indeed. Well, I used to be number 007. For now, I wish to be known and called Nana…Akwasi…Timber aka Chaka!

Abutu: (*shouts excitedly*) Chakaaaa!...Chakaaaa! Chak…

Gomido: (*angrily*) Hey…hey… Will you stop shouting like some castrated lizard?

Abutu: Can't a man exercise his freedom to shout? Why do you want to make me feel as if I am still in prison? By the way, who made you a Prison Officer over me?

Gomido: No one here says you can't shout. What you need to know is, your shouting must end where the other fellow's ear begins.

Basa: Na true.

Abutu: That's nonsense. That is most undemocratic.

Chaka: What is not democratic?

Abutu: If I should end my shouting just where the other fellow's ears begin, what guarantee is there that he has heard me?

Basa: Abi, you craze…Una want de eardrums break *Poooaaah*! before you sabey say him fit to hear you?

Abutu: Of course I don't blame you. You are an illiterate rural beg-your-pardon-nobody so…

Gomido: (*exasperatedly*) Oh No! Not again.

Basa: Me, I sabey say, beg your pardon, I no go sukulu before. But I no do tings like somebody wey just comot from inside bush. (Gomido and Chaka break into laughter) Hooooo! You be bush baby…Hoooo Bush Cat! Hoooo bush dog! (*Abutu and Basa begin to trade insults*)

Chaka: Stop it!

Basa: Hoooo! Bush-Fish like you!

Abutu: You unpolished illiterate rat.

Chaka: Will you stop what you are doing?

Basa: Me, I be rat ino be so? You, you be so foolish dat like you be goat wey dem kill you make pepper-soup and fufu, I swear, I go eat my fufu raw, I no go touch you self!

Basa & Chaka: Oh No, this is too much.

(*There is absolute confusion as Basabasa and Abutu trade insults by trying to out-shout one another.*)

Chaka: (*authoritatively*) Stop it, I say…Hey you folks, I say stop it. (*silence*) All this post-independence name-calling and undermining won't take us anywhere. It is most unhealthy for our post-prison life. We are a free people. What we do with our newly found freedom should be our major concern. Our collective future as brand new ex-convicts is what should engage every ounce of energy left in us. Do you understand?

Gomido: Well spoken Chaka.

Basa: So, de question be say, wetin man for do for life outsai prison, ino be so?

Chaka: Exactly. What do we do, now that we are free?

Gomido: That question, I believe, goes to all of us.

(*Breaks into a popular tune 'Now that we've found love what are we gona do with it?' All the others join in singing the first few bars in a capella fashion.*)

Abutu: I tell you guys, I wish to go into management.

Chaka: Managing what?

Abutu: A stable.

Gomido: Of horses?

Abutu: No, of sportsmen…I mean boxers and footballers.

Gomido: Any previous skills in that discipline?

Abutu: It's a job that requires no such extensive experience. Given the condition of things on this side of the global village, you can be a Sports Administrator once you know the rules of the game of Gutter-to-Gutter.

Gomido: And when you are in doubt, all you need do is consult.

Chaka: You consult the internet, isn't it?

Basa: Football na leather, boxing gloves na leather. But why una want to put money for inside leather? Abi, you craze?

Abutu: Show me any durable purse that is not made of leather. Besides, most of our footballers and boxers are highly talented …but, (*whispers*) very often, stark illiterate.

Chaka: So, you intend to exploit their illiteracy, I guess.

Abutu: (*protests vehemently*) That's most unfair! I am a businessman. All I do is scout for buyers on the foreign market and sell out the local boys. If I sell a player for 150,000 US Dollars, I pay the player 15,000 Dollars. But his money shall be kept in a joint account with me as the sole signatory. You see, most of these chaps cannot even sign their names. Do you call that exploitation?

Gomido: That's business.

Abutu: Thank you, my brother.

Gomido: A very crooked business at that.

Abutu: Nonsense.

Basa: As for me, whether ibi nonsense or no nonsense, de tin wey I wan sabey be say, which sai una for ged de boxers?

Abutu: Right here.

Gomido: Where?

Chaka: I don't suppose you mean...

Abutu: Exactly. Gomido and Basabasa here, will do the fighting, with you Chaka as the sole referee-judge, whilst I manage them. (*to Basa and Gomido*) You fight twice a year and you earn five million cedis per fight for the next ten years. How about that?

Chaka: It is cool with me!

Abutu: What about you two?

Basa & Co: Where is the money?

Abutu: After the fight. With thirty thousand people having paid to watch the fight, not to mention the pay per view Television rights, there's no way I can't pay your purse. (*Brings a sheet of paper from among his belongings and spreads it out before Gomido and Basabasa*) Please just sign on this dotted line.

Gomido: What's the paper for?

Abutu: Standard Contract. That ensures you two belong to my stable.

Basa: Beg your pardon! ...A stable? Who talk you say I want make horse my room-mate? Make you plus your contract go quench for sea.

Abutu: And you, Gomido?

Gomido: That's not the kind of fight I am interested in. I want to fight Satan from the pulpit.

Basa & Co: (*shocked*) Beg your pardon.

Gomido: I'll establish a synagogue.

Basa: Hallelujah!

Chaka & Co: Amen!

Basa: Abi wetin name na your... errmmm...errmmm... wetin dem call am self... ermm...Sy...na... sy na... what?

Gomido: Synagogue of Jesus Christ of the people, by the people for the people.

Chaka: The first Global Democratic Church of Christ. Let's all say Amen to that.

Basa & Co: AMEN!

Gomido: (*sings as a soloist*) Darling Jesus, Democratic Jesus

Oh democratic Jesus you are wonderful Lord!

I love you so, democratic Jesus

Oh my Darling Jesus you are democratic Lord!

(*The others join him in singing the song as if they are in a real charismatic church*)

Abutu: Announcements please. (*pause*) The congregation is reminded that there shall be a ten–day Holy Spirit Revival/Crusade from 8.30 am to 6.00pm everyday beginning from tomorrow. All church members must make it a point to attend. End of announcement Amen!

Chaka: Now is the time to hear the word of God. There is a man right here on whose tongue the Lord Himself has placed healing words of honey for His children, Amen!

Abutu & Co: Amen!

Chaka: If you agree with me let's give a great shout to the Lord as we welcome...

Basa: (*shouts*) De Honourable... Most Holy... Very Reverend ... Bishop ... Pastor... Evangelist ... Prophet ... Doctor ... Gomey!

Abutu & Co: Amen!

Gomey: Praise the Lord!

Basa & Co: Hallelujah!

Gomey: (*assumes the role of a charismatic Preacher*) The good book teaches us to lay up our treasures where?

Chaka & Co: In Heaven!

Gomey: Yes, in Heaven. But you can only get there through your Bishop. Your Bishop, is God's own chosen gatekeeper to the divine treasure throve of Heaven. The Bishop, is God's money-carrier from earth to Heaven. So, channel all your treasures here on earth through, whom?

Chaka & Co: THE BISHOP!

Gomey: I say through whom?

Chaka & Co: The BISHOP!

Gomey: Yes, The Bishop...If you want God to grant you prosperity in life, make sure you don't miss the coming ten-day power-packed Holy Spirit-filled Crusade. I know some of you might say the time conflicts with your work. Tell me, which is more important, God's work or man's work?

Basa & Co: God's work!

Gomey: Let me hear you. God's work or man's work?

Basa & Co: God's work?

Gomey: If your work is going to bother you, just report sick at the hospital. Ask the Doctor to give you five days sick–off. After the fifth day you go back for a review and request for additional five days or ask for a ten-day casual leave from your employers. Amen!

Abutu & Co: Amen!

Chaka: (*sarcastically*) No wonder productivity is so low.

Gomey: To tell you the truth, all I really want to do is to go into farming.

Abutu & Co: (*greatly alarmed*) Farming! Are you crazy?

Basa: Ma Brudas, I sure say someone has short-circuited de wires in de young man im brains.

Chaka: Why choose such a backbreaking labour-intensive occupation?

Abutu: May be he intends going into mechanized farming; tractors, combine harvesters and all that.

Gomey: Well, may be.

Basa: Beg your pardon, Wey kine crop you go plant, pine apples?

Gomey: Nah!

Abutu: Tomatoes?

Gomey: Nah, too perishable

Chaka: Cocoa

Gomey: Something quite close to that...

Basa: Coconut?

Gomey: Nah!

Chaka: Why not go into sugarcane production then?

Gomey: There's more money in my special crop than in sugarcane.

Abutu & Co: How possible? Prove it.

Gomey: Sugarcane, for example is harvested...

Chaka: Refined and packaged...

Abutu: Shipped, marketed and...

Basa: Dem sell am for supermarkets at...

Abutu & Co: One dollar or one dollar fifty cents per kilo.

Gomey: Excellent. My special crop goes through the same process of harvesting, refining, packaging, shipping, marketing and finally retailing.

Abutu & Co: Oh, I see!

Gomey: Except there's no supermarket overhead calculated into the price

Basa: (*eagerly*) Beg your pardon, how much you dey sell am?

Gomey: Wholesale price is between thirty to thirty five thousand US Dollars a kilo.

Abutu & Co: Whew! That is money!

Gomey: So, you see, given a choice, and the rudimentary knowledge of simple arithmetic, why would anyone in their right mind want to be in the sugar cane business?

Chaka: (*anxiously*) You still haven't mentioned the name of the crop.

Basa: I sabey de crop. Ibi cashew nuts.

Gomey: Nah! Come round let me tell you. (*pause*)

Abutu & Co: Cocaine!

Chaka: Arrest him! (*silence.*)

Chaka: (*to Gomey*) Tell me, where did you get that idea?

Gomey & Co: Jeffery Robinson, *The Laundryman*, page 171, at the prison library. (*They all break into laughter.*)

Abutu: Folks, I am off.

Chaka: Where does he think he is going?

Abutu: I wouldn't stay in this bishop-corrupted, cocaine-juiced and God-forsaken country Southside of the vast Sahara for one more day. I am going away.

Gomido: Away, to where?

Basa: You no sabey? De man him wan go for de bush.

Abutu: (*angrily*) Your mother!

Basa: (*retorts sharply*) You too your farda!

Chaka: Stop it! (*Basa and Abutu continue to trade insults to the annoyance of Chaka.*) Cease fire I say! (*silence*) Now, tell us, where are you off to?

Abutu: I am going abroad!

Gomido: Abroad, where?

Basa: Lagos, in Nigeria (*silence*)

Abutu: To Europe.

Chaka: Do you have a passport?

Abutu: That's no problem. (*pulls a passport cover from among his belongings*) Here it is. See this?

Chaka: What about this? (*pulls out sheets of paper from his belongings*)

Basa: Wetin be dat?

Chaka: Visa Application forms.

Abutu: May I have a look?

Chaka: Here, Basa, pass it over to him. (*Basabasa hands over the papers to Abutu*)

Abutu: What! Am I expected to answer all that?

Gomido: If you really want me to consider you for an interview to determine your suitability for an entry visa to Europe.

(*Takes a seat on a nearby tree stump and assumes the role of a female consular officer interviewing applicants for visa. Around his neck hangs a tag bearing a card with the inscription 'OPEN' on it. Soft classical music preferably, Blue Danube can be heard in the background.*)

Gomido: Young man.

Basa: Yes, Madam.

Gomido: You take this slip and come back at 1.30pm for your visa.

Basa: (*excitedly*) Thank you, Madam…

(*Basa and Chaka hold the frame of the unfinished doormat right in front of Gomido to give the impression of the latter being behind a glass cubicle.*)

Gomido: (*speaking with a false cockney accent. He pronounces the name as if he were a European being confronted with an African name for the first time.*) Francis Kokosiko Abutu, interview room number eight please… (*Pause*) …Francis Kokosiko Abutu, Interview Room eight, please.

Abutu: (*dashing to the window*) Good morning, Madam!

Gomido: (*confidently*) Good morning, you may sit.

Abutu: Thank you, but I prefer to stand Madam.

Gomido: May I have your documents.

(*hands the sheets of paper in his hands to Gomido through the window*)

Gomido: Your full name!

Abutu: Pardon me!

Gomido: Your name… full name,

Abutu: Abutu, Ayitey-Hewale Kokosiko

Gomido: Date of birth…

Abutu: 31st February 1936

Gomido: Place of birth…

Abutu: From Bukom, British Accra.

Gomido: Time of birth, if known…

Abutu: Not applicable.

Gomido: Mother's Name…

Abutu: Naa Amanua Gborbilorbi.

Gomido: Mother's place of birth…

Abutu: Amasaman.

Gomido: Mother's date of birth…

Abutu: (*hesitates*) Ermm… errmm… No idea.

Gomido: Father's name…

Abutu: Nii Kwartei Quartey alias Nokoko alias Something.

Gomido: Father's date and place of birth…

Abutu: Swalaba-Accra, but no idea about date.

Gomido: Parents' profession...

Abutu: Father is a fisherman. Mother is a fish seller.

Gomido: Monthly salary of father. (*pause*) Yes, your father's monthly salary.

Abutu: (*hesitates*) Eeerrrmm… No idea… I mean not applicable.

Gomido: Siblings…(*pause*)… I mean number of Brothers and Sisters.

Abutu: Oh that…I see, I have five brothers and three sisters.

Gomido: Names of brothers.

Abutu: Kpakpo, Nii MooLai, Ashong, Akwei and Papa Nii.

Gomido: Sisters…

Abutu: Ayorkor, Atswei and Naa Adaku.

Gomido: Married or not married?

Abutu: (*hesitantly*) Mmm… Well… some are married, others divorced… others too have remarried and separated…or are on the verge of separating.

Gomido: Do you have any family members living in Europe?

Abutu: My family members? …My family…living in Europe… Please madam, I don't get you.

Gomido: By a 'family member' I am referring to your spouse, Father, Son, Daughter, Great grandfather, great grandmother, niece or first cousin…

Abutu: First cousin?

Gomido: The son or daughter of your uncle or aunt.

Abutu: Oh I see. Now, I understand.

Gomido: Good, so back to my question. Do you have any family members living in Europe?

Abutu: By your definition of Family, I can comfortably say that all members of the West Indian community in the U.K. are my family members.

Gomido: What! (*pause*) Now, you, are you married?

 Abutu: Yes, Madam,

Gomido: Name of wife.

Abutu: Gbeebi Akley.

Gomido: Was it church wedding or…

Abutu: (*confidently*) Customary wedding.

Gomido: Date and Place of wedding.

Abutu: 24th December, at Kaadjaanor.

Gomido: Let me see your left hand. Why no ring on your finger?

Abutu: (*more confidently*) In customary marriage, we bear the oath of marriage on our hearts, where it is sealed in blood and flesh and stamped by two bottles of schnapps or local gin, as a sign of our total respect for our wives and their love for us.

Gomido: Quite interesting. What is your profession?

Abutu: (*confidently*) I am a Barrister.

Gomido: I see. Any letter of Support?

Abutu: Here you are. (*pushes more documents through the window to Gomido*)

Gomido: (*goes through the papers*) I see...So you are a solicitor

Abutu: (*baffled*) Excuse me.

Gomido: Which law firm do you work for?

Abutu: (*surprised*) Me... Law firm? I say I work with a bar... Chop Bar... Drinking Bar!

Gomido: What guarantee, is there that you will come back when you are given the visa to enter Europe? (*pause*) Any property?

Abutu: I don't get you?

Gomido: Any possessions of value?

Abutu: Oh yes. I have three cats, two dogs, one cutlass, and one cocoa-spraying machine still under repairs with the mechanic; Yes, and a pair of rain boots and a sizeable cassava farm cultivated under the Presidential Special Cassava Initiative.

Gomido: Is that all?

Abutu: I also have my pregnant wife.

Gomido: I see. Letter of invitation.

Abutu: It is among the documents I gave you (*pause*)

Gomido: Yes, indeed, it is here. Reason for seeking visa... VISIT.

Abutu: (*firmly*) That's right.

Gomido: Supposing you are offered a job in Europe during your visit, won't you take it?

Abutu: A job that pays well?

Gomido: (*enticingly*) A job that pays more than what you are receiving here.

Abutu: Euro or Pounds ... Sterling?

Gomido: Let's say 950.00 Euro a week.

Abutu: (*a bit undecided*) Mmmm...well... That's a handsome amount of money compared to what one can have here...950.00 Euro a week... Wow! Who'll offer me a thing like that?

Gomido: A company.

Abutu: A European company?

Gomido: You bet.

Abutu: I am afraid, I'll turn it down.

Gomido: (*surprised*) Why?

Abutu: Those people never offer anything for free. There's always some hidden string attached somewhere.

Gomido: Well, I am sorry, by the look in your eyes and the shape of your nose, I feel convinced you are not the type who'll return to this country if you ever stepped in Europe. So, I am denying you the visa. Here, take your passport.

Abutu: (*suddenly getting aggressive*) Then give me back my money... No delivery, no payment.

Chaka: What is he saying?

Basa: Him money. Beg your pardon. In dis country, No delivery–No payment. He want him money.

Gomido: No way. It is non–refundable. He can make an appeal.

Chaka: An appeal will take six months, Madam.

Gomido: Six months it will take and what of that? Good afternoon gentleman. (*Gomido removes the tag on his neck, turns the back of it to show the opposite side that bears the 'CLOSED' sign and hangs it on the frame and walks away leaving Chaka and Basabasa still holding on to the frame*)

Abutu: (*goes into a rage*) I don't want to appeal. Give me back my money. Hey you, I am talking to you. Give me back my money,

Basa: My bruda, dem close. Madam don go for lunch.

Abutu: (*angrily*) Cheats! You knew you were not going to issue me with the visa, and yet you deliberately subjected me to a humiliating interrogation as if I were a criminal under cross-examination in a court of law. Is that how you were interviewed at our national Mission in your country when you went seeking visa to come down here? (*screams*) Give me back my money! Where in your country is a man paid ¢900,000.00 for interviewing a person for less than fifteen minutes? (*Gomido returns to take his seat behind the frame sipping coffee from a cup*)

Basa: Abi, dis place na foreign embassy. Make una talk diplomatically.

Abutu: And what has been done to me is pure diplomatic extortion. Hey, you young woman sitting behind the glass door. I am talking to you! You are a Diplomatic robber. You are all a bunch of Diplomatic extortionists... Hoo! Ole! Jaguda! Hoo!...

(*Fade out classical music. Silence*)

Abutu: (*as they drop the frame*) Nine Hundred and Ninety Thousand whole Cedis gone down the drain.

Chaka: (*softly*) Five Hundred young people from this land of poverty apply for Visa and are denied everyday ...

Basa: Make we times 500 by ¢990,000.00

Gomido: (*gets down on his knees and does the calculation in the sand*) ¢495,000,000.00

Abutu: Multiply that by Monday, Tuesday, Wednesday, Thursday and Friday

Basa: Five days in a week.

Gomido: That gives you Two Billion Four hundred and Seventy Five Million Cedis only. (¢2,475,000,000.00)

Chaka: Again multiply that by the four weeks in a month! (*pause*)

Gomido: (*screams*) ¢9.9billion

Abutu: (*shouts*) Multiply by twelve months in a year. (*pause*)

Gomido: (*screaming*) ¢188.8billion... Oh my God! That can pay for over 500 bore holes to provide potable water for our rural folks in 300 villages... and re-gravel several kilometres of feeder road...

Basa: Beg your pardon... It fit to construct proper classroom blocks for 250

rural communities where the small small pikins go for school under trees!

Abutu: That is the unsolicited contribution by our poor folks from this God forsaken side of the Atlantic Ocean, to the economy of former colonial masters.

(*Chaka suddenly bursts out into laughter. He is unable to control his laughter*)

Gomido: What's funny? ... (*Chaka, still laughing*)

Chaka: Gomido come over. (*pause*)

(*Gomido and Chaka are laughing uncontrollably*)

Abutu: (*curiously*) Where is the joke?

Gomido: Abutu, come over. (*Pause. Abutu breaks into sudden laughter*)

Basa: Abi, wetin be de matter?

Abutu: (*trying hard to suppress his laughter*) Here, come over and let me tell you. (*Abutu whispers*)

Basa: (*shouting at the top of his voice*) Yes! Na true! Na true talk ... Ibi de same money dem take away from us, wey dem turn round give for we as medium term loan for development.

Chaka & Co: Hey! Sh-sh-sh-sh. Not so loud. Are you crazy? Don't you know that walls have ears? (*silence*)

Gomido: To be honest with you, what I really want to be is a Professor of politics. Stand for elections, go to parliament and fight for human rights. (*general laughter*)

Basa: Beg your pardon... Abi you booze or wetin? Who talk you say de hungry people for dis land dem want vote for somebody wey him ged prison record? You be big fool! (*long laughter*)

Gomido: (*coolly*) I don't blame you. You never entered a classroom, so you know nothing about history.

Chaka: What has history got to do with this?

Basa: Make una hask am now.

Gomido: (*confidently*) Everything.

Abutu: Such as?

Gomido: Joseph came out of prison to be the Prime minister to the Pharaoh of Egypt. That's number one.

Chaka: (*sarcastically*) Oh...I see, Chappie really did a thorough job on you. Why don't you rather be a preacher man? (*laughter*) On a more serious note, after Joseph who came?

Basa: I tink say after Joseph de next one go be Mary, Jesus him morda. (*laughter*)

Gomido: You are wrong. Rather it was Malcolm X. An African-American who came out of prison to give racist America of his time, a piece of mirror to take a good look at her conscience. That's number two.

Chaka: And number three?

Gomido: Abdel Gamal Nasser, came out of prison to lead Egypt...Number four, Dr. Kwame Nkrumah, The Osagyefo himself, came out of prison to lead the Gold Coast into Ghana.

Chaka: That's true.

Basa & Abutu: And number five?

Gomido: Nelson Mandela! Landed by helicopter from Robben Island to lead the ANC and South Africa through the narrow streets of SOWETO into freedom's rainbow highway singing *Nkosi kele le Africa! Malufaka yiso opondola yo!*

(*They all join in singing the Anthem up to a point.*)

Chaka: Okay...Okay! Any more?

Gomido: Yes, in Ghana, a certain Jerry John Rawl...

Abutu: (*vehemently*) Objection! (*pause*) Strictly speaking folks, that chap was in an army guardroom and not a real prison like you and I have been through.

Basa: Him too ino be thief like me plus you.

Gomido: Don't tell me what you don't know. That chap was a common criminal just like any of us here. He was arrested attempting to steal.

Basa: Wetin him go tif? Beg your pardon.

Gomido: Political power.

Chaka: I think, what you want us to understand is that, you are a potential parliamentary material, in spite of your Ex-Con record.

Gomido: Precisely, and more so when I am now a Born-Again Christian.

(*The rest burst out into laughter*)

Abutu: Please, spare us that unchristian anecdote.

Chaka: So, you want to become a Parliamentarian.

Gomido: That's right! A Senator.

Chaka: All right. Now, we invite our aspiring Born-Again Honourable Senator to address members of his constituency herein assembled. Silence everybody! (*pause*)

Gomido: (*baffled*) I don't seem to get you.

Chaka: You may mount the podium over there. You have two and a half minutes to address us on our present circumstances. Energy crisis, The Leopard called NEPAD, Indiscipline, corruption in the judiciary, The Presidential Special Gutter Cleaning Initiative, the depreciating currency, HIPIC and all. You may begin at the sound of the whistle. I shall be the timekeeper. You, Basabasa, will be my clock. At the sound of the whistle, begin ticking.

Gomido: (*confused*) Wait a minute... you mean I should.

(*Chaka blows his whistle*)

Gomido: (*Goes to stand on some two cement blocks put together close by*) You mean I should pretend this is some real political rally and...

Basa: Ke...ke...ke...ke...ke...ke. Half a minute gone! Ke...ke...ke... ke...ke...ke.

Gomido: (*suddenly realising the full import of the game*) Tsooooboee!... (*no response*) Tsoooooboe! (*no response*)

Abutu: Ke...ke...ke...ke...ke... Another half a minute gone.

Gomido: (*to no one in particular*) What do I do now? (*Pause. Clears his throat*) My people, do not fear circumstances. They cannot hurt us. It is not the circumstances in which we are placed that matters. It is not the circumstances enforced on us by the energy crisis that matters... But the spirit in which we as a nation, and as a people, meet them, as challenges, that constitutes our comfort. Above all, I want you to believe that there's NOTHING you cannot accomplish as a people by hard work and commitment. Therefore, let NO ONE, be he or she in or outside Government ever destroy that belief you have in yourself as a people. Thank you.

Basa: (*shouts*) Time Up!

Chaka: (*blows his whistle*) So far, so good. Remember this is an open forum and the electorate can ask questions, some of which you are obliged to answer and others you may ignore.

Gomido: Very well.

Chaka: Can we have the first question please? Yes you young man at the back there.

Basa: Thank you, Mr Moderator. Lucky Mphalele is my name and I represent the Sowetan, a community newspaper produced in South Africa. Please Mr Aspiring Senator, what in your opinion, do you think, is the cause for democracy being unable to thrive for long on the sub-Saharan political soil?

Gomido: Is that an optional question?

Abutu: (*angrily*) What a question. Don't you know that in every examination, the Question One is compulsory? Go check from the West African Exams Council.

Gomido: Thank you. The truth of the matter is that democracy is not a feasible proposition within any nation that is plagued by deprivation and grinding poverty. Sub-Saharan Africa remains the zone of the most desperate suffering in the post-cold war world. The answer to its multiple problems does not lie simply in good governance, or observance of human rights or positive defiance. It lies more in the developed world's response to Africa's genuine developmental needs. Sub-Saharan Africa's crisis is not an isolated issue. We must see it as the world's crisis.

Abutu: (*speaks with an American accent*) Well said, I am Joe Bush of the International Enquirer based in London. Must Sub-Saharan Africa wait perpetually for the slumbering Developed World to wake up whilst its children die by the hordes everyday?

Gomido: No.

Abutu: If no, then what must Sub-Saharan Africa do for herself?

Basa: Abi, dat one na Compulsory Question. I lie?

Gomido: (*confidently*) Never mind. Until sub-Saharan Africa accepts the blame for her predicament, we shall still be a long way away from a practical solution to her problems. So long as Sub-Saharan Africa produce what her children do not consume, and continue to consume what she does not produce, the sub-region and her children shall continue to be at the mercy of the developed countries.

Chaka: Can you please explain that a bit more?

Gomido: You see, the case of some of the Heads of State within the Sub-Region can be likened to that of an irresponsible person who fails to lead a sensible life and gets malaria. Instead of consulting a medical doctor in his own country, who specialises in tropical medicine, what does he do? He gets on the plane, flies from one country to the other... consulting foreign brain surgeons and turning round to blame the surgeons for prescribing what they know best.

(*Basabasa and Abutu burst out laughing*)

Chaka: Next! Yes... you at the back there. Please come forward. (*pause*)

Abutu: Thank you. I am Femi Olarigbigbe. I work for the Morning Star of Nigeria and I have two questions. One, what is going to be your party's position on culture?

Basa: Dat one na compulsory question. (*to Chaka*) Abi I lie?

Gomido: That's Okay. Well, if a people have no culture, if it has no worthwhile tradition, it becomes a negligible factor in the thought of the world, and it stands in danger of being exterminated. On the basis of this assertion, we shall strive to supply the necessary inputs to the relevant institutions to ensure a vibrant and sustainable national culture.

Abutu: Question number two. What is your party's position on the regular fracas arising out of the enforcement of the ban on drumming and noise making within certain traditional areas of our land, and the refusal of certain Christians to abide by it?

Chaka: I believe that is an optional question.

Abutu & Basa: Yes it is an optional but he may answer to earn a bonus point.

Gomido: (*very gently*) The path crosses the stream,
The stream crosses the path.
Which is the elder? (*pause*)
The path was created by man to meet the stream.
The stream has been there since creation.
Even though they cross each other's path,
The stream has never quarrelled with the path,
They have learnt to coexist peacefully
In the bosom of nature's harmony.

Basa: (*mimicking a woman's voice*) Me too I wan hask two question. My name na Angelina Obolo. I be de General secretary of de West African Association of Housewives. An NGO. Tell me, Mr. Senator-to-be, wetin you go do give de plenty housewife wey dem dey dis country inside? Dat one na question number one.

Gomido: For us, the term *Housewife* shall not be part of our political lexicon. DOMESTIC ENGINEERS shall be the replacement. That, I think, is much more dignifying, even if semantically.

Basa: (*confused*) Beg your pardon... Wetin be dat sementic.... You mean you go give de housewife cement make dem take build house?

Abutu: (*sarcastically*) No, he'll give them Cement for the building of gutters in your mouth.

Basa: Beg your pardon!

Abutu: Beg your illiteracy. That is why I say go to school.

Basa: Your Morda im mouth. Hoo! Bush baby! Look, if you joke wid me I go wound you.

Chaka: (*sternly*) Basabasa, are you ready with your second question or not? Time is running.

Basa: Question number two. If you go for power, wetin you go do for women wey dem husband dem beat dem by heart, for de sake of say dem no do notin?

Gomido: That's a good question. Violence against women. We shall introduce a new concept of women empowerment that shall require all women to be trained in martial arts and equipped with boxing gloves to be worn over their minds in self defence.

Chaka: A sort of mind shield.

Gomido: Precisely. Much better than a Domestic Violence Bill that was violently dragged through parliament like a cow to the abattoir.

Chaka: The last question, and I ask it. I am Nick Lancey from the BBC. African Service, London. How do you intend to help lift this dark poverty curtain off the sub-region?

Abutu & Basa: (*Abutu and Basabasa murmur*) Compulsory question please!

Gomido: (*heaves a sigh*) Let me refer you to something General Colin Powell said to me many years ago. He said, and I quote.

'The worst kind of poverty
Is not economic poverty
It is the poverty of sharing
It is the poverty of love' unquote.

Let us therefore love one another and treat one another as human beings and not as Anglophone, Francophone, Christianphone, Muslimphone, Gramophone, Microphone, Telephone and what have you. It is only when we stop these senseless balkanisation of humanity that we shall find ourselves on the road to making life better for the people in the sub-region. Thank you and may God bless you.

(*all the ex-convicts applaud Gomido*)

Chaka: (*still clapping*) Well... well... What a mind he has. Isn't it a shame how as a nation we cry for a saviour and yet lock up such brains behind all sorts of artificial prison bars? We are quick to accuse others of draining our best brains, but fail to see the internal brain drain we are carrying out very subtly on ourselves by the use of our prison systems. My brother, Gomido, note down my name as your Campaign Manager.

Gomido: Thank you.

Basa: Me too.

Abutu: All of us can't belong to the same political party. Somebody must be in opposition just to oppose issues. That is the beauty of democracy. I choose to be in the opposition.

Chaka: That's your choice. By the way, which constituency are you going to be standing for.

Abutu: Need you ask? Prison constituency of course.

Chaka: And the name of the party?

Abutu: P.G.P.P. of course.

Basa: Beg your pardon... P.G.P.P. wetin be dat?

Abutu: Prison Graduates Popular Party.

Basa: Wetin go be de party him slogan?

Gomido: That is in the pipeline.

Basa: Too bad, by de time de slogan reach here ego make wet. (*general laughter*) Why you dey laugh?

Abutu: Instead of going to school you were catching crabs by the stream (*derisive laughter*) You can't appreciate a simple idiomatic expression.... A figure of speech. All you know is "Beg your pardon"

Basa: (*takes offence*) Your Morda... Hoo! Bush baby!

Chaka: (screams) Cease fire! We are all tired... we need to rest. Let there be peace.

(*Abutu and Basabasa suddenly stop trading insults and go to lie down using their belongings for a head rest. Lights fade out on them.*)

FOURTH LEG

Abutu: Folks, we've rested enough. I suggest we get on the move.

Basa: Beg your pardon... Why?

Abutu: I don't feel too comfortable here.

Chaka: That is natural.

Abutu: What is?

Chaka: Considering the fact that you've been in prison for all these years. It is only natural you won't be comfortable with your freedom.

Basa: If de Comfort wey ino good, make una try Mercy.

Abutu: Listen to that beg-your-pardon-illiterate. As for you... you are just like a... a... a... a...

Chaka: (*firmly*) Please... please... no more insults. Please (*pause*)

Abutu: All right. I forgive him.

Chaka: Now, tell us what your worries are.

Abutu: This idea of living too close to a prison, long after you've been discharged, gives me the creeps.

Gomido: What do you mean?

Abutu: It is like hanging around the graveyard long after the funeral party had gone away. It has its own temptations and wrongful interpretations.

Basa: Wey kine application be dat, abi? Application for employment in a cemetery? Beg your...

Abutu: Spare us the beg-your-pardon nonsense. As for you … you are… I am even lost for adjectives to colour you.

Basa: You fit colour me in charcoal, I don't mind.

(*general laughter*)

Abutu: That is why I keep saying you should have been to school and….

Chaka: Hold it! (*pause*) No more insults. This new commonwealth of ex-cons has no place for cross-boarder insults. Have I made myself clear?

Abutu: Yes, Chaka.

Chaka: Good. Now explain yourself on the issue regarding your discomfort with our present location and its comparison to the graveyard.

Basa: Na so!

Abutu: You see, in the case of the graveyard, we could be mistaken for grave looters…

Basa & Chaka: (*shocked*) What!

Gomido: Considering the way we are dressed.

Chaka: Yes, that's possible. And the other?

Abutu: We could be mistaken for escaped inmates and hurled back inside to do a time-added on.

Gomido: That is impossible.

Chaka: Never ever use the word IMPOSSIBLE here. This is a sub-Saharan democracy. Everything and anything is possible. The Attorney General could call for a judicial review of the amnesty that set us free.

Abutu: And before you can say *Jack-where-are-you?* You'd have been arrested at church on Sunday morning, processed by Monday morning and fast tracked into jail by Tuesday dawn..

Basa: (*really scared*) Abi make we comot from dis place before wahala come take we for inside jail yard again. Yoo!.

Gomido: (*angrily*) My brother relax, nothing is going to happen to us. We have our discharge papers on us.

Abutu: Supposing the discharge papers turn out to be fake.

Basa: (*suddenly gets hysterical*) Walahi…somitin serious go hapin. Kai… I swear… Somebody go die… Allah!

Gomido: Or may be we deciding to go back into prison voluntarily.

Abutu: Impossible! … God forbid!

Basa: To go back in side? Never! (*suddenly turns his back to the penitentiary*) Forward EVER! Backwards NEVER!

Chaka: Let us rather celebrate our freedom in song. (*pause*) What do you say?

Abutu: I am not in a singing mood.

Chaka & Co: What at all is the matter with you?

Abutu: Folks, my stomach. I need food. I am hungry!

Basa: (*shouts excitedly*) I ged am! Oh yes! I ged am. Now I sabey de job I want do.

Chaka: He wants to be a civil servant.

Basa: (*protests vehemently*) Beg your… Abi I no want to be nobody him servant. I be free person. I comot from prison. I be my own master. Free body!

Gomido: Then you join the IRS.

Basa: IRS? Ibi some new F.M. Radio Station?

Gomido: Internal Revenue. Services. (*enticingly*) That is where you make all the big bucks. A guy is supposed to pay a tax of twenty thousand Cedis. You arrive at a gentleman's agreement with him. He pays only twenty cedis and he gives you a gift of ten thousand cedis.

Basa: (*contemptuously*) Dat one na bribe… Beg your…

Chaka: Shut up. Everyone in the civil service does it, one way or the other.

Basa: (*shocked*) Na so? Me I no sabey.

Gomido: That is the lubricant that keeps the engine of the African civil service running *chuku-chaka-chuku-chaka* like a locomotive train, carrying only the rich and leaving the poor behind on the tracks.

Abutu: Have you forgotten the civil servants' prayer?

Chaka & all: ' …and give us this day our daily bribe as we receive from all those whose jobs pass through our hands.' (*general laughter*)

Basa: De Civil Service no be good place for my heart. Ibi Evil Service. I go work for Japanese restaurant.

Gomido & Co: As what?

Chaka: As the Chef, perhaps.

Basa: Not the Chef. As a Waiter.

Abutu: (*not amused in the least*) Why that?

Basa: Because I love am. Look, if I try to explain to you, you no go fit to understand.

Chaka: (*sudden burst of anger*) This is one thing I still can't understand about my people.

Gomido: (*showing genuine concern*) What is it my brother?

Chaka: (*fuming*) Why is it that we would always want to work for someone else but never for ourselves? If we are not working for a former colonial master, you can bet we are working for a former colonial master's *skin-mate.*

Abutu: How dare you say that? That is most unfair. You sound racist.

Gomido: Forgive me, If you think I do, but that is the global fact.

Abutu: It still beats my mind though. (*pause*) Well, come round, two of you, Basabasa and Gomido. (*pause*)

(*Abutu and Gomido break out into laughter.*)

Abutu: Now, you, Chaka.

Chaka: Me? What of me?

Basa: Wetin you go be, after Prison? Beg your pard…

Chaka: I am going to be an Abusua Panyin.

Gomido: (*baffled*) What is that?

Basa: A traditional title. A big family head. Sometin like a big chief in a small village.

Chaka: That's right. It is an established post in our traditional set up.

Abutu: What is the job description attached to the designation?

Chaka: Can't tell you now, but at the appropriate time you all shall get to know.

Gomido: Very well, that leaves you Abutu to tell us how you intend celebrating your emancipation.

Abutu: Well, I intend to approach one of these foreign NGOs for assistance to enable me set up.

Chaka & Co: To set up what?

Abutu: What a question, my business of course.

Basa: And de name of de business? (*laughs*) Beg your pardon...

Abutu: Ku Enye Ga Enterprise. Or Death is Money Enterprise.

Gomido: Dealing in what?

Abutu: Coffins and caskets.

Basa: Beg your ... Why coffins and caskets?

Chaka: I tell you, our brother is suffering from Cemetery cocidiosis. (*laughter*)

Basa: Who gave you this silly idea that what society needs most is coffin and caskets?

Abutu: De tin people want be food, clothing and roof over dem head.

Gomido: And Medicare.

Abutu: (*goes to pull out some old news paper from among his belongings*) Read this. 'Over two hundred people infected with the deadly HIV/ AIDS virus everyday in our land.' What does that tell you? Don't be daft. What it means is that there is a future for coffin makers and gravediggers here in sub Saharan Africa than there is for Accountants and I.C.T professionals.

Gomido: I am still not convinced.

Basa: Make you prove de *Ku- enye- Ga* theory.

Chaka & Co: Yes, prove it to us that indeed Death brings wealth.

Abutu: I'll do so on one condition.

Chaka: And what is that?

Abutu: That one of you is prepared to die.

Chaka & Co: What?

Basa: I beg your pardon. I no dey inside.

Gomido: Not me either. I don't want death for a companion.

Abutu: Cowards that you are. You desire the fruits of death and yet would not dare venture into death's orchard.

Gomido: How dare you call me a coward? Don't you know who I am? I am Sortorme, Gomido Tsorgali. Great grandson of Torgbuiga Whenya of Wheta. The man who dived under water and fought two live crocodiles with his bare hands whilst still smoking a lighted pipe. I don't fear death. I volunteer to die. (*Drops down and feigns death.*) Look I am dead!

Chaka: Yes, Gomey is dead. Look his eyes are shut.

Basa: De man die, now where de money dey?

Abutu: I am afraid that is too cheap a death to die.

Chaka & Co: Too cheap you said?

Abutu: You heard me right.

Basa: All closing eyes no be die?

Abutu: Since there is an expensive way to live, naturally, there ought to be an expensive way to die.

Chaka: So, tell us, how does one die expensively?

Abutu: First, you fall sick as a result of high blood pressure, or some Cardio Vascular Arrest and be rushed in a Mercedes Benz, C. Class, to either Nyaho Clinic or SSNIT Hospital.

Basa: Or Korle-Bu Teachers Hospital.

Abutu: If you don't mind medical students using your body as a teaching aid, then go to a Teaching Hospital.

Gomido (*pretending to be short of breath*) I prefer to be taken to the Military Hospital.

Basa: Beg your pardon… You be soldier?

Gomido: (*feigning severe chest pains*) Adjiiiiiiiiiiii. Mmmmmm! (*screams*) Aaaaaoooo! … Somebody help me!

Chaka: (*showing great concern*) What's the matter Gomey?

Gomido: (*with difficulty*) My chest! … Aaaaoooo! … the left side of my … Aaaaa oooo! (*panting*) Ao God, am I really going to die?

Basa: (*with urgency*) Abi make we carry am go throw way for hospital. Oya!

Abutu: Let me get a taxi then.

Chaka: With what are you going to pay for the taxi? (*Gomido is groaning loudly*)

Abutu: (*To Chaka*) Abusua Panyin… please lend us some money for taxi to…

Chaka: (*angrily*) Me? My money, for you to take this man to the hospital. What has he ever done for me? I am sorry. I don't have a dime.

Abutu: So what do we do? Leave him here to die because we have no cash to carry him to the hospital?

Basa: Abi make una improvise. Make una use una head.

Abutu: Why don't you use your back instead?

Basa: True-true, make I use my back… Oya, Gomido make you come sit my back make I give you free ride… (*groaning Gomido is carried on the back of Basabasa who takes him in a wide circle using his mouth for an ambulance siren. Meanwhile Abutu and Chaka with the help of a few items from their belongings transform themselves into nurses*)

Basa: (*desperation in his voice*) Auntie Nurse, we go fit to see de doctor?

Nurse 1: (*saucily*) You cannot. Join the queue.

Basa: (politely) Beg your pardon…Please nurse, Dis one na emergency.

Nurse 1: (*flares up*) Beg your pardon, which of us is trained to determine when a situation is an emergency, you or I?

Basa: (softly) Beg your pardon, Na you, madam of course … I very sorry, Madam Nurse. Make you no vex, Madam.

Nurse 1: (*sucks her teeth loudly*) Where is your card?

Basa: Ibi nyim dis.

Nurse 1: National Health Insurance card, mister. Not voters ID card.

Basa: We no ged am Madam.

Nurse 1: Take him to the OPD.

Basa: Whosai de…. Errmm… PWD dey.?

Nurse 1: Hey Mister, do you have timber in your ears? I said OPD not PWD. Over there. (*points towards the direction of Nurse 2*) Put him in that wheel-chair and push him away. Just follow the arrow. The nurse at the other end will take his temperature and write his history and refer him back to us.

Basa: Tank you, Madam (*pause*)

Nurse 2: Next!

Basa: Gudu morning Auntie nurse.

Nurse 2: Name!

Basa: Basa into Brackets Squared.

Nurse 2: (*a bit baffled*) Whose name is that?

Basa: (*confidently*) Dat my original name, madam.

Nurse 2: Are you the patient?

Basa: Beg your pardon…

Nurse 2: Are you the sick person coming to see the doctor?

Basa: (*with an air of self-importance*) No, Madam, Ibi my broda here who sick. Me, I be him Ambulance driver. Na me, carry am. Him no fit to speak correct English. So, I be him 'terpretator'.

Nurse 2: (*Not in the least amused*) I want the patient's name.

Basa: Him name be, Kweku Nyankomago Menyawo-a Meyewo- Gomido D'Omingo.

Nurse 2: What is that?

Basa: Dat one na him full compound name.

Nurse 2: Doesn't he have a shorter version of that jaw-breaking tongue-twister? Ask him.

Basa: Gomido! (*pause*) Gomido! You fit to hear me?

Gomido: (*feebly*) Yes… I can… (*coughs*) I can… (*coughs*)

Basa: De madam-Nurse want sabey if say your compound name him ged revised standard version?

Gomido: (*coughs with great difficulty*) Kweku… (*coughs*) Duah… Kweku Dua… (*long cough*)

Basa: (*to Nurse 2*) Him revised standard name na Kweku Duah. Simple.

Nurse 2: (*begins to write*) Kweku…Dua…tell me, is it Duah with 'H' at the end?

Basa: (*calls out*) Gomido! you fit hear me?… Good. Your Duah, him ged 'H' for him back side?

Gomido: (*feigning great pain*) No, it has horns at the front like a cow.

Basa: Madam Nurse, Him say eno carry tail for him backside.

Nurse 2: Age!

Basa: (*hesitantly*) Mmm… well… make we say roughly… about 58 years old... Yes, somitin laka dat.

Nurse 2: (*angrily*) I don't need you to guess. This is a hospital. We don't do somitin-laka-dat *guestimations* here. We deal with facts and figures. Ask him for his real age and stop the guesswork.

Basa: (*shouts*) Gomido! How old you be!?

Gomido: Tell her I'm old enough to be her father.

Nurse 2: (*curiously*) What was that he said?

Basa: Him say, him tink say him ged de same age plus your Papa.

Nurse 2: No problem. (*pause*) Is he married?

Basa: Of course, him ged wife plus plenty man and woman pikins.

Nurse: (*screams in anger*) Let him answer for himself.

Basa: (*shouts*) Gomido! ... De Madam-Nurse ewan to marry you. But efear say your wife go beat am well-well.

Gomido: Tell her if I marry her and take her home, my wife will faint on account of her ugliness. If she wouldn't mind being a sixth mistress, I may consider her unsolicited proposal. (*Basa tries hard to suppress his laughter*)

Nurse 2: What was that he said?

Basa: (*stifling his laughter*) Him say... Him say... if na marriagement you want, he sorry. You are too late. Him hands already full...

Nurse 2: (*contemptuously*) God forbid! Peuf!... See my finger? See this? It is a diamond ring. I am properly married... Church wedding!... I am somebody's missus!...okay?

Basa: Yes, madam.

Nurse 2: (*contemptuously*) Take your card and vanish from my sight. What impudence!

Basa: Tank you, madam. Make you no vex, madam. Na so de world be. Some want, dem no ged am. Some too gedam, dem no wantam. Make you no vex at all.

(*puts Gomido into a wheel-chair and pushes him back towards Nurse 1*)

Nurse 1: ...As I was saying, when you hear your name you come for your card and go home and come next week. The doctor has gone to join his colleagues on the picket line to fight for better conditions of service. Georgina Johnson ... Albertina Quagrine...

Basa: (*almost out of breath*) Madam Nurse, we ged de card.

Nurse 1: Let me see.

Basa: Here him dey.

Nurse 1: Good.

Basa: We fit to see de Doctor now?

Nurse 1: Not yet. Your deposit first.

Basa: Deposit... why? Dis one no be maternity case. My bruda is not pregnant.

Nurse1: The choice is entirely yours.

Basa: All right, how much be de deposit?

Nurse 1: Only fifty dollars... U.S. or its equivalent in the local currency according to the inter bank exchange rates for the day.

Basa: Beg your pardon... You be Nurse or you be forex Bureau operator?

Nurse 1: What did you just say?

Basa: I wan ask say no reduction for de deposit?

Nurse 1: Reduction? This is a hospital ...A Government Teaching Hospital and not a street side Market.

Basa: Sorry, Madam-Nurse. So how much does that work up to in the local currency?

Nurse: Let's see. (*pulls out an calculator from somewhere and computes the figures*) Here you are.

Basa: (*explodes*) Ewoooo!

Nurse 1: Hey what is that? Don't you know this is a hospital and you are not to shout?

Basa: I sorry Madam, but de money. Whosai I for ged dat kine money? Gomido,

Gomido: (*feebly*) Hmmm...

Basa: Where we for ged dis American dollar money? (*shows the computed figures on the calculator to Gomido*)

Gomido: Even if you write '*for sale*' on my body and send me to Salaga market, with all my value added sickness, I'll not be able to fetch that much.

Basa: So, wetin we for do now, Gomido my bruda?

Gomido: Talk to Abusua Panyin.

Basa: (*resentfully*) Beg your... Man wey no fit give money for taxi to carry you to hospital, how he go fit to give 50 American Dollar?

Gomido: May be we have to solicit for aid and donor support from international NGOs.

Basa: Na true. Make we sit by the road side with cup in hand and make music. Who knows, some of the International Donor Agencies passing by, may be kind enough to drop in some coins .

(*Basa manages to prop Gomido to sit up next to him. The two sing a beautiful duet. During the course of the singing they pass a rusty metallic bowl around the front section of the audience soliciting for alms. When the music is over and the bowl is retrieved, they count the money they have been able to collect and run with it to the nurse.*)

Basa: Auntie Nurse . . Auntie Nurse...

Nurse 1: What is it?

Basa: De money is ready.

Nurse 1: Let me have it... (*re-counts the money given to her*) Good. You can now transfer him unto this hospital trolley and bring him in. But you'll have to wait here. I'll call you when the Doctor arrives from the picket line.

Basa: Tank you, madam. I hear.

(*long pause*)

Nurse 1: By the way, this is for you.

132 *Efo Kodjo Mawugbe*

Basa: Tank You. Dis be de chit for de collection of de medicine?

Nurse 1: No, that is for Lab Test.

Basa: Beg your pardon... Lab text?

Nurse 1: (*smilingly*) Sure, It is the results of the tests that would assist the doctor in determining what medication to prescribe for you. You can go now.

Basa: (*quite satisfied*) Tank you Madam-Nurse, you be very kind woman. Gomido, let's go.

(*Basa pushes the trolley to one end, stops and pretends to be whispering to someone. He excuses Gomido.*)

Gomido: (*weakly*) Where are you off to again?

Basa: Wait here. I need to clear sometin wit de Madam-Nurse. (*pause*) Madam, just one more ting.

Nurse 1: (*exasperatedly*) What is it again?

Basa: Dem say make we pay for de Lab. Text.

Nurse 1: (*sternly*) Of course, what do you expect?

Basa: But Madam Nurse... I ...tink say all dat charge dey inside de American fifty dollars. I lie?

Nurse 1: I am afraid you are wrong. The fifty dollars was for the doctor guessing which lab tests you probably needed to undergo

Basa: Allahu Akbar! 50 dollars just for guess work?

Nurse 1: Shh..shh...sh..It is not my fault. (*whispers*) Cash and carry.

Basa: (*shouts*) Cash and Carry!

(*There is a loud scream from Gomido*)

Basa: (*dashes back to the trolley and calls out for help*) Nurse my bruda dey die o. ...Nurse... Oh nurse...make una help ma bruda! Gomey...Gomey... Make you no die o, Gomey... Nurse!..nurse!....

Nurse 1: (*shouts*) Orderly...Orderly!

Voice: Yes, Sister.

Nurse 1: Come here quickly.

Voice: Yes, Sister! (*pause*)

Nurse 2: Sister, here I am .

Nurse 1: (*with great urgency in her voice*) Hurry, help the young man over there send the patient to Ward 'D'. Be quick! Go!

Orderly: Ward 'B'?

Nurse 1: I said Ward 'D' ... 'D' for Death. Quick ... Be gone!

Basa: (*despondently*) Ao...my bruda don die finish.

(*Orderly run to assist Basabasa with the trolley. They push the trolley through an improvised crowded hospital corridor and stop at a point close to two cement blocks.*)

Orderly: Well, So, here we are.

Basa: Whosai?

Orderly: This is Ward 'D'.

Basa: Beg your pardon... But abi dis one, na corridor.

Orderly: Yes, but it is Ward 'D'... Side ward.

Basa: If dis na ward, whosai de hospital beds dey?

Orderly: Hospital what? (*laughs*) Haven't you heard that these days Hospital Wards are like Boarding Schools? Once you are through with your lab tests and you are given admission, you go to the Hospital Administrator for your prospectus to know the items you have to buy.

Basa: So, me I no ged prospectus some, wetin I for do?

Orderly: You improvise.

Basa: Impro...impro... wetin?

Orderly: Don't worry, I'll show you. Just help me arrange these cement blocks. (*Basabasa assists the orderly to arrange the cement blocks place a plank over it and cover the plank with some dirty old rug retrieved from their belongings.*) Now, here you are. Help me carry him unto the....

Basa: (*shocked*) You wan put de live person for de top of hard wooden plank, as if say ibi cow meat una dey put for butcher table! Abi?

Orderly: This is a bed sitter.

Basa: No blanket...

Orderly: With blanket then man you are asking for P.I.S. Presidential Initiated Suite. (*laughs*) Look, you should be grateful to God that your brother has a bed sitter. I wish you could take a trip to the Maternity Block and see things for yourself.

Basa: Wetin dey dere?

Orderly: Come over (*whispers*)

Basa: (*frightened*) Wetin be dat?

Orderly: Over there you'll see both mothers and their newly-born babes fortunately and comfortably sleeping on the bare cold terrazzo floor. Six newly-born fine babies sharing one cot. And you know something?

Basa: Wetin?

Orderly: They don't even complain. The babies and their mothers don't complain. They are happy. Can you imagine that? The day-old human babies being treated less than day-old chicks on a poultry farm hatchery are happy.

Basa: Na so?

Orderly: Oh yes! They are very grateful for the generosity and magnanimity of the charitable medical system we operate.

Basa: I see... make I hask my broda if he wan make we take am go for de labour ward. Gomey!... Gomey... (*pause*) Gomey, de orderly nurse say, if you dey here, you go labour in vain. So, I want take you for Labour ward proper. Abi, you go go? Gomey! Gomido! Talk to me Gomey! (*getting hysterical*) Gomey! (*screams*) Gomey!

Orderly: No need shouting. He won't hear you.

Basa: Because of why?

Orderly: He's long gone.

Basa: Beg your pardon... Long gone for where?

Orderly: I am afraid he is... I... I mean... he is...

Basa: (*screams*) Oh No! Gomey why you for do dis to me?

(*silence*)

Basa: So, what do we do now?

Orderly: We wheel him away to the mortuary.

(*Orderly pulls the rug to cover the face of Gomido and begins to wheel him away*)

Gomido: (*suddenly sits up on the trolley and speaks through the nose*) Hey, be careful. No one is forcing me into any ice-cold fridge to share a narrow chamber with some real corpse I never knew during my lifetime.

Orderly: Will you keep quiet and die nicely like a gentleman…Please.

(*Pushes him back and pulls the cover over him*)

Gomido: (*protesting*) Don't I have a right to decide where I should be taken?

Orderly: Your freedom of choice ended the moment the Doctor declared you clinically dead.

Basa: Whosai de mortuary dey?

Orderly: This way.

Basa: Oya, make we go quick before dis dead body begin to smell.

Gomido: (*pleading*) Please, make sure the temperature in the mortuary is so regulated that I don't freeze…

(*Basa, assisted by orderly, pushes Gomido back unto the trolley and wheels him away. There is a flute dirge as the trolley is slowly wheeled away. Fade lights*)

FIFTH LEG

(*The house of Abusua Panyin-Chaka. It is dawn. Sound of distant cockcrows, barking of dogs and chirping of birds to signify a new dawn. Traditional dirge on flute creates a solemn atmosphere. Enter Abutu and Basa as family members*)

Chaka: (*sitting on the tree-stump*) Well, you are most welcome.

Abutu & Basa: Thank You, Nana.

Chaka: As the elders say, even though there is trouble, we say there is no trouble. As you can see, I am sitting in my house, it is you who have journeyed. It is you who might be having a load-bearing tongue. You may unfold it.

(*Abutu and Basa whisper*)

Abutu: (*to Basa*) The Abusua Panyin has laid the path. With your permission, I wish to tread on it.

Basa: You fit to walk for top.

Abutu: Nana, our mission here this early morning is very brief. Our presence here is in response to the call you sent out to all members of the bereaved family of which you are the Abusua Panyin, to meet and plan the funeral for our departed Royal. I am done.

Chaka: I am deeply touched by this show of friendship and brotherliness on your part. To think that you woke up around 3.00 am, licked the dew off the grass along the winding footpath, all the way from the mountains to this place. Once again, I say you are all welcome.

Abutu & Basa: Thank you, Abusua Panyin

Chaka: (*clears his throat*) Errm…errrmm. Abutu, why not be my *Okyeame* on this occasion.

Abutu: With all pleasure, Nana. Spit into my mouth that I may spit.

Chaka: Okyeame, are you there?

Abutu: Nana, I am all ears.

Chaka: Get it across to all family members who have come from far and near, that today marks the seventh day since our Royal poured salt away. As tradition demands, we are gathered here to discuss how we are going to perform those customary rites that are necessary to conduct him safely through the gates that lead to the village of our ancestors.

Abutu: So says Abusua Panyin. That it was time the late Royal was found a fitting resting place and not left to freeze in a refrigerator as if he were a piece of edible carcass.

Basa: Somitin like mad cow beef, ino be so? (*pause*) I sorry…very sorry.

Chaka: This would mean going for the most expensive casket on the market.

Abutu: So says Abusua Panyin, that the Royal remains should not be interred in some cheap wawa casket.

Basa: Never!

Chaka: And I…. Abusua Panyin Chaka-Timbo! don't care how much the best casket shall cost.

Abutu: Nana, *Mmo ne kasa!* Well-spoken. The eagle that lays its eggs where no human eye can see has spoken. The eagle that flies straight towards the sun and fears nothing in this world except the gun and the snake, has spoken. (*pause*)

Basa: So, Beg your pardon... who go pay for de coffin?

Chaka: Mr. Beg-your-pardon, please leave everything to me. I shall bear the full cost of the golden casket. And the full cost of the ten day-long funeral. I have spoken!

Basa: But whosai we for ged de casket. De body still dey for inside deep freezer.

Chaka: The casket?

Basa: Yes, Nana. (*Abutu breaks into a long laughter*)

Abutu: No need worrying yourselves. You are right at the entrance of *'Ku-Enye Ga Enterprise'*. Yes, gentlemen, may I please help you? (*general laughter.*)

Abutu: Well, since we are operating a cash and carry system, you have to bring the cash to carry the casket else your corpse shall start decomposing and…

Gomido: I refuse to decompose! (*laughter*) But on a more serious note, I think Abutu's point is well-proven.

Chaka: Indeed, proven beyond all reasonable doubts.

(*sudden lightening flashes and loud thunderclaps mixed with strong blowing wind*)

Abutu: Folks, we have to hurry and get out of here. The weather is changing.

Basa: Na true-true. Emake like ego rain.

(*more thunderclaps*)

Chaka: I think so too. Let's look for a hiding place before we are soaked to our underwears.

Abutu: Let us simply get out of here.

Gomido: Out of here to where?

Abutu: To somewhere... anywhere...Just somewhere we can get some shelter and...

Basa: And Food!... Food! Some of we de hungry.

Gomido: So, where do we go? (*silence*) Are you all quiet? We want to move. Someone suggest where we should be heading from here.

Chaka: Well, may be, we go back to the palace.

Basa: Palace...which palace be dat?

Chaka: What a question. Don't you know who you are? You are Princes....

Basa & Abutu: Princes?

Chaka: Yes, Royals!

Basa & Abutu: Royals?

Chaka: You are a peculiar people. A chosen generation. A generation belonging to the Palace Reserved for Important Sons of the Nation. (*pause*) Check out the acronym.

Basa: Wetin be acronym... beg your pardon... idey like crayon?

Abutu: No, beg your ignorance, it tastes like rainwater.

(*Sound of gentle rain-drops on the roofs around*)

Basa: Your morda. Hoooo bush baby!

Chaka: (*spells it*) P...R.... I...S.... O...N. stands for, Palace Reserved for Important Sons of the Nation.

Abutu: (*vehemently*) Back to Prison? No way. (*emphatically*) It shall be over my dead body. You'll need a bulldozer and a forklift to carry me from here back to prison. In fact, you shall need a helicopter to fly me over these walls.

Basa: (*excitedly*) Ma bruda, why you dey shout-shout so? Look de time enack, by now dem dey serve prison ration... Food!...

Gomido: (*very excited*) Yes, that is true. We can be sure of getting some warm clothes, even if it is second-hand. See how we are all shivering. Over there, in Prison, we shall become assets of the State and receive free medical attention.

Basa: Cash and carry go be history.

Gomido: Exactly. We shall have free shelter in Prison.

Abutu: Stop It... Stop it, I said!

Basa: No rent, no land lord coming to harass we.

Abutu: (*screams*) I say stop it! (*silence*)

Chaka: We are in a democracy. Let us put the issue to vote. (*pause*) As many as are IN favour of going back into the Palace Reserved for Important Sons of the Nation, say 'Aye'!

Gomido & Basa: Aye!

Chaka: Those NOT in favour, say 'Nay'!

Abutu: (*screams*) Nay!... Nay ... and Nay! A thousand times.

Chaka: One abstention, which is I. A two-to-one decision. I think the Ayes have it.

Basa: (*desperately*) Make we go quick-quick. Abi, I hungry too much. Make we go. By now dem dey share de ration for insai.

(*The rain intensifies.*)

Gomido: Yes. It is far better in there than out here in this rain and cold weather, where we could easily catch pneumonia in a society that practices Cash and Carry medical system without a human face. Let's go.

Abutu: (*resolutely*) I am a free man. I am heading for Canaan. I am never going back to Egypt.

Basa: We no dey go to Egypt. Dat place na too far. We dey go for de PALACE, over dere. Oya, (*with his back towards the prison*) Forward NEVER, Backward EVER! Make we go now. As for me I dey hungry. Let me begin to pack our belongings for the trip back to the palace.

(*They start packing their belongings and when they are all set Chaka approaches Abutu*)

Chaka: Abutu, for the very last time, are you sure you are not coming along with us back into the palace?

Abutu: My mind is made up. I am determined to stay out of your so-called PALACE by every means possible.

Gomido: The rains will beat you.

Basa: Cold go catch your body and hungry go catch your belly.

Abutu: The rains will come.
The cold, the hunger
and even the pain may come,
but they are mere circumstances
that cannot hurt me forever.
They all shall pass.
I shall hang on outside here
and set up my coffin and casket business.
With 200 people being infected with the
HIV/AIDS virus a daily,
very soon I shall be experiencing a boom
In my business.
I am off.

(*Exit Abutu*)

Chaka: Good luck then.

Gomido & Basa: (*excitedly*) Bye-bye…We're off to dine in the Palace… Bye-bye!

(*Chaka, Gomido and Basabasa with their belongings slung behind their backs move towards the prison gates. They start banging on the gates.*)

Voice: Who is there?

Chaka & Co: (*shivering voices*) It is we.

Voice: You, who?

Chaka & Co: We were once members of this Royal family.

Chaka: We belonged to this palace. (*The peephole on the gate is opened*)

Voice: Your IDs, please.

Chaka: (*confidently*) I am Royal PT 007.

Voice: Yes, you were here for murder.

Gomido: That is correct

Gomido: (*proudly*) I am Royal number WWW dot 96

Voice: You were sent here for internet fraud.

Gomido: Well, something like that.

Basa: (*excitedly*) I be Royal KW66.

Voice: You were sent in here for stealing electrical cables meant to supply several kilowatts of power to 66 rural communities.

Basa: Ibi so dem put for de charge sheet.

 Voice: And your mission here this evening?

Chaka & Co: We have come to re-register. Sah!

Voice: Re-register for what?

Gomido: For re-admission into the fraternity of the PALACE as prodigal Royals. Sah!

Voice: Why?

Basa: (*in a whisper*) Abi, make you tellam say we be Hungrily Indebted Poor Ex-Cons. Tell am say our freedom make us Hipic. (*shouts*) Abi, I say tellam quick-quick! Beg your pardon...

Chaka: (*shouts at the top of his voice*) We have not been able to handle effectively the freedom we gained from you. Sah!

Gomido: (*whispers to Chaka*) That's a lie and you know it. (*shouts at the top of his voice*) Rather, it was the freedom that couldn't handle us. Sah!

Voice: I am afraid you are all suffering from an acute form of Acquired Prison Traumatic Syndrome. The health of other inmates could be jeopardised if you are allowed in. But first, wait and let me discuss it with my Commandant. We might have to quarantine you for a few months if you don't mind...

Basa & Co: (*happily*) We don't mind at all.

Gomido: Once we'll be given free meals during the period of quarantine, that's okay.

Voice: But I'll first have to clear it with my superior officer. Wait for me, I'll be right back. (*violently shuts the peephole*)

Basa: (*earnestly*) Make we pray.

Gomido & Co: (*They get on their knees and start praying*) We lift up our eyes unto the prison... From where cometh our help!... Our help Cometh from the lord who made the prisons and its officers... He'll not suffer our stomach to go hungry. Behold, He that keepeth the prisoner will not slumber He that keepeth...

(*The main gates open. Out steps a Prison Officer in full uniform. The Ex-convicts stop praying and stand up on their feet facing the Officer.*)

Officer: I am the new Prison Officer assigned to escort you inside. Here are kneepads you are to wear on your knees as you crawl back into the palace. And you shall remain confined in solitary on your knees, till the Commandant is satisfied you are completely cured of the Acquired Prison Traumatic Syndrome you are suffering from.

Chaka: Please, Officer, may I ...

Officer: (*roars*) Shut up, you may not. Get down on your knees, NOW!

(*They hurriedly pick up the knee pads, put them on and get down into crawling position*)

Officer: By the left quick march...

Abutu & Chaka: Please allow us to walk upright on our own two feet.

Voice: Too late. You forfeited that right by applying for readmission into the palace.

Abutu & Co: Oh No!

Officer: Too bad. You must crawl back inside since you came voluntarily

Basa: (*defiantly*) Beg your pardon. If I no go walk for my own leg then me I wan go back outsai.

Officer: Too late. Now march on your knees. Left-right...left-right...left-right...left-right...

(*As they crawl back into the prison, the rains get intensified there are thunder claps and lightening flashes. The gates begin to shut, suddenly there is black out. We hear the sobbing of the ex-convicts in the background.*)

THE END

21 March 2002

Book Reviews

Bernth Lindfors, *Ira Aldridge*. Vol. 1, *The Early Years, 1807-1833*; & Vol.2, *The Vagabond Years, 1833-1852*
Rochester NY: University of Rochester Press
ISBN 978 1 58046 381 2: Vol 1, 2011, 387 pp. + 13 illus.
ISBN 978 1 58046 394 2: Vol 2, 2011 244 pp. + 18 illus., $99/£55

Ira Aldridge 'became' Senegalese (allegedly the grandson of a Fulah prince) in Manchester at the age of twenty-three, five years after leaving his native New York to reinvent himself as an actor in England. The year was 1830, and Aldridge, who had had himself billed as the 'African Roscius' since 1826, was banking on the British appetite for abolition three years before Parliament finally passed the Abolition Act. As Lindfors' painstaking research makes abundantly clear, if opportunism was a survival tactic for any jobbing actor on the road in the 'Age of Reform', it was a *sine qua non* for an isolated black one. It may have been Aldridge's enthusiastic reception in Hull (William Wilberforce's home town), in 1829 that inspired the Senegal fiction, which Lindfors neatly labels 'an illicit but entertaining form of ethnological show business' (1: 184).

Obversely, running through the author's narrative of Aldridge's (mostly provincial) theatrical experiences in Britain, there is a bolder argument: 'He dressed in borrowed robes to prove a point about human equality' (1: 1). There is every reason to hope that Aldridge's admirers found their prejudices challenged, but, much as he would like it to be the case that the African Roscius was on an ethnic mission from the start, Lindfors has not uncovered clinching evidence that he was. Rather the reverse. 'Ethnological show business' is one thing, the quest for universal equality another. Aldridge's imaginary migration from North America to West Africa was initially undertaken in order to upgrade his publicity material. It can certainly be argued that his success, particularly in Europe after 1852, upset the myth of white superiority, but to present his Manchester self-translation as the birth of a missionary is, I think, fanciful.

This is a small blemish in a work of monumental scholarship. The first of these handsomely produced volumes (£55 for more than 600 pages in hardback counts as almost a snip these days) makes the most of shifty sources in an attempt to reconstruct Aldridge's American boyhood and early youth. The suggestion is that his father wanted him to become a preacher, and that the boy toyed with the prospect of a career as a sailor until he was fatally bitten by the theatrical bug after associating with (working for?) either, or both, of the visiting stars, James and Henry Wallack. It is likely that one or other of the Wallacks helped him to make the astonishingly bold decision to try his luck in London. There was little hope for him on the institutionally racist American stage, but his prospects in Britain were far from bright. It is here that Lindfors makes the first of a number of telling historical points. Aldridge made his London debut (at the Royalty) on 11 May 1825, a little over a year into the stage-life of Charles Mathews the Elder's *A Trip to America*, the latest of his immensely popular one-man 'At Homes'. One of the characters featured by Mathews in this comic narrative of his American tour was a 'black tragedian' whose soliloquy he claimed to reproduce: 'To be or not to be, dat is him question, whether him nobler in de mind to suffer or lift up him arms against one sea of hubble bubble and by opossum end em.' Enthused by his reception, the tragedian abandons the role of Hamlet to sing 'Opossum up a Gum Tree' (1: 56). Aldridge was not yet eighteen when he played Othello at the Royalty, but audiences schooled by Mathews were surprised to find him a comparatively competent 'black tragedian'. That Aldridge was conscious of the favour inadvertently done him by Mathews is shown by his subsequent willingness, eagerness even, to sing 'Opossum up a Gum Tree' as a curtain-piece to *Othello*.

It may be that Aldridge had naively hoped so to captivate London audiences as Othello that he would be able to sustain himself with that part alone, but there was no chance of that. The story Lindfors unfolds in the first of his two volumes is that of a tyro who gradually took possession of enough roles to last for one week in small towns (Kendal, Tewkesbury, and Ledbury) and two weeks in larger centres (Manchester, Glasgow, and Hull). Evidence of versatility was the key, and Aldridge was a quick learner. He constructed an unusually prosperous touring career in Britain on a foundation of the twinned roles of Othello and Mungo (in Bickerstaff's *The Padlock*): tragedy today, comedy tomorrow. Over time, he added many more, whiting up for several of them, but his ambition, like that of any would-be star, was to secure an engagement at one of London's patent theatres (the few licensed to perform serious drama). Lindfors's first volume builds towards the anti-climax of Aldridge's appearance as Othello at Covent Garden in 1833. Some reviewers were respectful, but audiences were thinned out by an influenza epidemic and further discouraged by critiques that read now as vitriolically racist. 'In the name of propriety and decency', the *Athenaeum* took exception to Ellen Tree's being subjected to 'the indignity of being pawed about by Mr. Henry Wallack's black servant' (1: 267). More cruelly, the clever young journalist Gilbert Abbott à Beckett relaunched the vilification of Aldridge he had begun in 1831 as editor of the comic paper, *Figaro in London*.

Lindfors has much of value to tell us about à Beckett. He is one of many minor contributors to the Aldridge story who are brought to fuller life in these generous volumes. A willingness to digress – just a little – in pursuit of a good subject adds valuable colour to what might otherwise be a travelogue. I know of no account of a nineteenth-century actor that has followed its subject's itinerary in such detail. Aldridge acted in towns and villages from Penzance to Aberdeen, at a probable average of over twenty venues per year, and Lindfors has tracked down responses in most of them, not least during the Irish years of 1833-39. This was 'perhaps the happiest period of his life' (2: 51). Irish audiences warmed to him, and their support gave him the confidence to compile a one-man show, which was part of his repertoire from 1835 to 1845. Just how good an actor Aldridge was will never be known. There were many in the second rank who, like him, might shine for a week in Shrewsbury or two weeks in Limerick, but who never secured a hold in London. A similar story might be told about Edmund Kean before 1814 or Irving before 1871. The difference is skin deep. Lindfors is knowingly contributing to black history, and knowingly leaving that history a volume short. Aldridge toured British theatres for twenty-seven years before sailing to Brussels in 1852. 'The triumphant Continental phase of Aldridge's career were [*sic*] his glory years, demonstrating what he was able to achieve both as an accomplished actor and as a distinguished representative of his race' (2: 181). What we need now is a scholar as excitable and as scrupulous as Lindfors to write Volume 3.

Peter Thomson
University of Exeter

Austin Asagba, (ed.) *Cross-Currents in African Theatre*
Ibadan: Kraft Books, 2008 [first published by Osasu Publishers, University of Benin, 2001].
ISBN 978 978 039 121 5 np.

Austin Ovigue Asagba (ed.) *Theatre & Minority Rights:*
Perspectives on the Niger Delta
Ibadan: Kraft Books, 2010
ISBN 978 978 8425 36 6 n.p.

African Theatre has the good habit of reviewing books often unavailable in the retail and marketing circuits of the global North; studies brought out by university presses or general publishing houses on the African continent with relatively small or no international distribution. Although Kraft Books is a participating publisher of the UK-based African Books Collective (ABC), with some of their works available through the ABC website (http://www. africanbookscollective.com), the two books under review are currently not offered for sale. It is thanks to the extraordinary personal connections of the review editor that I received my copies. (I am still trying to get two other Nigerian books favourably reviewed in *AT 10: Media and Performance*. They, too, are unavailable through the usual channels; a helpful graduate student is now hoping to obtain them for me on her current research trip to Nigeria.)

What I am trying to say – and what I keep saying in the classroom – is that we, as students of African theatre based in the North, need to make an effort to read and recognise the plethora of academic work done on the African continent, and that we need to acknowledge it in our own critical thinking. That the mysteries of the market-place sometimes hinders us from doing so in a timely fashion can be made clear with the first collection of essays under review. *Cross-Currents in African Theatre* grew out of the First Annual Conference of the University of Benin on African theatre – in April 1990. It is important to point this out because this review is written exactly 22 (!) years after the papers were initially presented. The book seems outdated before you open it, which makes me wonder whether I will able to do justice to the contributors. In the meantime, some of them have made an international career – I am thinking of Onookome Okome (University of Alberta, Edmonton), for example – who might not be too keen on having an early work scrutinised. (Okome's article on language and ideology in two of Tunde Fatunde's plays is still readable today, a youthfully passionate critique of Fatunde's dramaturgy said to fail the playwright's claims to revolutionary commitment). While some of the sources, terminology, and critical approaches read indeed somewhat old-fashioned today, the collection still has its uses for theatre scholars and teachers of African theatre.

Asagba's idea at the time was to put a book together that would help alleviate the 'dearth of teaching materials in the theatre discipline [...] provide a cross-current of ideas on African theatre and hopefully, encourage an annual discourse and workshop among theatre practitioners, scholars and students' (6). Ultimately, so the Foreword by Dapo Adelugba suggests, the collection is hoped 'to begin to articulate a theory of African Theatre in broad ideological terms' (9). It should be made clear that 'African Theatre' translates largely into 'Nigerian theatre' in this collection, with one article on Ghana – a cogent paper by Chinyere G. Okafor (now Wichita State University, Kansas) on the relationship of setting and thematic realisation of change in Aidoo and Sutherland – and Asagba's own comparative analysis of revolutionary rhetorics in Osofisan and Ebrahim Hussein. Asagba provides a solid reading of *The Chattering and the Song* and *Kinjeketile*, even if his concluding suggestion that playwrights draw on applied theatre techniques to create more 'popular' plays is somewhat forced. All in all, the book comprises twenty-one contributions, covering issues as varied as Nigerian popular music (Josephine Ngozi Mokwenyei), community theatre experience in Kwara State (Ayoola Akinwale) and television broadcasting

(Barclays Foubiri Ayakoroma). The majority of chapters, however, focus on the close reading of plays by established dramatists such as Soyinka, Sofola, Onwueme, and Rotimi. It is striking that there is relatively little on productions and performance, though I found those dealing with performative and practical aspects of theatre the most interesting (for an example see Taiwo Adeyemi's 'Towards Bridging the Gap Between the Academic and Professional Theatres in Nigeria'). Fascinating are also the occasional historical tidbits that emerge. Ahmed Yerima, in his overview on 'Colonialism and the Development of Drama in Nigeria', comments on drama by colonial administrators and local radio programmes in the 1950s, all of which fascinating moments of Nigerian theatre history which call for more scholarly attention.

As for the idea 'to begin to articulate a theory of African theatre in broad ideological terms', this book is a child of its time. While many contributors stress the relationship of theatre and society, Femi Osofisan, in his opening keynote on 'The Political Imperative in African Dramaturgy and Theatre Practice', sets the tone. Despite the crumbling of the Eastern bloc in the late 1980s, playwrights of the left should not abandon their thinking and continue to see their craft as part of the struggle for the 'common people' (20) to create a theatre that serves as their advocate.

The plight of the common people is also the overarching theme of Asagba's second collection, *Theatre and Minority Rights*. The book emerged out of an eponymous conference by the Society of Nigerian Theatre Artists (SONTA) in 2008, again at the University of Benin, and is both timely in terms of publication date and topic. The majority of the 18 chapters revolve around plays, theatre projects and government schemes in and on Nigeria's troubled Niger Delta. Oil exploitation in the Delta region fuels the nation's economy, but local communities have long suffered from the loss of control of resources and revenues, and from enormous environmental damage. This has led to social unrest, violence and militancy. Many articles reflect the view that performance in its many forms – from theatre-for-development projects to dance theatre, from literary drama to video film – can help alleviate the region's plight through conscientisation, education and reorientation in search of a resolution to the conflict. The idea of theatre as 'an instrument for social, economic and cultural change' (33), however, remains largely a projected ideal. Canice Chukwuma Nwosu, for example, in an informative article on youth restiveness in Bayelsa State and the failings of the National Economic Empowerment and Development Strategy (NEEDS), proposes a 'Theatre on the Raft' programme to reach riverine and estuarine communities completely surrounded by water. The project is meant to 'sell to the people, the philosophy and ideology of peaceful coexistence, unity in diversity and dialogue' while to 'the government and its agencies, it will emphasise true federalism that will enhance control by the states' (30). Though the idea of putting theatre on rafts is ingenious and rather intriguing, the question remains whether the conflicting parties will 'buy' this programmatic approach so easily. Similarly, Tor Iorapuu argues for a Theatre for Transformative Change (TfTC) which he sees as a 'counter-revolution' (208) to theatre-for-development (TfD), being apparently less self-reflexive and effective than the new method he proposes. The following sketch of a TfTC project in Plateau State (central Nigeria), however, lacks the very self-critical reflection requested earlier on, and the supposed difference to TfD does not really become clear. The overall impression of this collection, then, is that of an idealistic goodwill from artists and academics alike mixed with certain helplessness in the face of the gravity of the Niger Delta crisis.

The remaining articles are again close readings of play-texts (by Yerima, Clark, Sofola, Onwueme) and video films (*Igodo: Land of the Living Dead*), participant insights into dance drama ('A Nation at Crossroads'), and thoughts on the importance of costume and make-up for the promotion of minority cultures in a production of Sam Ukala's *Break a Boil*. A potentially interesting form of performance, that of ordinary women's nude protest against the dire consequences of environmental pollution – '"Our weapon is our nakedness"' (93) – is unfortunately little explored beyond a moralistic concern for the 'virtues of womanhood' (94). I am tempted to think that the performative power of such simple acts of resistance is much greater than that of many educational theatre projects.

With contributors from all sides of the divide – community activists, artists and government officials - the collection highlights the many-faceted conflicts and contradictions emerging from the Niger Delta. We should expect more publications on the region to come.

Christine Matzke
University of Bayreuth

Michael Etherton and John Reed, *Chikwakwa Remembered: Theatre & Politics in Zambia, 1968–1972*

Dublin: Original Writing, 2011, 176 pp.
ISBN 978 1 908477 31 6, €25

As its title suggests, this memoir is as much about politics as it is about theatre. The two authors, colleagues at the University of Zambia in the immediate post-independence years, were devoted to the interests of the new nation, excited by the possibilities of a new drama articulating its concerns and ambitions, and full of a creative energy and determination to create a performance space in which these dreams could be realised. The result was the Chikwakwa Theatre, built brick by brick by the authors, their colleagues and students out of a derelict tobacco barn close to the end of the garden of Reeds' house outside the university campus. The intriguing story they tell is a mixture of triumph and disaster – the former in the theatre's building and operation, the latter in the expulsion from Zambia of Etherton and his colleague Andrew Horn in the genesis of Chikwakwa, and the consequent constraints placed upon Reed.

The authors set out their manifesto. Beyond the need for a 'good' theatre building offering its audiences and players 'a feeling of inclusion' was a greater imperative:

> The building, the theatre space, must reflect societal values. We want Chikwakwa to go much further with the idea of inclusiveness. The theatre must reach out to those folk for whom the idea of a theatre building is, within the cultural structure of colonialism, an alienating place. The architecture has to say to them, if, as we intend to, we bus in citizens from the surrounding townships, this is *your* place, be comfortable here, relaxed – even before they hear a dramatic word spoken by the actors standing before them. (52)

All this was against the background of the colonial amateur theatre in the old Northern Rhodesia, as elsewhere in southern Africa, where plays from a traditional European repertoire were performed by expatriate casts in competitions before adjudicators flown in from London. It was a head-in-the-sand attitude that continued well into independence and offered no opportunity or encouragement for a growing indigenous theatre.

The authors explain that the derivation of the name of this new theatre is from the Nyanja, '"*Chikwakwa*": this the metaphor for the theatre we want to create: a grassroots theatre, a theatre that slashes grass down to the roots which will thrust up green shoots at the next rains.' But behind all the idealism is the very practical business of designing and building. Greatly achieved through volunteers, with the authors themselves deeply involved, the creation of this innovative African performance space – one to place alongside, for instance, Efua Sutherland's Ghana Drama Studio at Legon, Duro Ladipo's Mbari Mbayo in Oshogbo, Ola Rotimi's Ori Olokun Theatre in Ile-Ife – is chronicled and illustrated in detail. (A slight digression at this point. Those of us who were involved in university theatre in other parts of Africa often had to break out of the architectural facilities generously provided for us by expatriate university architects and find more liberating performance space through the creation of, for instance, the Makerere Free Travelling Theatre and the University of Ibadan Travelling Theatre. We can envy Etherton and his colleagues starting from scratch!)

From early productions of Mario Fratti's *Che Guevara* (the subject of a fascinating chapter in its own right, generously illustrated) and an adaptation of a radio play by the Zambian writer Andreya Masiye, *The Lands of Kazembe*, Chikwakwa went on to develop new Zambian (often student) work and its own travelling theatre. This aspect of their work caused Chikwakwa to consider the crucial matter of language. Etherton writes:

> As Chikwakwa emerged from the bush around John's house as a place for new Zambian theatre...the issue of what language or languages should be used becomes increasingly important. Our first travelling theatre experiment... showed us how important it was to perform in the main language of the locality. We rehearsed play scripts that are in English; then let the cast members use their mother tongue to capture the idiom of the dialogue in the local language.

For several years the 'mud theatre' (illustrations in the volume show how modest a description that was) thrived, striving to produce an authentically Zambian theatre, radical and politically engaged. When Etherton and Horn were deported (ostensibly for involvement in student demonstrations), Chikwakwa's work was carried on by others – specifically Fay Chung, David Kerr, and Mapopa Matonga – increasingly travelling, creating workshops and new work.

Etherton's final comments sum up both the achievement and the agenda of Chikwakwa's founders.

> What was started in Zambia in 1969, with the building of Chikwakwa Theatre, was a physical expression of a new kind of drama and theatre. Zambian drama then broke out of that particular building, which today lies unused and cramped by encroaching housing. Theatre moved into the countryside – then came back into the middle of city slums, into essentially non-theatre spaces. It joined similar innovations in performance and action among communities in different parts of the world. It is part of a movement which, despite the problems of a world dominated by overwhelming macroeconomic realities, continues to struggle for fairness, justice and change for those impoverished by global economic growth.

This is an important and moving record of a great – if fraught – achievement.

Martin Banham
University of Leeds

Kene Igweonu (ed.), *Trends in Twenty-First Century African Theatre & Performance* (Foreword by Temple Hauptfleisch)
IFTR/FIRT African Theatre and Performance Working group: Amsterdam/ New York: Rodopi, 2011, 474 pp.
ISBN 978 90 420 3386 3, €94/ US$127/ $85

This new collection of eighteen critical essays is more ambitious than the title suggests, extending beyond broad descriptions of trends in 21st-century African theatre and performance to offer innovative approaches to how theatre in the African context may be conceptualised and practiced. The essays challenge European paradigms of theatre that have long dominated African theatre practice without resorting to counter-discourses that perpetuate binaries. Rather, they suggest concrete ways in which we can rethink approaches to intercultural practices, expand definitions of applied/ community theatre and redefine approaches to specific practices that extend beyond the African context, insofar as they also engage with the implications of increasing globalisation.

The first section on general trends, which again is not a particularly helpful sub-title, addresses the issue of how African theatre practitioners could approach interculturalism in the postcolonial context, without reinforcing binaries, or ignoring cultural hegemonies. The chapters by Samuel Ravengai, Kene Igweonu and Petrus du Preez engage provocatively with post-colonial and intercultural theory in the contexts of multicultural and intercultural engagements in African urban contexts that are becoming increasingly cosmopolitan. Each chapter offers significant critical engagement with theory against specific practical examples. Ravengai explores the issues of theatre training in styles and techniques of western realism for a specifically African body. Ravengai's argument about culture being embodied is something that is increasingly emphasised in current discourses on culture and performance studies, and thus is particularly pertinent in the context of intercultural practice. He explores various limitations of Stanislavski's psycho-technique, given the specifics of both a rural and urban African body, and suggests how these limitations may be addressed. This chapter is challenging and engaging. At times the theory gets in the way of the solutions offered, but the examples cited are provocative and suggest real potential for moving intercultural theatre practice forward.

Kene Igweonu's chapter on identity construction in Africa and the African-Caribbean looks at the complexities of interculturalism in the context of imposed cultural interaction, particularly for previously enslaved cultures, and proposes 'transculturation' as a more accurate description of these particular intercultural interactions. The chapter makes for an interesting comparison with Kadiatu Kanneh's (1998) analysis of *African Identities* in the context of the black literatures of Sierra Leone, the United States and the Carribbean. Petrus du Preez provocatively pits intercultural and intracultural issues against one another, suggesting that the tricky terrain of negotiating aesthetics and hegemonies is not limited to collaborations between the north and south, but extends to cultural hierarchies when artists from different African contexts collaborate, as was the case with the Handspring and Sogolon Puppet Companies' production of *Tall Horse*.

Chapters in this first section include two specific to South African theatre. Temple Hauptfleisch's chapter maps out how Theatre Studies developed in South Africa from a predominantly European literary perspective, gradually widened to include ways of engaging with African performance forms and the syncretic forms that emerged from the radical theatre of the 1970s, finally engaging with everything 'from trance dance to Performance as research'. Although not strictly focused on the 21st century, this chapter offers a useful overview of the periods, organisations, research centres and shifts in focus in theatre criticism in South Africa, which facilitates an understanding of why particular methodologies, theories and approaches define contemporary South African theatre.

Johann van Heerden's analysis of trends in post-apartheid South African expands on the 'confusion in post-apartheid theatre institutions' suggested by Loren Kruger (1999:195), exemplified in his analysis of the restructuring of Performing Arts Councils and the gap between government funders and practising arts communities in South Africa. He offers an insightful analysis into the way festivals function in South Africa, particularly in relation to English and Afrikaans theatre, with a question hanging over the development of African-language theatre, given the Macufe festivals which has run since 1997. Van Heerden highlights issues that dominate post-apartheid theatre; namely, social reconciliation, identity – particularly for people who feel that they belong to a minority group – the reinterpretation of recorded history, engaging with the 'Africanisation' of culture, and issues related to gender, sexuality and equality.

The five essays in the second section emphasise how applied theatre has retained a central place in the African context. They outline different issues and projects in Tanzania, Zimbabwe and Nigeria. Both Vicensia Shule and Ola Johnsson critique the way applied theatre is mobilised in Tanzania. Shule specifically criticises the effects of neo-liberalism and the consequences, for Tanzanian theatre and culture, of donors' emphasis on funding theatre that is tied to development. She perceptively assesses how institutions are implicated in the donor culture. Like many other critics cited, Shule stresses that effective TfD is dependent on sustained theatrical activity that has a strong grassroots base that defines local aesthetics and theatrical integrity. Ola Johnsson is similarly critical of the efficacy of Community-based Theatre (CBT) in Tanzania, suggesting that 'AIDS has turned CBT into one of its symptoms'. Despite offering suggestions for how CBT can be more effective, given the complexities of the sociological and theatrical contexts which are fraught with various levels of politics, and with stakeholders who have contesting agendas and views, this essay remains pessimistic. Johnsson ends his analysis by provocatively suggesting that CBT 'has played out its role as opener and mediator in HIV prevention and now needs a political mandate' (284). This statement offers a very real challenge to theatre practitioners working in applied theatre, as well as to governments and their agencies who are dealing with a pandemic that threatens the future of the continent.

The other three articles in this section look at how theatre is mobilised for wider cultural action, extending the usual application of community and applied theatre. Praise Zenenga explores how popular theatre in Zimbabwe between 1998 and 2008 was used to imagine a new social order and provided an alternative form of expression to political protest. Using specific examples, Zanenga points to satirical comedies that became known as Panic or Urgent Theatre as they drew attention to post-independent nationalist failures, and underlined the urgency for national and international intervention. She argues for theatre's potential both to provoke change and to facilitate national healing and reconciliation. This chapter suggests a real shift in applied theatre which still draws on local popular forms to engage local communities, national and international audiences. Vibeke Grøstad's analysis of how citizenship is being explored in specific Zimbabwean plays evidences a similar expansion of the usual approach to applied or community theatre. This is also true of Gladys Akunna's suggestion that dance movement analysis be mobilised as a psycho-diagnostic tool in contemporary Nigeria.

The third section of this book focuses on analyses of specific practitioners or performances. Five of the seven chapters focus on Nigerian examples: Osita Ezenwanebe and Adebisi Ademakinwa both analyse Ahmed Yerima's *Hard Ground*, which dramatised the Niger Delta crisis in Nigeria. Ngozi Udengwu offers a provocative analysis of the reasons for Stella Oyedepo's success with delivering performance on demand. This, he argues, highlights how contemporary Nigerian practitioners could restore waning public engagement with live theatre. Jeleel Ojuade looks at Nigerian Yoruba Bàtá and Dundun dance in the diaspora, and asks to what extent these create identity for Nigerians, or 'Africans' living outside the continent, and what relevance they have in the age of globalisation. Chris Ugolo traces Nigerian dance as a cultural form, and explores to what extent celebration is used as an aesthetic device in Herbert Ogunde's *Destiny* (1986), while exploring its potential role in contemporary performance practises.

Awo Asiedu argues for the need for indigenous theorising of contemporary theatre practices in African terms. She specifically focuses on two terms coined by Ghanaian playwrights: *anansegoro*, by Efua Sutherland and *abibigoro* by Mohamed ben-Abdullah. South African Alude Mahlali analyses her process for creating a memory play by drawing on the 'girlfriend aesthetic' of Kevin Quashie. This chapter looks at the complexities of finding a practical methodology that addresses the specific experiences of black girlhood. It draws on the work of African-American feminist critics, bell hooks and Toni Morrison, Zimbabwean novelist Tsitsi Dangarembga and Gcina Mhlope's play *Have you Seen Zandile?* while highlighting issues of memory and nostalgia in contemporary South Africa.

This collection is a rich resource for Anglophone African theatre scholarship. Each chapter includes a bibliography, and the editor has included a selected bibliography on African theatre scholarship which, although not comprehensive, does point to key texts that have become available between 1990 and 2011.

Although these chapters are diverse in focus and theoretical approaches, they are all profoundly engaged with issues of methodologies, aesthetics, the relationship between European and African forms, ideas and practices in the context of increasing globalisation. The collection also reveals how economic hegemonies affect academic research in the African context, insofar as the research is dominated by South African and Nigeria scholars, with a few international scholars and one chapter from a Ghanaian and Tanzanian scholar respectively. While the collection underlines the important contribution of the IFTR working group in facilitating discussion and dissemination of research, Kene Igweonu highlights some of the challenges involved in enabling this research group in his introduction. This raises the question of how more scholars from diverse backgrounds, beyond Anglophone Africa, can be involved in these important dialogues, debates and innovations in theory and practice. Overall this is an exciting collection that suggests a vibrant generation of theorists and practitioners who are moving theory and practice in the African context forward in ways that engage theatre practitioners from any context.

Yvette Hutchison
University of Warwick

Austin Ovigue Asagba (ed.) *Sam Ukala: His Work at Sixty*
Ibadan: Kraft Books Ltd. 2008, 265 pp
ISBN 978 485 44 2 9, n.p.

Duro Oni & Sola Adeyemi, (eds) *Developments in the Theory & Practice of Contemporary Nigerian Drama & Theatre: A Festschrift in Honour of Dapo Adelugba*
Rochester, UK: Alpha Crownes Publishers, 2011, 382 pp
ISBN 978 0 9566837 0 0 n.p.

Sam Ukala: His Work at Sixty celebrates the life and work of Nigerian scholar, dramatist, poet and humanist, Professor Samuel Chinedu Ukala. It is, however, his achievement as playwright, director and general man of the theatre that is interrogated and evaluated by a broad field made up of his colleagues, associates, former students, friends and members of his family on the occasion of his turning 60. I know Sam very well: we were undergraduates together for a brief year (he in his final year and I in my first) at the University of Nigeria, Nsukka; we again were MA students together in 1982-83 at the University of Ibadan where incidentally we were taught by Professor Dapo Adelugba, the subject of the other book being reviewed; and lastly we met again at the Workshop Theatre, University of Leeds when he and his family came for a one year stay as Commonwealth Fellow in 1994. Thus, for myself and others familiar with the author, this book succeeds very well in presenting a composite picture of this scholar-artist and political-humanist whose passion for the theatre and the arts is very strongly matched by his love for and abiding faith in his country, Nigeria. His plays and other writing are about Nigeria, her numerous problems, the frustrations faced by its peoples because of failed and corrupt leadership, and his hopes of the future for the country when the masses have risen to toss out the pathologically miscreant politician-thieves and thugs who have been ruling Nigeria since independence in 1960.

The book is divided into four parts. Part One focuses on Ukala's concept of folkism – a fusion of elements of traditional African theatre with Western dramaturgical elements – and its application to his works and those of other dramatists. Part Two consists of critical engagements with individual plays by Ukala, while Part Three concentrates on his foray into the video movie genre with his adaption of his apparently most popular play, *Akpakaland*, for the screen, with the same title. Part Four is a combination of four poems by Austin Asagba, the editor of this collection, all dedicated to Ukala followed by tributes from the many people who have worked with, been taught by, interacted with or whose lives have been touched upon or influenced by him.

A central element of Ukala's scholarship and creative endeavour much mentioned and celebrated by many of the contributors is his theory of *folkism* – an idea he developed as part of his doctoral dissertation at the University of Ibadan in the 1980s. Ukala has adopted folkism as the dramaturgical and performance philosophy underpinning his own practice since completing his doctorate in 1986.

Although the collection does its job of presenting Ukala, not all the essays in this book have any business being in the public domain given the poor scholarship and even poorer writing abilities displayed by some of the contributors. Many of the essays in the collection should have been 'killed off', thereby saving the reading public the irritation which encountering such mediocre scholarship and writing elicits. Having said this, some essays are fine and should be commended for competent scholarship. One would like to acknowledge essays such as the first three in Part One by Austin Akpuda, George Enita and Best Ugala which in their respective ways focus and interrogate/explicate Ukala's folkism. In particular, Ugala takes issues with folkism by identifying three key problems which plague the concept. Other contributors worthy of mention are Daniel Omatsola, whose essay, despite its many weaknesses, remains one of the really intellectually engaging essays of the collection; Chukwuma Anyanwu and Elo Ibagere whose essay on the challenges of adaptation demonstrates the authors' understanding of the film medium, its use and/or lack of in Ukala's adaptation of *Akpakaland* for the screen.

Any work which celebrates Professor Dapo Adelugba, the eminent African theatre and performance teacher, actor, scholar, director and mentor, can only be a good and welcome thing, and *Developments in the Theory and Practice of Contemporary Nigeria Drama & Theatre* is certainly that. For the many hundreds of Nigerian and African students who have been taught or mentored by Dapo Adelugba over the forty-something years that he has been teaching in higher education, directing for the stage or contributing to learned journals, the essays, tributes and interviews in the book provide a rounded picture of the man, the scholar and the theatre artist that is this complex human being, 'Baba Dapo', 'Uncle Daps', 'Prof'… 'Opelenge'. The wonder that is Professor Adedapo Abayomi Olorunfemi Adelugba leaps out from every essay, every interview and every tribute in this book!

Developments is divided into three parts: essays, interviews and tributes. There are 19 essays in Part One, four interviews in Part Two, and 21 in Part Three. While not all the essays are 'gems' of scholarship – in fact, some should not have been published at all – there are a few that in their erudition and substance capture the depth, versatility and passion of Dapo Adelugba. Although personally taking issues with Chukwuma Okoye's swipe that 'It is not the well-fed African academic, permanently domiciled in comfortable Western institutions, marketing alterity and waging a war of identity in/ against the centre, even as s/he has already somewhat become "centred"' (44), the essay's reading of the postcoloniality of contemporary African theatre gives one much food for thought. Other essays worthy of mention are Ahmed Yerima's on Adelugba's ideal of a national theatre and the assessment of how contemporary Nigerian theatre has measured up in that regard; Matthew Umukoro on the relationship between a national theatre and the idea of the nation; Sunday Ododo's essay on gender ambiguity and iconic paradox in Ebira Ekuechi 'facekuerade' performances. The two essays on practice and research and practice-led research by Chris Dunton and Patrick Ebewo are interesting, although both authors' distinctions between the two terms are rather confusing and thus unhelpful. Ebewo's conclusion, however, that '[t]he battle should be on the pressure for the recognition of the artistic output as equivalent in full or proportional value to publication' is a valid call for assessing advancement within the academy. Other essays that impressed are Olakunbi Olasope's reading of Euripides' *Trojan Women* and Femi Osofisan's *Women of Owu*, especially the theme of war and the fate of women who are left behind by defeated husbands, fathers and brothers. I particularly liked Ekundayo Simpson's 'Translation Problems of the African Film Maker…' which progressively became quite lucid in the way it delineated its arguments. So also is Chika Anyanwu's contention that extending Mohammad Yunus' 'social business enterprise' based on his microfinance model of rural development will enable an appreciation of Adelugba's contribution to the development of the Nigerian economy as 'social capital development' (205). Muyiwa Awodiya's 'Dapo Adelugba at 70…' rightly asserts that Adelugba's life history as theatre teacher and scholar 'signposts a clear picture of Nigeria's theatre history and its present day practice' (259) and the essay also captures the many qualities which make Adelugba the brilliant man of the theatre that he has been these many years. Outside these essays are others that the editors might have offered further guidance on and exercised some severe pruning.

Finally, three interviews by Adelugba and one by Wole Soyinka give the reader a flavour of who Adelugba is; his take on his work and Soyinka's point that 'Adelugba is a finer teacher than I am. I am a very impatient teacher. He was patient almost to a fault.… He was not selective and he was very p-a-t-i-e-n-t!' (297) says it all about Adelugba. But it is in the tributes that 'Prof.' comes alive 'before our very eyes'; each adding to the character tapestry of the man that we have all come to know, respect and love. This collection is a worthy celebration of this wonderful human being, Dapo Adelugba.

Osita Okagbue
Goldsmiths, University of London

Barclays Ayakoroma, *Dance on his Grave*
Nigeria: Kraft Books, 2010, 94 pp.
ISBN 9788425335, n.p.

Barclays Ayakoroma, *A Matter of Honour*
Nigeria: Kraft Books, 2010, 73 pp.
ISBN 9788425328, n.p.

Greg Mbajiorgu, *Wake Up Everyone*
Nigeria: Kraft Books, 2011, 79 pp.
ISBN 9789180059, n.p.

Jonathan Desen Mbachaga, *Widow's Might*
Nigeria: BookWorks Publishing, 2011, viii + 40 pp.
ISBN 9789140121, n.p.

I picked up all the plays included in this review during a trip in late 2011 to the Society of Nigerian Theatre Artists annual conference. Unlike most other African nations Nigeria does have a local play publication mechanism, but it is small scale and distribution is extremely weak. The conference was held at Nigeria's largest university, Ahmadu Bello, but the university bookshop had very few books of any kind and most of those had been lying around long enough for the pages to curl. These books were being marketed by the playwrights and their friends within the conference auditorium, and this was apparently the major means of book distribution even though prices were modest. Getting the voices of Africa's newer playwrights into the public arena remains an ongoing problem for all concerned with the theatre.

Barclays Ayakoroma is the most experienced of the playwrights under consideration, and both of his plays reviewed here were first performed around twenty years ago. They have also both had tiny publications before, but have now been reprinted by the major current publisher of Nigerian drama, Kraft Books. Ayakoroma says that he learned his craft under the tutelage of the great Nigerian playwright and director, Ola Rotimi, and this is apparent in the stagecraft evident in these texts. Both plays are theatrically fast-paced, entertaining and rooted in the communities they speak to in southern Nigeria.

A Matter of Honour deals with the issue of where a man should be buried. In a number of African cultures the location of burial is seen as hugely important, and can become a matter of major dispute between communities, each arguing they have the strongest claim to see the deceased as 'their' son or daughter. In his 'Author's Note' Ayakoroma sees such disputes as a major distraction; one that can sometimes lead to multiple deaths as a result of fighting among rival factions and which distracts from the more fundamental problem of addressing corrupt government.

In *A Matter of Honour* we never meet the central character, Oweibi, because he is already dead. Rather we witness a dispute between his fatherland, the village of Amabiri, and Angiama, the motherland where Oweibi spent most of his life and died. Amabiri has never shown any interest in Oweibi, but the elders are determined to uphold a tradition which demands that all males must be buried in their father's village. The 'honour' in the title relates to this traditional demand over which both sides prepare for virtual war until wise council in Angiama prevails and Oweibi is buried in secret, presenting Amabiri with a *fait accompli* which is reluctantly accepted.

A number of factors give this play more theatrical vigour than many equally didactic pieces. It begins with a vibrant, happy marriage scene giving much scope for music, dance and audience involvement, before introducing a central, engaging character. Egberi is the local drunk who demands a liquid fee for all information, but who stirs up the whole situation by telling the Amabirians about Oweibi's death and then needling them into action. When the play moves to Angiama we see another traditional ritual in the 'wake-feast' for Oweibi which can again draw an audience into the action of the play. Ayakoroma has something of an ear for pithy and engaging language and makes liberal use of proverbs. *A Matter of Honour* is interesting in that it uses many traditional performance forms to question a blind adherence to cultural forms which are seen in this instance as simply a matter of pride and honour and not in the community interest.

Dance on his Grave is also set in a 'traditional' ambiance in a community centred on the court of the King of Toru-Ama, but this is a play about gender relations. There seems to have been a fascination in recent years in Africa with plays about mass action by women; a notable exponent being Ayakoroma's fellow countrywoman, Tess Onwueme. However Ayakoroma chooses not to take the female side in a play he says was inspired by August Strindberg's misogynistic masterpiece, *The Father*. At the centre of *Dance on his Grave* is a women's strike led by the Queen. In order to prevent the resumption of a war that the women see as unnecessary and wasteful of their sons' lives, they come together and agree to refuse both domestic and sexual services to their husbands. As is to be expected the men are hopeless at domestic tasks and much humour is milked from their sexual frustration, but stalemate is reached with the women continuing the strike even after many of them have been severely beaten by their menfolk. The men say tradition cannot be breached and women must remain subservient. The play climaxes when a taunt of the Queen's that men can never be sure if they are the father of their children causes such angst for the King that he publicly drinks poison and dies. The court is devastated, the Queen repents and 'proper' gender relations are restored.

Ayakoroma says there have been numerous popular productions of this play and I can well imagine he is right. The leading characters are strongly drawn; as with *A Matter of Honour* the crowd scenes are vibrant and fast moving; the humour over sex and domestic roles is predictable but would undoubtedly draw roars of laughter, and the plot really does leave one wondering which side will prevail right up until the end. I cannot, however, conclude this review without registering my distress at Barclays Ayakoroma's casual scorn and mockery towards women. This reaches right back to the 'Authors Note' where he mocks a real Women's Day event, and continues throughout the play, including apparent endorsement of serious assaults on many women. The feminist in me would say that this originates in what appears to be a deep insecurity about the idea of any challenge to the surely boring dominance of the missionary position in all sexual congress in his culture. As for the king who commits suicide: that man needs to realise that certainty is only for the gods.

Widows' Might by Jonathan Mbachaga is another play about women, but this time the message is much more progressive. This play deals with a specific tribal custom where a widow is supposed to go through a series of ritual, humiliating 'purifications'. These include drinking the water the husband's corpse has been washed in, stripping naked in front of a group of male elders, and then seeing the family goods redistributed among the husband's family. The widow, Ifeoma, refuses to concede to any of these demands. Once again tradition is seen as reactionary and destructive, and once again the women come together to support their sister. In a straightforwardly didactic play Mbachaga sees the tribal elders roundly condemned by their own king for holding on to outdated aspects of tradition, and order is restored along with improved women's rights.

Finally, *Wake Up Everyone* by Greg Mbajiorgu is a hugely ambitious and wide ranging environmental play. Set in the Niger Delta where oil companies have wrecked terrible devastation over many years there are plenty of obvious targets, and not content with listing environmental dangers Mbajiorgu also lays into the corruption by companies and government that allows this environmental degradation. Whilst one cannot but admire the ambition of the playwright who experiments with the meta-theatrical use of a theatre company operating within the play to make a great list of green demands and has his play culminate in a devastating flood, the range of issues raised is simply too much for one work to carry. Action is overwhelmed by information which results in too many passages of indigestible fact-laden prose. There is a real theatrical intelligence here; it just needs to resist the temptation to deal with all the evils of the world in a single play.

Jane Plastow
University of Leeds